Navigate the Noise

Navigate the Noise
Investing in the New Age of Media and Hype

Richard Bernstein

John Wiley & Sons

New York • Chichester • Weinheim • Brisbane • Singapore • Toronto

Published by John Wiley & Sons, Inc.
Published simultaneously in Canada.

Library of Congress Cataloging-in-Publication Data:

Bernstein, Richard, 1958–
    Navigating the noise : investing in the new age of media and hype / Richard Bernstein.
      p.   cm.
    Includes bibliographical references and index.
    ISBN 0-471-38871-8 (cloth : alk. paper)
    1. Investments.   2. Investment analysis.   I. Title.

  HG4521 .B445 2001
  332.6—dc21   2001017840

Printed in the United States of America.

10 9 8 7 6 5 4 3 2

To Chris and Sara

Contents

Acknowledgments

If I thank anyone for their help in producing this book, it must be my team at Merrill Lynch: Kari Bayer, Lisa Kirschner, and Lynette Phillips. Their efforts have been invaluable in making us the top-ranked quantitative strategy team in the United States for the past six years. Many of the graphs and tables produced in this book are the result of their tremendous research efforts. The newest member of our group, Kevin Lui, should also be recognized for his recent contributions. Other members of the department whose thoughts are included in this book in various forms are Nigel Tupper, Carrie Zhao, Satya Pradhuman, Markus Barth, Steve Kim, Diane Garnick, and the late Kevin Augustine.

To thank every colleague at Merrill Lynch who has somehow helped with this effort would require an entire separate book. There are some, however, who deserve special recognition for their help, support, and ideas: Jasper Boersma, Patrick Brady, Mallory Bradshaw, Don Bronstein, Trish Burger, Chris Burns, Bob Ciullo, George Clark, Gerald Cohen, Zee Crocker, Tim Cross, Alastair Coutts, Dan Dolan, Bob Farrell, Sr., Bob Farrell, Jr., Marty Fridson, Frank Gorke, Mike Heffner, Brian Hull, Richard Klein (you still have to pay for a copy though), Steve Lamon, James Lamont, Dick McCabe, Bill McIlroy, Marthe McLinden, Bob Malloy, Andy Melnick, Steve Milunovich, Peter Mitsakos, Jeff Peek, Stan Rubin, Deepak Raj, Jose Rasco, Mason Rees, Susan Riordan, Mike Rothman, William Russell, Ron Santangelo, Stan Shipley, Steve Spence, Bruce Steinberg, John

Sullivan, John Svolos, Tom Truckenmiller, Paul Van Cura, Dave Webb, and Scott Weisenberger.

Thanks also to the many clients who have taught me a great deal about understanding the financial markets. I am particularly grateful to John Raphael and Joe Higgins at Swiss Re, Stan Dinsky and Eli Salzman at Lord Abbett, Bahaa Fam at Fidelity, Bernie Tew at QED Investments, the entire crew at Alliance Capital Management in Minneapolis and Chicago, and Jean Ledford at Evergreen. The "Fun Bunch" deserves special mention: Bill Peterson, Bill Riegel, and Bob Nemeth. In addition, thanks to all my friends and associates in the Chicago Quantitative Alliance and in the Q Group. Thank you to my colleagues on the Hamilton College Endowment Committee whose diverse opinions I always enjoy.

Last, but proverbially not least, I sincerely thank Bill Falloon, Jennifer MacDonald, and Alexia Meyers at John Wiley and Sons, and Bernice Pettinato at Beehive Production Services. Their prodding, patience, and guidance have been wonderful.

I want to emphasize several things. First, the thoughts and ideas expressed in the book are my own and not necessarily shared by the people I have mentioned or by my firm, Merrill Lynch. Second, a critic of my earlier book, *Style Investing*, pointed out that I spelled some of the names incorrectly in the acknowledgement section of that book. That was particularly careless on my part, and I hope I have given a better effort this time. Because of that experience, I specifically remind readers that any errors in the book are mine.

Introduction

"Content is king" is a hackneyed phrase used by firms to rationalize their information strategies. Some firms believe there is so much information available today that only the most relevant or important information will attract viewers, listeners, or readers. Major corporate strategies have been planned and executed based on the "content is king" theory because many firms apparently believe only they offer important information. They take extraordinary measures to get information users to notice and appreciate their superiority. However, have you ever heard a firm admit that their content is a waste of time?

Equity investors today are on the receiving end of all this "content is king" craziness. There are probably too many investment magazines, too many investment websites, too much stock research, and too many investment-related television and radio shows. It is questionable whether investors are getting better investment information today than ever before as many believe. However, regardless of whether or not the quality of information has improved, the price to receive information appears to be high. In exchange for a few bits of important facts, investors are being smothered by useless information. Although some information may indeed rate "king" status, the vast majority of it probably ought to be classified as "junk."

Because of the overwhelming amount of information, "king" is not content but rather the ability to sift the overwhelming amount of data and information that bombards investors today to determine which data are actually relevant. Investors are showered with so much irrelevant information, or noise, that the truly relevant information gets quickly buried or overlooked as being too obvious to be important. Investors probably need a great deal less information than is available to make an informed investment decision. More important, they need less information than they think they need.

Although there is clearly no way to prove this, I believe an increased number of bad investment decisions are being made because of the increased availability of information. Every day I see investors make significant decisions based purely on noise and not on good investment fundamentals. Rumor, innuendo, chat rooms, whisper numbers, and stock price momentum have replaced strategic planning, fundamental research, disciplined investment approaches, and risk analysis. So much information seems to be moving so rapidly that many investors are afraid to be idle because they believe the opportunity cost of not reacting is exceptionally high. Just as the drug addict believes life is impossible without a daily fix, today's investors find it inconceivable that life might be better without so much information. Investors find it hard to believe that ignoring the vast majority of the investment noise might actually improve investment performance. The idea sounds too risky because it is so contrary to their accepted and reinforced actions. (Author's note: As I was reviewing a version of this manuscript on a commuter train to work, I realized that an advertisement for an online investment news service directly opposite me was specifically targeted to reinforce that fear. Its tag line read, "Ignore us at your own risk.")

Sifting information for the few nuggets of gold is certainly important, but so is slowing down the entire investment process. Information seems not only to be abundant, but its flow seems torrential. Investors sometimes seem to be fighting to keep up with the flow, forgetting to stop to understand what is flowing by them. Events appear to happen so fast these days that investors feel the urge to act quickly and frequently. It may be impossible to find the golden nuggets if you do not take the time to examine your sifter. When I was a child, my grandmother thought everyone drove too fast. "Slow down. I want to smell the flowers," she would always say. I think that is good advice for today's investors as well: "Slow down and smell the flowers."

"You have to see the forest through the trees" is an old Wall Street saying. It refers to situations in which we are so bogged down in minutiae, that we do not see the obvious. Today, investors focus on the leaves, and do not even realize that there are branches, trees, and a forest. I see portfolio managers whose desks are covered with more and more quote machines and computer screens as they attempt to keep up with every bit of information produced that might even remotely affect their stocks. In my mind, the more they try to keep up with the flow of information, the further behind they fall.

Let's take a noninvestment example from everyday life to demonstrate how we allow unimportant, trivial, and sometimes inaccurate information to control our lives, while we ignore information that has a high probability of being correct because it *seems* obvious and unimportant. I find that weather forecasts have much in common with Wall Street forecasts. Both sets of forecasters claim to have superior forecasting and timing skills and to utilize improved technology that makes today's forecasts better than in the past.

Every Monday night, a lot of people watch the five-day weather forecast to get a first glimpse of the upcoming weekend's weather. We know the probability is low that Monday's forecast for Saturday will be correct, but we still want to know the forecast. We feel we need the information even though we basically know it is worthless. In fact, we consider those five-day weather forecasts so important that television program directors like to tease us with bits of them and hold the forecasts until the end of the show. (Quite good for Nielson ratings but not for going to bed early.)

In addition, most television stations now advertise the advanced technology their weather forecasters use with the implication that better technology leads to more accurate weather forecasts. If they wanted to truly impress viewers, they would show statistically how inaccurate their forecasts were before the new technology was installed and how much improved the forecasts are subsequent to the installation. I am all for technology, please do not miss the point here, but useful technology should improve our lives. I still cannot set firm plans on Monday for the weekend, and weather-related delays still hamper my travel plans.

There are other weather-related forecasts that are accurate 100% of the time, but we generally consider them worthless or obvious. For example, I can say with nearly 100% accuracy that sane people will not be outdoors wearing shorts, T-shirts, or bathing suits in Minneapolis in late January. An obvious statement, but I bet my prediction is more likely to come true than will this Monday's forecast for Saturday regardless of what new computer or Doppler technology the weatherperson uses.

There are basic conditions that have a very high probability of success in the stock market but are considered mundane or obvious, just as is my forecast for late January in Minneapolis. Instead of paying attention to the obvious routes to success, investors are chasing after every new bit of information produced by every new technology.

This example characterizes the stock market more than most might think. Everyone wants to know how the stock market is going to perform for a finite and typically short period. Often, when I have been interviewed for television, I am steered away from comments that are longer term and have a higher probability of being correct and toward comments regarding what my view is on the stock market's return for the next week or month. The probability of short-term market forecasts being consistently correct is probably no higher than is that associated with Monday's forecast for Saturday's weather.

Some television stations now post reporters on trading floors at exchanges, and they report investment information measured in minutes. Such reporting is very similar to the poor reporters who must give hurricane reports from the waterfront. In one case the reporter is being buffeted by 100-mile-per-hour winds and by traders in the other. In both cases, the reporters tend to report eye-catching but probably worthless information. Yes, there are high winds and strong surf during a hurricane. Yes, stock trading becomes more frantic when unexpected news is announced.

Imagine if an analyst were interviewed on television and simply said a diversified portfolio of stocks outperforms over the long term. The interviewer would most likely comment that everyone knows that fact, but viewers are interested in the analyst's outlook for the market during the next week or subsequent to the 9:30 A.M. open. Whether it is weather (it will be cold in Minneapolis in January) or the stock market (a diversified portfolio of stocks outperforms over the long term), the obvious is rarely good entertainment.

Go one step further with my analogy. Similar to all the new technology used to predict Saturday's weather on Monday, think of all the new technologies being employed to predict superior stock returns: neural networks, quantitative models, Brownian motion, oscillators, behavioral finance, optimization algorithms, options theory, game theory, and on and on. Yet portfolio performance has generally been no better than before these investment technologies existed. Some would argue performance might even be worse than before.

I am often asked what the key is to successful investing. Because I am a so-called quantitative analyst at a major Wall Street firm, people expect me to describe some technologically advanced method. However, my response is nearly always "buy low, sell high." This response gets polite giggles, and people generally ask the question again reminding me that their question was indeed a serious one. My response to their question is indeed somewhat tongue in cheek, but, realistically, I have not met many investors who can consistently buy low and sell high. I do know many whose computer and information budgets are growing exponentially.

This book attempts to help both professional and individual investors sift through all the noise and hype to find true investment information. This is not a how-to book. It will not provide readers with the Holy Grail for picking stocks. This is not a book for day traders who have become information junkies and are so addicted to Wall Street's noise that they have quit their regular jobs. This book will, however, provide simple, and in some cases obvious, concepts of investing that will help investors determine the difference between noise and true investment information.

The book begins by giving the reader some basic background. Chapter 1 defines investment noise and demonstrates how ubiquitous and insidious it is. Chapter 2 discusses noise and the do-it-yourself syndrome that is invading investing. Not everyone will agree with the term *syndrome*, but, regardless, the do-it-yourself mentality is changing the industry. I will state the following right up front: In my opinion, investing by yourself *and* attempting to decipher and digest all the investment noise and hype is a plan for failure or at least for subpar results. Certainly, you can invest by yourself. However, I would suggest that individuals wishing to do so take a boring route with a proven track record: index funds. Chapter 3 outlines how expectations change and, more important, how noise influences investors' expectations.

Chapters 4 through 7 discuss planning, diversification, risk, and risk perception. Investors tend to recklessly bandy these terms with little understanding. Therefore, this group of chapters is as appropriate for professional investors as it is for individual investors. One of the main points of these chapters is that it is virtually impossible to assess your own risk tolerance. Very few people can objectively critique themselves, and the psychological aspect to investing should never be ignored. For example, when asked whether you like to take risk in your investment portfolio, you might respond differently depending on who asked the question. You might not want to appear too wimpy if you had already portrayed yourself as an expert or appear too aggressive if you don't fully trust the person who asked. Also, risk is a relative term. What you might consider extremely risky, someone else might consider very conservative.

Investors' risk tolerances tend to change according to their time horizons. Strategic plans should consider both the time horizon and the timing of future liabilities. If you are saving for a child's college education, your attitude toward risk might be completely different when the child is 3 than when the child is 18 and entering college in several months. Similarly, a pension fund for a very young workforce should be managed quite differently, in my view, from one that has a steady stream of retirees.

Most investors think of diversification as a tool to enhance returns. They are shown charts that imply that mixing assets not only produces higher returns but also helps us sleep at night. One rule that is nearly always true when investing is that there is no "free lunch." Those charts that seem to offer higher returns with less risk generally are based on very long time periods and fail to outline how consistent the returns are year by year. Over a 20- or 30-year period, the combination of assets might indeed yield higher returns with less risk, but that says nothing about shorter-term results. Thus, people diversify and often quickly become disenchanted with the strategy. "If I had only left all my money in XYZ stock, I would have made more than if I had split my investment into three different companies' stocks," they might say. Diversification is a risk-reduction tool, not a return-enhancement tool. If you want to sleep at night, then you diversify. If you want higher returns, then strap on your seatbelt. History has shown that it is extremely rare to achieve very high returns *and* sleep at night. Perhaps more important, I have never seen a study that indicates you can achieve higher returns with less risk by listening to noise and trading more frequently. Noise traders can indeed achieve higher returns but typically must do so while incurring higher risks.

Here is a quick check to see if you have assessed your own risk tolerance correctly. Have you ever been very worried or not been able to sleep when the stock market tumbled on a particular day or when a stock's price was cut in half before you blinked? Do you worry so much that you cannot decide whether to sell the stock because it is going down or to hang on because you think it will rebound? (Be honest!) If you even consider answering these questions affirmatively, then you should familiarize yourself with the risk assessment chapters of this book because the odds are you have incorrectly assessed your own risk tolerance. If you had assessed it properly, then the day-to-day gyrations of the stock market or of a particular stock should have no impact on your ability to sleep at night.

Different investors actually have different concepts of risk. Some consider risk to be the uncertainty of an outcome. Traditional academic studies use this definition and base risk on a statistical measure called *standard deviation*. Others simply define risk as the probability of losing money or the probability of the investment falling short of some goal. Most risk/return studies incorporate the academic definition of risk. However, I have tested many investors to uncover their definitions of risk and more than 95% of them more closely associate risk with the probability of losing money. Later in the book, you can take some simple tests to determine how you define risk.

In addition, we examine time horizons. One of the simplest methods for filtering noise is to extend your time horizon. This technique is probably appropriate for many individual investors, but they tend to ignore it. Individual investors are increasingly saving for their future retirement and should be significantly extending their time horizons unless they are close to retirement. Ironically, their time horizons are getting shorter and shorter. A short time horizon for a long-duration liability does not make a lot of sense. I rarely monitor the performance of the mutual fund in which I invest my IRA. I know they are good managers, so why worry about every gain or loss for an investment I cannot touch for nearly 20 years? This chapter also shows why day trading is a sure route to investment failure.

Next, chapters 8, 9, and 10 examine how to actually filter noise to advantage. These chapters examine what makes a good analyst, outline the differences between a good company and a good stock, and define what makes a good investor. You can filter much noise simply by better understanding the adjective "good."

Truly insightful analysts are rarer than most think. There is a thin line between analysis and reporting, and many analysts simply report. Analysts and portfolio managers tout stocks on television or expertly assert a stock's "story" in the printed financial media. Putting it simply, the story is typically noise. It helps the successful investor very little. You might hear the same story from every analyst who follows the stock, and some might even just parrot a story that the company wants Wall Street to believe. However, research has shown that truly insightful analysts can add tremendous value to the investment process. I outline in Chapter 9 several methods to objectively search for such true insight.

Investors often talk about "good" companies with good management, good products, and good growth prospects. However, believe it or not, "bad" companies significantly outperform "good" companies over the long term. Your focus, then, should probably be on "good" stocks rather than "good" companies. After all, if you know it is a good company, and I know it is a good company, most other investors probably know as well. The odds are the current stock price already reflects the company's quality. Contrary to popular belief, bad companies actually make good stocks. Investors are so afraid of bad companies that they tend to ignore those companies' improving fundamentals. Investors generally become interested only after the consensus asserts that a bad company has turned into a good company.

Chapter 10 examines style investing and what truly drives style rotation. Growth managers tell you growth outperforms over the long term. Value managers tell you value outperforms over the long term. My research suggests that they basically perform the same over the long term, but there are tremendous cycles of style investing that can be used to advantage.

Finally, Chapter 11 is a summary that offers a simple checklist for filtering noise based on the 10 previous chapters.

I try to recognize my potential biases. Some will criticize my views expressed in this book as biased because I work for a major brokerage firm. They might claim I have a vested interest in people believing the playing field cannot be leveled, and there is too much information for individuals to digest. First, I make no assumption that professionals can decipher investment information from noise and hype any more successfully than can individual investors. Even Chapter 2 on do-it-yourself investing is geared toward plan sponsors, portfolio managers, and trust officers as much as toward individual investors. Second, my opinions about investing were what originally led me to work for a major brokerage firm. My firm has not molded my opinions regarding investment strategies and investors' abilities to implement them. Rather, my beliefs have molded my career. The significant changes to our industry during the past five years or so have had no impact on my views regarding what makes an investor successful.

The bull market of the 1990s made many investors feel smart, but it was a false sense of security. Few investors I have met, whether professional or individual, understand the difference between noise and true investment information. Those who do understand the differences are generally quite boring. They are not day traders who overreact to every tiny bit of information, and they don't get their investment ideas from interviews on television. They realize true investment information does not come in two-minute sound bites or tips in a chat room. Rather, they understand that true investment information is relatively rare, but when discovered leads to years, not minutes or days, of outperformance. They would rather sleep at night than trade after hours. They would rather spend time with their children or grandchildren than update price charts every minute. They would rather fish in a stream than watch streaming quotes. They realize that if they have invested intelligently, today's news will probably have little impact on their retirement account or portfolio performance. They generally have a strategic plan, and they stick to it.

I do expect investors to enjoy reading this book, but my guess is few will ultimately follow its guidance. The ever-present noise in the financial markets is very powerful and insidious. There are too many entities selling noise for an investor not to eventually succumb. If readers remember only one thing from this book on navigating noise, I would hope it would be the following: The more investment information there is, the less of it one needs to listen to.

Chapter 1

What Is Noise?

Noise (physics): A usually persistent disturbance that obscures
or reduces the clarity of a signal.

—*American Heritage Dictionary*

We can make more intelligent and informed decisions in today's media,
Internet, and information age than we ever could before. For example, we
can shop more effectively and efficiently by using the Internet because it
provides us with the potential savings of buying an item at lower cost, and
allows us to avoid the time, frustration, and fuel costs of comparison shop-
ping in person. If you are buying a CD by a specific performer on the Internet, the facts are pretty clear. You want the specific CD by the specific
artist. It is easy to decipher the information. There are no intangible issues.
The CD is identical regardless of where you buy it. One online store might
charge $15 with free shipping, whereas another might charge $14 for the
same CD, but charge $5 for the same shipping. The choice is obvious: $15
is cheaper than $19. This discussion would be the same whether it con-
cerned a CD, a car, a TV, or groceries. The goods under consideration are
essentially commodities and are identical regardless of where purchased.
The prices paid, and perhaps follow-up service received, are the primary
discriminating characteristics. Multiply this analogy by the number of
catalogue stores and physical stores, and it is no wonder why Americans
have become so price conscious.

It is arguable, however, whether today's tremendous amount of information regarding investments is similarly beneficial. Most would say it is indeed beneficial because the abundance of information levels the playing field between professional investors and individuals. No longer do select groups benefit from information others do not have. The barriers have been broken down. By using the information on the Internet, in financial magazines and newsletters, and on television and radio, most individual and professional investors now have equal access to investment information.

FORGET "LEVELING THE PLAYING FIELD"—ARE INVESTORS ACTUALLY PROFITING FROM THIS STUFF?

Contrary to what most people believe and many advertisements claim, there have never been barriers that prevented individual investors from obtaining the same information to which professionals had access. Everyone has always had equal access to investment information. Of course, I am referring to legal information. Inside information, stock manipulation, selective disclosure and the like are illegal because they specifically hinder a fair and open market. Legal information has always been available to both the professional and individual investor. Admittedly, it was not necessarily easy to obtain, but it was always available to the investor who wanted to spend the time acquiring the information. Even professional investors had to work harder to obtain information before the invention of computers, financial databases, stock quote machines, and financial television channels (although some would loathe the inclusion of the latter!). The media and information age and the Internet have not broken down some romantic David and Goliath notion of a barrier between individual and professional investors. They have simply made it easier for *everyone* to obtain information.

The point is not whether the playing field has been leveled and whether individual investors have the same tools as professionals. Rather, it is whether all this information is actually helping people invest more profitably regardless of whether they are professionals or individuals. In other words, is anyone actually making money from all this stuff? Some investors might indeed be benefiting, but my guess is the vast majority of investors' portfolios are not performing better because of the increased availability of information.

Investment information is easier to obtain, and there certainly are many more sources of investment information than there were only a short time ago. That, in and of itself, is actually a problem in my view. The more information available to us, the more we must necessarily understand to make the information worthwhile, to extract useful information from the noise. The more numerous the sources of information, the longer we must search for one having the best answer to our inquiry. There is a tradeoff between the time needed to understand and digest information and the incremental benefit derived from it. Thus, the spreading abundance of information means the marginal benefit of additional information may be negative. It is not a problem that people have greater access to information. The problem is the greater availability of information may be hurting the investment process instead of helping it. We no longer have to search for information, but we now must spend more time assessing its relevance and hoping we have analyzed the important issue correctly.

Information is increasingly easier to obtain regardless of an investor's level of sophistication. Everyone has greater access to information. The advantages that exist for professional investors, and will always exist if you ask me, are attributable to the simple fact that they are professionals and not because they have privileged access to information. The professional's advantage did not disappear as news dissemination evolved from the town crier to the nightly news, yet it is curious that everyone now thinks the playing field has miraculously been leveled. Personally, I think it is impossible to completely level the playing field. We might be smarter investors to admit it. People do not attempt to remove their own gall bladders. Few of us would attempt to defend ourselves in an important court case. However, it is odd that an increasing number of people believe that professional advice is unnecessary to manage their wealth despite the financial markets' increased complexities.

The persistence of a professional advantage does not mean that the problems associated with Wall Street's media and information age are any different for professional investors than they are for individuals. In fact, the pressure portfolio managers feel today to perform well may make it more important for professionals to correctly decipher noise than it is for individuals.

THE AVAILABILITY OF INFORMATION IS CONSTANTLY EVOLVING

Some might view the current availability of financial information as something new, but the availability of investment information, and of all information for that matter, is constantly evolving. Realistically, today's media and information age is no different from any period in history in that information is easier to obtain today than it previously was, and is presently harder to obtain than it will be in the future. Unless we live in a society in which town criers still give the news, the odds are that investment information has consistently been easier to obtain through time. Before the widespread distribution of financial newspapers and telephones, individual investors needed to physically go to the exchange to get timely information. Professional investors would send runners and messengers. Later, with the spread of news services and ticker tapes, investors only needed to telephone their brokers or go to their brokers' offices. When I was a child, many retirees would sit for hours in brokerage offices to watch the ticker. Some brokerage offices even had chairs arranged as in a theater for customers to be comfortable while staring at the ticker. Today, tickers are personalized so you can watch on your computer only the stock symbols about which you care. The communal ticker is obsolete and is basically used today for decoration and effect.

The ticker may be a simple but very good example of the evolution of information dissemination. The original tickers were based on the telegraph/teletype. A stream of paper would flow from a machine that deciphered code. Only one person at a time could read the flowing ticker tape. That technology eventually evolved into the electronic streaming ticker that fostered the theater motif I mentioned earlier. Many people could stare at the ticker at the same time. Next came the streaming ticker that appeared on the bottom of your television screen, and now it is the streaming ticker on a website. However, the rapid spread of quote machines during the 1970s made the streaming ticker obsolete. No longer did investors have to watch the ticker to see how their stock was trading, they could monitor only the stocks they chose. The electronic streaming ticker evolved from high technology and a leap in information availability to a commodity of relatively little value.

THE INTERNET IS MERELY PART OF AN EVOLUTION

Information has become a commodity, but the Internet is not solely responsible. As mentioned, information has always increasingly become a commodity. The Internet is simply the next phase of improved information flow. Roughly speaking, from Pony Express to telegraph, from telegraph to telephone, from telephone to radio and television, from radio and television to computer, from computer to timesharing, from timesharing to personal computer, and from personal computer to Internet, an individual's access to information increased every step of the way. Think of all the sources of information that you have access to in your home: potentially hundreds of television stations, magazines, newspapers, radio, Internet sites, and, of course, word of mouth.

Has the Internet actually changed things? Of course it has and of course it will, but we should keep in mind that each generation at some point believes they are reliving some form of the industrial revolution. The Internet appears to be our generation's iteration. At the risk of being repetitive, the Internet is merely the latest stage of the evolution of information dissemination. It provides us with more information than we previously had, but less than we will have. In this respect, there is little that is different today.

IF THE PLAYING FIELD HASN'T BEEN LEVELED, THEN WHY HAVE INDIVIDUAL INVESTORS' PORTFOLIOS PERFORMED SO WELL?

Chapter 2 discusses the irony of how nonprofessionals believe they know as much or more than professionals almost regardless of the industry, but let's touch on it briefly here.

Because of the odd construction of the bull market during the last few years and the resulting outperformance of some individual investors' portfolios, some might disagree with the preceding statements regarding the inherent advantage that professionals have over individual investors. An increasing number of investors believe they are smarter than their mutual fund manager, and have decided to liquidate their mutual fund holdings in order to trade individual stocks. During 1998 and 1999, many individual investors' portfolios performed well, which seemed to justify their decisions to liquidate their mutual funds.

Some self-managed portfolios might have outperformed during that period, but it might have been attributable to luck rather than to skill. Figure 1.1 shows that nearly 70% of the technology stocks in the S&P 500 outperformed the index itself during 1999, while a vast majority of stocks underperformed in most other sectors. The odds of investing in an

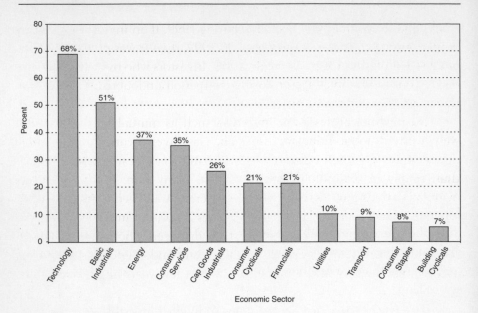

Figure 1.1   **Percent of Stocks by Economic Sector That Outperformed the S&P 500 Index in 1999**
Based on data from Merrill Lynch Quantitative Strategy.

underperforming technology stock in 1999 were quite low because almost all of them outperformed. Individual investors and day traders tended to focus primarily on the technology sector during 1999, and their portfolio performance during the year was generally quite good. With 70% of the stocks in the sector outperforming, though, it is very hard to attribute to skill such stock selection that led to outperformance. Given that nearly the entire sector outperformed, it was probably a waste of time for investors to attempt to pick the best technology stock. They probably should simply have bought a basket of technology stocks or a technology mutual fund and gone to play golf with their free time.

Concentrating a portfolio in the technology sector was the correct strategy. I don't mean to belittle that strategy as it worked very well. However, few investors probably understood the risks of not diversifying into other sectors. Few cared about diversification when the technology sector outperformed, but everyone cared when it subsequently underperformed.

At the other extreme, the probability of picking an underperforming consumer staples stock was quite high because 92% of all consumer staples stocks underperformed the S&P 500 during 1999. If an investor picked an outperforming consumer staples stock in 1999, then it was probably attributable to old-fashioned stock picking skill. Investors who overweighted the entire consumer staples sector during this period undoubtedly found that their portfolios performed miserably.

Meanwhile, professional investors, such as mutual fund managers, were worried about fiduciary issues such as diversification and capital preservation. They felt obligated to invest in a broader universe of stocks than simply in technology stocks. In fact, many were prohibited from overconcentrating in a specific sector or were not allowed to invest in the technology sector at all. Hindsight is always 20/20, but imagine how critical investors would have been of portfolio managers who had put 80% of their funds into technology stocks had the sector underperformed instead of outperformed? Many of the heroes of the past few years might have been goats.

The 1999 experience has led many individual investors to think they are better investors than are mutual fund managers. I have overheard many discussions in which someone laments that some fund manager just doesn't get it and that the manager should be investing in technology stocks and nothing else.

Sellers of information have quickly jumped on the idea that individual investors can compete with professionals and have encouraged a strong do-it-yourself attitude. We also discuss in Chapter 2 whether the do-it-yourself trend is really in individual investors' best interest, or whether the promoters of the trend might actually benefit more than do investors. Also, as some investors subsequently learned, they were taking considerably more risk than they anticipated by investing in only one sector. In many cases, their large positive returns of 1999 turned into large negative returns in 2000, while the mutual fund managers who were so derided only several months earlier either posted gains or did not suffer losses of nearly the same magnitude.

NOISE IS MORE INFORMATION WITHOUT BETTER INFORMATION

The media and information age and the Internet have brought us more information but not necessarily better information, a subtle but extremely important distinction. Investors ideally want better information rather than more information. However, in this new age we have seen the increased quantity of information pretty much without any consistent improvement in quality. To make matters worse, some might legitimately argue that the advent of the Internet allows any quack to provide investment advice. Thus, there could actually be an increased flow of information with a worsening of quality.

More information without better information can result in a lot of wasted time and poor decision making. It might actually take more work to uncover worthwhile information if there is more information without better information. We would all like to read one investment report, act on it, produce large returns, and go about our business. Instead we are flooded with information we really do not need. It is conceivable, therefore, that investors might actually be worse off today than they were 5 or 10 years ago despite Wall Street's new information age.

More information without better information is noise. As aptly demonstrated in many commercials for headache remedies, it is sometimes hard to think when your children are yelling at you, the phone is ringing, and the television is blaring. Drivers turn down the volume on their car radios when they get lost because the noise makes it more difficult to concentrate on the directions and street signs. The same things happen to investors. There is so much commotion that they have trouble concentrating on the important facts. Investors seem increasingly pressured and befuddled as more and more information becomes available.

If the volume of information were negated by its new superior quality, then investment performance should have demonstrably improved. As noted, however, performance has not really improved. It appears as though the new age of information, media, and hype has not been clearly beneficial. It may be interesting to know more facts and learn about more companies than before, but why should we care about all this new information unless it improves portfolio performance?

MORE TIMELY INFORMATION ISN'T NECESSARILY BETTER INFORMATION

Investors make the common mistake of confusing more timely information with better information. Timeliness of data is completely independent of the quality of the information. It is sometimes easier to issue information of poorer quality more rapidly than it is to issue high quality information. Information can be disseminated much more rapidly if we do not have to check facts or check for editorial consistency, for example. My own research reports would go out to clients more quickly if they did not have to be approved by my firm's legal and compliance departments. When it comes to disseminating information, being first does not necessarily mean being best.

We must certainly differentiate between delayed data and stale data. Clearly, reports issued today about events that occurred weeks or months ago are not very helpful to investors unless they offer some unique insight that relates to today's events or provide a different historical perspective. I think most readers will agree with me on this particular point.

However, today there is a rush to get information minute by minute, second by second, tick by tick, and revision by revision. The implicit assumption is that investors' returns will suffer if they do not keep up with the market's "real-time" data. Many believe market leaders pay very close attention to real-time data. However, suppose the leader is the first lemming ready to jump off a cliff. Should we define the leader's actions as insight or foolishness?

In my experience, I have found that more timely investment information is often just noise. This comment may sound very strange to some. As I mentioned, investors today assume that more timely information is necessarily better, and it may be inconceivable to some investors that I would want to ignore the most up-to-date (up-to-the-minute?) information available. If the market discounts information quickly, how could one possibly get in front of the market using old, stale data? Perhaps "old" and "stale" are not synonyms. The following example might prove helpful.

I have a stock selection model, called the EPS Surprise Model, that is based on analysts' earnings estimates. I have been running the model since June 1989, and it was back-tested to early 1986. The long or "buy" portfolios produced by this model have consistently outperformed the overall market, while the short or "sell" portfolios have consistently underperformed. The long portfolio alone (ignoring the hedging potential of the short portfolio) has historically outperformed the market while incurring less risk. Keeping in mind that past performance tells us little about future results, the model has historically been a terrific stock selection model. The long portfolio has outperformed its benchmark during 11 of the past

14 years, while the short portfolio has similarly underperformed during 11 of those years. Figure 1.2 shows the historical performance of this model relative to its benchmark. We discuss the details of this model in Chapter 9.

Despite the outstanding performance depicted in Figure 1.2, some still find it odd that the data used within the model is updated only monthly. The model uses month-end earnings estimates, and we do not incorporate intramonth estimate revisions. I am often asked why we ignore the availability of real-time earnings estimates and run the model on old, stale data.

An investor once quite effectively incorporated this particular model into his investment strategy using our month-end data, but he got greedy. His performance was so successful using month-end data that he fell into the trap of assuming more timely data was necessarily better data, and more timely data would improve his performance beyond his already excellent returns. He rebuilt our model to incorporate the latest available earnings data on a real-time basis. He ended up losing a lot of money for two reasons. First, his trading costs began to escalate because the increased flow of infor-

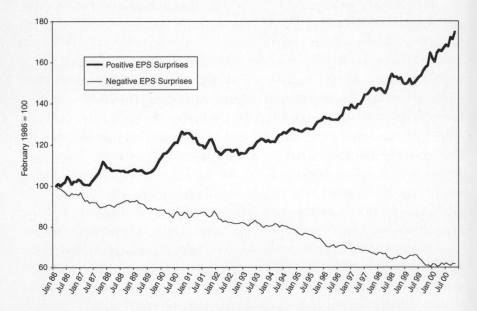

Figure 1.2   **Relative Performance of Earnings per Share Surprise Model**

mation made it difficult for him to determine what was noise and what was true investment information. As a result, he traded much more frequently and haphazardly. He hurt his performance by trading more on noise than on investment fundamentals, and to make matters worse his transaction costs began to escalate as well. Second, he now had a larger number of decisions to make, and the simple probability of making poor decisions began to rise. He turned a successful and disciplined investment strategy based on well-measured forecasted information into an unsuccessful, random, high-turnover trading strategy that reacted to noise.

NOISE OBSCURES INSIGHT

Users of real-time earnings data may actually ignore the information of insightful analysts. I do not have a particularly positive opinion of some real-time data because it seems to me we get to watch those investors who generally have no particular insight catch up to those who do. For example, let's assume an analyst has great insight regarding the earnings of company XYZ. She makes a forecast on January 1st for the full-year's earnings and never changes the estimate during the year. Further, let's assume that the estimate turns out to be correct. The analyst has made one estimate for the company's earnings, never changed the estimate, and forecasted correctly. Sounds like a very good analyst to me.

However, the earnings estimate of such an incredibly insightful analyst might actually be dropped from some real-time databases because she did not update the estimate within a certain number of months. The estimate, simply because it has not been changed, is considered stale. The earnings estimates of other analysts who could not forecast well the company's earnings would probably remain in the database because they frequently update their earnings estimates. By year-end, all analysts might have the exact same estimate, but who really provided the value? The analyst who correctly forecasted the outcome one year before it occurred or the analysts who repeatedly changed their estimates while trying to understand the factors that caused the final outcome?

Perhaps more important, the analysts who constantly changed estimates and buy/sell/hold ratings were probably the ones who were interviewed in the press, appeared on television, or more frequently spoke on their firms' morning calls. Imagine an interview on television in which a reporter interviews an insightful analyst regarding company XYZ:

Reporter: "You were on our show at the beginning of the year. Your above-consensus estimate for company XYZ was $1.00 and you had a buy rating on the stock. What has changed since we last spoke?"

Insightful Analyst: "Nothing, actually. It remains our favorite stock in the group."

Reporter (incredulously): "Nothing?"

Insightful Analyst: "No, nothing. The company is progressing as we thought it would."

Not exactly a scintillating interview and certainly not good for ratings. The interview might sound much more exciting and might be better for ratings if the reporter interviewed the following analyst. Keep in mind that we have the advantage of knowing the company eventually earned $1.00 as the insightful analyst originally predicted.

Reporter: "You were on our show at the beginning of the year, and your estimate for the company was $0.75. In addition, you had a neutral rating on the stock. What has changed since we last spoke?"

Analyst: "A lot has changed. The company reported a positive earnings surprise in the latest quarter. We subsequently raised our earnings estimate to $0.85 based on the company's stronger-than-expected order trends and international growth. In addition, we raised our rating on the stock to a buy. It is now our favorite stock in the group."

The second analyst *sounds* more interesting, but the story that the analyst is telling was already uncovered by the insightful analyst months before. In fact, given the hindsight we have in this example, the second analyst is going to raise estimates at least one more time. Although the second analyst might appear quite informed about the story associated with the stock and certainly promotes interest in the stock, listening to the insightful analyst from the beginning of the year might have been better for investment performance.

This example may seem simplified, but it is remarkably close to what frequently happens. Real-time data added excitement to the scenario, but it also added noise. The noise distracts us from the fact that the analyst who was repeatedly altering estimates may not be very insightful, while the analyst who is indeed insightful gets ignored or, worse, is considered boring.

HYPE: THE GOALS OF INFORMATION PROVIDERS AND INFORMATION USERS ARE NOT NECESSARILY THE SAME

The goals of information providers and information users are sometimes very different. As information increasingly becomes a commodity, the competition intensifies among information providers to gain information users' attention. Providers must differentiate their information from the pack.

The journalist Daniel Schorr recently noted that reporters must differentiate between events and what he calls pseudoevents.[1] According to Schorr, there are true newsworthy events, but there are also staged or hyped productions made to resemble events. In the particular commentary to which I refer, Schorr discussed political conventions and the attempts by political parties to direct or control the news flow from the convention to their advantage.

Investors must similarly differentiate events from pseudoevents. We should not merely assume the information flow in the financial markets is truly made of important events. Many sources of information create pseudoevents to attract or direct our attention (not necessarily maliciously). Nonetheless, sources of investment information are hardly objective. Each source wants to prove its importance and relevance versus its competition.

In a simple sense, there are two methods for differentiating one source's information from that of others. Information can be truly more insightful, accurate, and useful. The focus of the information could be on quality. However, as I have pointed out, quality does not always make good entertainment. Alternatively, the information can be hyped to make it seem more exciting. For example, the goal of an eye-catching headline of a tabloid newspaper might be to increase readership and not necessarily to convey accuracy. The advertising for the nightly news tends to accentuate aspects of news reports the network believes will entice viewers to watch the news program later that evening.

Users of the information might want accurate information, but the primary goal of the provider of the information might be to gain more users, readers, or viewers. Consider the following anecdote. Several years ago my wife and I hosted a holiday party. The night before the party the New York area had a rather severe winter storm. The following day, I drove all around the area in which we live to check the roads, knowing we would get calls from our guests inquiring whether the party was still on and if the roads were safe to drive. The roads were not only clear by midafternoon, but they were also generally dry thanks to a clear sky and plenty of sunshine. As it turned out, 14 of the 16 couples invited to the party did attend. I thought it was odd that the two couples who did not attend the party both gave the identical reason for not attending (in fact, nearly word for word). They both said they had been watching a cable television weather channel, and the weather forecasters were saying that the roads in the New York area could be excessively slippery and driving could be hazardous.

Most people probably watch a weather-related channel thinking they will get the most accurate and unbiased weather information because the channel employs experts. They forget, however, that the channel has only one thing to sell to viewers, namely, the weather, and the channel is competing for viewers' attention with potentially hundreds of other channels. If on the day of the party, the weather anchor had said "bad storm last night in the New York area, but things are clear and fine now," then my friends probably would have quickly channel surfed to some other cable channel or turned off their television and attended our party. However, the weather anchor probably said something like "bad storm last night in the New York area. Are the roads safe in the aftermath? Stay with us and after the break we will fill you in on all the potential hazardous driving conditions." My guess is that embellished teasers and comments such as these kept my friends watching the channel. They made their decision based on potentially exaggerated (although technically accurate) reporting, and they missed what I consider to be the premiere social event of the holiday season.

The main point to this example is that my friends, the users of the information, assumed their goal was the same as the goal of the information provider, the cable weather channel. That assumption led them to make a poor decision. The goal of the channel's management was to keep my friends watching that particular channel and to sell more advertising time. However, my friends' goal was to get an accurate portrayal of the road conditions in the New York area.

Most investment strategists would suggest an appropriate benchmark for asset allocation is something close to 60% stocks, 30% bonds, and 10% cash or perhaps 65% stocks and 35% bonds. These figures are based on historical studies that indicate such combinations offer a combination of risk and return most investors would find safe and appealing. Actual asset allocations differ from these figures depending on an individual's or a pension fund's risk tolerance and asset/liability issues.

If those asset allocation benchmarks are appropriate for the broad range of investors, is it unreasonable to ask why the news flow is not divided 65% on equity market information and 35% on bond information? I can get a tremendous amount of information about investing when I watch television, read the daily financial pages, read business periodicals, or log on to investment websites. However, it is disproportionately focused on equities, with very little information regarding bonds or money markets.

As noted, quality information does not always make for good entertainment, and bonds just are not as exciting as stocks. A discussion of government versus agency versus mortgage debt might be important to investors, but I doubt that it will ever be as exciting as the initial public offering of a new genetic engineering or Internet company. Ladder, bullet, and barbell strategies should be important considerations for nearly every fixed-income investor, but a discussion about those topics will never be as eye-catching as is the daily measurement of the gain or loss in technology CEO wealth caused by NASDAQ's gyrations.

The media will correctly argue that readers and viewers prefer stories about stocks rather than about bonds. However, the users of such news flow should understand that equities dominate the news not because of their importance in the financial markets (global debt markets are bigger than global equity markets), but, rather, because the providers of the information realize equities are better entertainment. Information providers may skew the information toward equities because it is in their best interest to do so regardless of what might best benefit investors.

A reasonable consideration is whether any information provider's management has a greater interest in keeping information users glued to the information than in providing accurate and straight reporting. There have always been conflicts between editorial interests and business interests, but my guess is such conflicts are becoming more numerous in a broader range of media. A recent newspaper report highlighted the conflict between a well-respected television anchor and her network as the network attempted to leverage her reputation to add "reality" to a new show. Evidently, the anchor thought the demands made on her by the entertainment division of the network were compromising her status as a respected journalist. The report compares the demands made on her by the entertainment division to the criticism given by her colleagues in the news division.[2] Most investors do not seem to be considering such issues when using information to make their investment decisions. They assume everything is news and nothing is entertainment.

Investors should also skeptically view information that comes directly from companies. Many companies now employ sophisticated investor relations departments whose purpose is to attempt to put a positive spin on every company event. Figure 1.3 highlights the increased proportion of positive earnings surprises reported by S&P 500 companies during the late 1990s and 2000. The unusually strong U.S. economy is certainly responsible for some of that positive news. However, adroit investor relations officers might be behind some of those surprises as well. I would not be surprised to find some companies guiding Wall Street analysts toward expected earnings outcomes, and then reporting earnings that beat the targeted figures. Positive surprises come more easily if you work to lower expectations.

I am constantly amazed that investors do not question a company that reports positive surprises quarter after quarter despite frequent communication with Wall Street analysts. It seems to me a company that constantly surprises either is doing so because they know investors like positive sur-

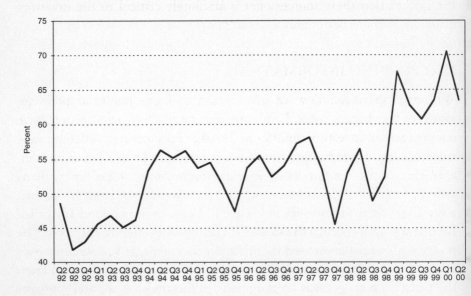

Figure 1.3   **Percent of S&P 500 Companies That Reported Positive Earnings Surprises**

prises and they have lowered the hurdle, or because management does not have adequate control mechanisms to monitor the company's businesses.

I have advised some companies to provide clear and consistent information regarding their business prospects. Although all companies want their stock to outperform the market, ultimately they should also worry about the volatility of their stock. The ability to attract investors and capital depends not only on stock price performance but also on the consistency of that performance. A company that manufactures earnings surprises could see its stock price repeatedly jump up on the positive news, but such price movements could potentially increase the longer-term volatility or risk of its stock, which, in turn, raises its cost of capital. Thus, while some companies have chosen to play the short-term, noise-producing game of manufacturing positive surprises, that choice might someday come back to haunt them.

In this latest version of the information age, we must be increasingly critical of the investment information we receive. The investment information business has become so competitive during the past 10 to 15 years that it has become difficult to find a source of unbiased or accurate investment information. It may be in the best business interests of the financial media, whether it be print or television or website, to have investors believe the information these sources offer is absolutely critical to the investors' future investment performance. As in many cases, it is *caveat emptor*.

DECIPHERING INFORMATION

With this increased flow of information and the potential problems investors face because of it, I am somewhat surprised that few people have commented on investors' abilities to decipher information. Differentiating true investment information from noise is difficult. I know a portfolio manager who got his first taste of cable television financial programming many years ago when he was at home sick one day. While watching, he heard a story about one of the stocks he owned in his portfolio and quickly called his trader to find out how the stock was trading in reaction to the news. The trader was somewhat amused that the portfolio manager was so concerned about a stock that was actually trading quite normally. A short while later, the portfolio manager was on the phone to the trader again and was concerned about a second stock. The trader again told the portfolio manager that nothing special was happening. The trader suggested that the manager get some rest, for it seemed as though the manager's virus was doing something to his thinking. After another short period, the manager was again calling the trader. This time the trader hung up.

The lesson from this story is that even experienced, professional money managers have trouble deciphering true investment information from noise when they do not know well the source of the information and therefore cannot determine the information's importance and accuracy.

Perhaps the best example regarding investors' inability or unwillingness to decipher information, and their willingness to trade purely on noise involved an error in reporting. A television station reported that a brokerage firm was upgrading its recommendation on a stock with the ticker symbol MACC. Unfortunately, the correct symbol was AMCC. MACC is the symbol for MACC Private Equities, Inc., a company with a market capitalization of only $17 million, while AMCC is the symbol for Applied Micro Circuits Corporation, a company with a market capitalization of roughly $20 billion at the time. Not a single Wall Street research analyst followed MACC, while AMCC was covered by 16 analysts. Regardless, investors watching that particular station began to buy MACC based on the station's reporting without checking to see if the reported information was correct. To better understand the magnitude of this example, MACC typically did not trade more than several hundred shares per day and did not trade at all on some days. However, there were 344,000 shares traded on the day of the inaccurate report (see Figure 1.4). The stock nearly doubled before everyone, including the television station, realized a mistake had been made, at which time the stock nearly halved back to its original price. I would guess the folks who traded those 344,000 shares did so purely on noise and did not base their buy orders on good fundamental research or even a technical chart. These traders clearly did not confirm the information, or even look to see if anyone actually followed the company. It would have taken only a few seconds to filter noise from information to determine that the report was inaccurate.

We can identify less visible cases of investors who trade on noise by tracking activity in chat rooms. It seems as though investors do not differentiate whether the person making a statement about a company in a chat room is a Wall Street analyst, a 12-year old having fun, or someone trying to manipulate the stock to his or her own advantage. An experienced NASDAQ trader once commented to me that he occasionally traded during the

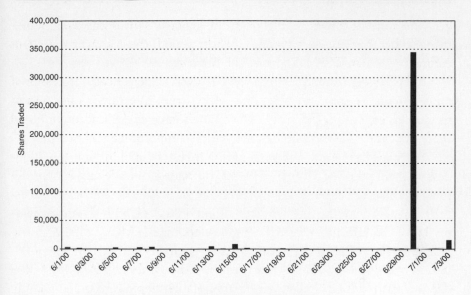

Figure 1.4 **Daily Volume of MACC Shares Traded**

day by watching the chat rooms. By simply watching what was being said in the chat rooms each morning he was able to anticipate how day traders would act. He would then get better prices on his trades given the transparency of their actions. If investors truly believe that the playing field has been leveled between individual investors and professionals, they should talk to this trader to learn why it may not be so. He is aware of the noise, understands well how others will act given its presence, and then uses that knowledge to his advantage.

It is becoming increasingly important for investors to fully understand how information is hyped even about seemingly mundane issues. The media will sometimes comment that the market seems to be taking a certain economic statistic "in stride," and that the reading of this important statistic must have been "already discounted." Television might quickly cut to their reporter on the floor of the T-bond futures pit, only to hear that the bond market is having a "muted" reaction. One should question whether the market has indeed taken the economic statistic in stride or whether it never cared about the statistic in the first place. Was the media giving us important insights regarding the market's reaction to an important economic statistic, or were they creating noise regarding a statistic that few care about?

Many of the chapters in this book look specifically at different methods for deciphering true investment information from noise. Most have a common theme: Ignore most of the available information, slow down the investment process, and trade less frequently.

NOISE IS EXPENSIVE

Investors often neglect transaction costs when compiling investment returns. They typically take the percent change between the price at which they sold the stock and the price at which they bought the stock. Such calculations ignore the costs involved in trading a stock. Of course, the investor must take into account broker commissions, bid/ask spreads, processing costs, market impact, and, perhaps most germane to this book, the costs of acquiring and processing information. Commissions are only one part of transaction costs although they get the most attention.

Noise can be very expensive for two reasons. First, we tend to trade more frequently when noise is prevalent. Second, we must pay for the information and the opportunity cost of deciphering it. Let's examine both reasons.

As I described in my example about the investor who altered my stock selection model to incorporate noise, noise tends to make us believe events are changing more rapidly than they really are. The perception leads us to trade more often in order to attempt to keep up with the changing markets. If we were to ignore noise and pay attention only to the true investment information, then we would tend to trade less frequently. Investors who do not trade on noise are more likely to realize events do not change very quickly, and the allowable time to trade an outstanding investment is probably quite long.

Perhaps a larger component of transaction costs is called *market impact*. There are debates on how to properly measure market impact, but a common simple definition used is the difference in performance between a paper portfolio and an actual portfolio. Market impact is typically higher if you are a noise trader because you are trading with a herd mentality. If everyone were attempting to sell a stock based on a bad earnings announcement or the like, sell trades would swamp buy trades, and the stock's price would obviously go down. If you placed an at-the-market trade in this example, your paper portfolio might significantly outperform your actual portfolio. A sell might be entered at $30 but might get executed at $27,

$25, or $23, depending on the magnitude of the negative surprise and the general liquidity in the stock.

Consider this example in the context of the insightful analyst discussed earlier. The insightful analyst might have seen the company's problems months earlier than consensus, and she might have been selling the stock when everyone else was still buying. Market impact could conceivably have been positive if she had entered the trade with proper instructions. Thus, noise trading and its resulting market impact can be expensive because they can significantly hurt portfolio performance.

Noise can also be expensive because we must pay for all the information that seems so valuable. Quote services, research services, newsletters, databases, and various software subscription fees are just a few to name. It is common for institutional investors to spend hundreds of thousands of dollars on database subscriptions alone.

Momentum investors are today's well-known noise traders, and good ones tend to have huge technology budgets. They buy stocks on good news and hold them until the first hint of bad news, at which time they eliminate or significantly reduce their positions. One of the only ways to digest noise faster and get in front of other noise traders is to have a bigger and better computer system than anyone else. Sophisticated voice mail and e-mail, real-time databases, and huge computers to wade nonstop through all the information are mandatory for the successful institutional momentum investor.

Meanwhile, old-fashioned value investors are at the other end of the spectrum. They rarely trade on noise, and have the computer budgets to prove it. Their buy-and-hold mentality makes the real-time data arsenal rather superfluous. After all, placing a trade five minutes earlier or later is rather meaningless if your average holding period is three to five years.

I do not mean to imply that value managers are necessarily any smarter than momentum managers. There are successful and unsuccessful managers within both clans. My point is that computer budgets and portfolio turnover tend to be lower for value managers than for momentum managers.

Once you have information, there is an opportunity cost that must be assumed to decipher all the information for which you now pay. This is impossible to measure, but I attempt to measure it with respect to my own needs by how much I learn from a source. People are often surprised to hear that I do not regularly read certain daily financial newspapers. They are shocked that I do not want to keep up with what is going on in the markets. I don't subscribe for two reasons. First, I rarely learn anything insightful from these particular newspapers. If you subscribe to a lot of data or information providers and believe that all of them provide insight and are invaluable because you are learning from all of those sources, I suggest that you leave your investing up to someone who might know more about investing than you do. This remark is not meant to be disdainful at all, but the inability to determine expertise is typically a sign of a novice in any industry.

Second, I do not necessarily want to *keep up* with the market. The more you attempt to keep up and be aware of everything that is going on, the more susceptible you are to trading on noise. I would rather willingly admit that there are short-term topics in the stock market about which I am unaware, than not to understand more fully the major events in the market. Using a previous analogy, I prefer to see the forest rather than the trees.

NOISE IS MORE FUN

For some, paying attention to noise makes investing more fun and exciting. Trading floors, the centers of noise, tend to constantly buzz with excitement as traders react to the ebb and flow of noise. Traders run from post to post, shout to be heard, and sometimes even get injured. Television reporters prefer to interview analysts from the trading floor because it sets a more dynamic background for the interview than does a studio or someplace quiet. Many investors want to feel the same excitement.

Let's face it, noise is fun. It keeps us entertained. We like talking about our recent gain in a stock we picked, or telling someone else about a hot stock with which they are not familiar. We like trading frequently because it is more fun, not because we have to do so. After all, a diversified portfolio of stocks tends to outperform over the long term, so why not buy a diversified portfolio and simply hold it? It is boring.

Unfortunately, noise turns investing into a hobby. Some people build model airplanes, some travel, some golf, but more and more people *play* the stock market. Again, I may be biased, but I do not think building wealth should be treated as a hobby. Noise may be fun, but I would rather do other things in my spare time and get higher returns.

TUNE OUT THE SIREN'S SONG

In the musical and movie *Tommy*, characters put on blinders so they cannot see, put in ear plugs so they cannot hear, and put corks in their mouths so they cannot speak in an attempt to tune out the world. The show is actually a pretty good analogy for successful investing. Many of the subsequent chapters describe methods for filtering noise and deciphering true investment information from hype. In a way, these are the blinders, earplugs, and corks of successful investing.

Noise is the siren's song of investing. Like the siren's song of mythology, its allure is irresistible and its promises great. However, once you succumb to the temptation, the reward never matches the promise.

Chapter 2

The Risks of Do-It-Yourself Investing: What You Don't Know Could Hurt Your Performance

It is ironic that we think we understand other peoples' businesses better than they do, but get terribly defensive when other people say they understand our businesses better than we do. Personally, I think I would be a better CEO than are most companies' CEOs, would be a better Congressman than is my Congressman, and would be a better coach of the New York Knicks than is their coach. However, dreaming and doing are different things. I might think I know a lot about medicine, but I am not about to repair my own hernia.

The do-it-yourself (DIY) attitude is growing in society. From home improvement to nutrition and health to legal issues, we increasingly feel the advice of an expert is unnecessary. As a result, some of the country's most successful consumer-oriented companies during the last decade or so have been based on this growing DIY trend.

Some jobs can be adequately done without professional help. With little detailed training, you can adequately paint a house, build a new bookshelf, tend a garden, or cook a tasty meal. With a little more training, you could adequately tune your car or sew a gown from a bolt of cloth. With considerably more training, you could go into business to do these things for others.

The key word in the preceding paragraph is "adequately." Rarely are DIY projects of the same quality as those done by professionals. Most of us have other jobs and responsibilities and cannot spend the time or effort needed to produce a top-quality DIY job. Of course, there are exceptions. I have a friend whose hobby is construction, and the quality of his work is excellent. He is completely renovating a second home with the help of only his construction-conscripted wife. However, the overall project will take him more than 10 years to finish. There is obviously a tradeoff between the quality he wishes to achieve and the time it will take him to reach that goal doing it by himself as a hobby.

ARE YOU REALLY AN EXPERT? WHAT YOU DON'T KNOW CAN HURT YOU

We will all admit that professionals must do certain things. However, it seems as though we increasingly consult those professionals only as a last resort, or we decide that an alternate route is preferable to the traditional course of action. The use of alternative medicines is growing in the United States, for example. Some of these remedies may truly provide benefits beyond those offered by traditional medicine. However, some may be beneficial for reasons other than those advocated by providers, or they may have absolutely no remedial effect whatsoever. To my knowledge, the Food and Drug Administration (FDA) has tested only a few alternative medicines, and users typically do not know the alternative medicines' side effects or drug interactions. Yet, when traditional doctors question the use of some alternative medicines, they are maligned as trying to protect their own businesses and profits. I am certainly not naive enough to believe that doctors and their supporting associations are completely altruistic. However, it is curious that simple advertisement is proof enough for some people to trust their health to such alternative products or supplements, and that such advertising is sometimes considered more honest and trustworthy than is rigorous FDA testing. I am surprised that people with whom I discuss this issue often say the companies selling some of these alternative or supplement products could not make the claims they do if the products did not provide the benefits advertised. In other words, as good consumers they know more about health than does a doctor, and a doctor is simply moti-

vated by profit maximization. I suppose these self-proclaimed good consumers also believe that those who sell alternative medicines are not the
least bit interested in making a profit.

A recent article in the popular press pointed out that, because of the
Dietary Supplements Health and Education Act of 1994, the FDA does not
regulate alternative medicines or supplements. Thus, "supplements don't
get the same premarket safety and efficacy evaluations that drugs get, nor
does the FDA set standards to ensure that labels accurately reflect con-
tents." (Admittedly, the author of the article is a traditional doctor.[1])
Given that more than one-third of the ginseng brands tested in a particular cited study were found to contain pesticides and lead, both of which are
obviously harmful, it is pretty clear that we are not always the experts we
think we are. What we don't know can sometimes hurt us.

The DIY trend has certainly not ignored financial investments. Some
investors hear, see, or read the noise described in Chapter 1 and immediately believe they are experts. Similar to my ginseng example, it is possible
that DIY investors do not know as much about investing as they think they
do. Admittedly, I may simply be the person offended by others who believe
they know my industry better than I do, but I strongly doubt that noise-
induced DIY investing is a sure route to success.

THE BUSINESS OF DIY: THE SIREN'S SONG

As pointed out in Chapter 1, many entities have a vested interest in producing noise that encourages DIY investing. Book sales, newsletter distribution, television ratings, website "eyeballs," and newspaper circulation (to
name only a few) all could potentially benefit from DIY investing gaining
in popularity. If booksellers, magazine publishers, television producers, and
others can get investors to believe they can invest on their own, the more
investors will need the services these people offer.

These entities do not suggest that DIY investors do not need help.
Rather they argue that the DIY investor does not need *traditional* help.
Providers of alternative medicines admit that we do need medicines to get
well, but just not the traditional ones (i.e., you don't need theirs, but you do
need mine). Similarly, some information providers argue that their website,
book, TV program, or magazine will provide you with more and better
information than can traditional Wall Street research and money managers. (Why listen to those bad analysts on Wall Street, when you can

listen to me or use my website? I'll help you more than they ever could.) In my view, you should be as skeptical of advertisements supporting the need for an alternative source of investment information that will allow you to invest successfully by yourself, as you might be of the claims of a supposed miracle drug.

An article in the *New York Times*[2] described the growing use of tailored portfolios, and how investors now have alternatives to mutual funds. The article mentioned how disgruntled mutual fund investors could now form and invest in self-tailored portfolios that better match their investment goals and objectives. One individual investor quoted in the article commented that he did not like all the stocks that were in his mutual fund, and that a tailored portfolio gave him better control.

I counted six firms mentioned in the article willing to help investors design and buy tailored portfolios. The article mentioned several other firms that would be offering such services in the near future. This presents an interesting problem. How does an investor decide which one of these new portfolio-oriented firms is the right one to use? In addition, other than the transaction itself, what is the difference between tailored portfolios bought as a single investment and a tailored portfolio bought as series of individual stocks? The investment issues are identical for both despite the claims made by the companies offering tailored portfolios of a new (read superior) investment service.

However, as discussed in Chapter 1, noise is a siren's song. Its lure is hard to resist. So, if you insist on doing it yourself, here are some issues about investing that most investors probably have not considered. I do not offer any sure method for successful investing, lest I be as guilty as those I criticize. However, I think the following information will improve your ability to deafen your ears to the noise that encourages investors to blindly DIY.

I am certainly not claiming that professional investors have the definitive key to success. Just as in science, new theories of investing are always being studied, and earlier theories are determined to be obsolete. Using my previous analogy, we should remember that doctors once thought bloodletting was a cure for many diseases. No professional investor has a foolproof strategy for outperformance, but I hope professionals do have the experience so that they don't make the same mistakes that novices might make.

If by the end of this chapter you still believe you know someone who has a foolproof method of investing and are ready to follow that lead and invest by yourself, I might suggest snake oil to relieve the headaches that might follow.

PAST PERFORMANCE DOES NOT NECESSARILY REFLECT FUTURE RESULTS

In Chapter 1, we examined why many individual investors believe they are smarter than their mutual fund managers, and the subject deserves a quick recap here. In 1999, a very large proportion of the stocks within the technology sector outperformed the overall market. Because most individual investors focused only on that sector, their stocks tended to perform quite well. However, such stock-picking prowess proved to be luck rather than skill when NASDAQ corrected in 2000. Many individuals' self-managed portfolios began to underperform as the technology sector performed poorly. In extreme cases, some of the stocks that were considered stars in 1998 and 1999 became the dogs of 2000. Ironically, given my earlier medical analogies, one such stock carried the name of a very famous doctor.

Meanwhile, many mutual fund managers performed poorly during 1998 and 1999 because they did not concentrate their portfolios in the technology sector. Their concerns regarding fiduciary responsibility and diversification weighed heavily during a period in which the stock market paid attention to only one sector. As pointed out earlier, if the technology sector had performed poorly during 1998 and 1999, the portfolio managers who concentrated their portfolios in one sector would have been considered fools. I am not attempting to use one or two years' examples as an excuse for many managers' poor performances through time. However, it is that rather unique one- to two-year period of performance that made many nonprofessionals believe they can invest better than professionals can. The legal phrase "past performance does not necessarily reflect future results" applies to all investors. In this chapter, we examine why this statement is true.

PERFORMANCE: RISK TAKING VERSUS SKILL

Professional money managers' fiduciary responsibility is extremely important and is not merely an excuse for underperforming. Most portfolio managers know well that performance tables are based solely on absolute returns of the portfolio and that they could take an inordinate amount of risk to "juice up" the portfolio in order to outperform. Similarly, they could load their portfolios with investments that are outside their stated realm of expertise (i.e., a large capitalization growth stock manager might buy small capitalization value stocks if the latter group of stocks are outperforming despite the strategy advertised to investors). Taking extreme risk or changing strategy may be impossible for some professional investors because of the investment charters to which they and their clients have agreed. Some portfolio managers also understand that taking extreme risk will provide only short-term rewards and may not be in their clients' best interests. High levels of risk will ultimately cause more volatility in the portfolio's returns, as significant outperformance caused by higher levels of risk taking is typically followed by significant underperformance. Although risk/return relationships are the basic tenets of finance, it appears as though some well-known investors of recent years have chosen to ignore them. Investors should be careful not to confuse excess risk taking with skill.

That being said, fiduciary responsibility is not an excuse for poor *risk-adjusted* returns. There are simple methods for calculating returns on an apples-to-apples basis so that the returns of portfolios that incorporate different levels of risk are comparable. Without these measures it would be difficult to tell whether the manager of a capital preservation fund was better or worse than the manager of an aggressive growth fund. Poor risk-adjusted returns through time simply mean poor investment management.

Whether professional or nonprofessional, investors would like to believe that they are skillful investors when their portfolio performance is good. In my opinion, investors who consistently produce superior returns are either extreme risk takers (in the case of many current hedge funds and aggressive growth funds, whether investors know it or not), are naive and lucky, or have an extremely rare skill. When our portfolios perform well, we would like to believe that we have a very rare skill that others do not possess. However, the following section attempts to explain why most investors are probably either lucky or taking more risk than they think they are.

IS THERE A FREE LUNCH?

Figure 2.1 shows a risk/return scatter diagram for the roughly 40 equity strategies my group regularly follows. The horizontal axis shows the volatility of the strategies' rolling 12-month returns from 1987 to June 2000. The

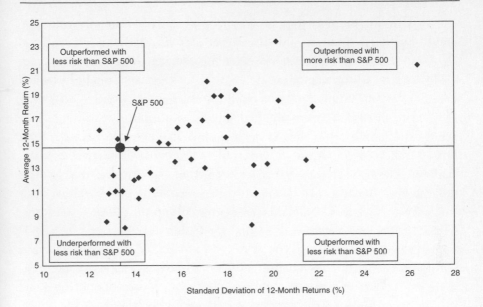

Figure 2.1   **Risk/Return Tradeoff of Selected Equity Strategies**

volatility is measured using the strategies' standard deviation or inconsistency of returns. In Chapter 6, we discuss the benefits and drawbacks of using this particular statistic to measure risk, but for now the inconsistency of returns will suffice as our risk measure. The vertical axis represents the average 12-month return during the time period. The S&P 500 is highlighted as a benchmark because the strategies generally incorporate stocks only in the S&P 500.

The quadrants in the chart demonstrate the relative risk/return combinations that are possible. Strategies that ended up being superior to simply investing in the S&P 500 by the end of the 14-year period are those northwest of the S&P 500 in Figure 2.1. By investing in such strategies for the full time period, you would have received higher returns than the S&P 500 (north) but would have incurred less risk (west). Those strategies that outperformed but necessitated taking more risk than the overall market are northeast of the S&P 500. These strategies can be dangerous in that they entice investors with a history of superior performance but then disappoint because the outperformance is inconsistent. The southwest quadrant contains those strategies that underperformed the S&P 500 but did so without requiring incremental risk. There is nothing necessarily wrong with these strategies simply because they underperformed. Some of these strategies might have been appropriate for investors who simply do not like taking the risks inherent in equity investing (e.g., capital preservation strategies would tend to fall in this quadrant). Strategies that successfully short or sell stocks will also fall into this quadrant because they are specifically designed to underperform. If they fall into this quadrant, then their low level of risk implies that they underperformed consistently, an excellent trait for a short-selling strategy. Bad strategies tend to fall in the southeast quadrant. These are strategies that underperformed and incurred more risk than the overall market. These are truly irrational strategies, for why would you desire to have a risky *and* underperforming portfolio? For fun, look for these statistics for your favorite mutual fund, and see where it falls in the diagram.

Only two of the strategies analyzed are northwest of the S&P 500. There are very few strategies that outperform the overall equity market without requiring investors to take more risk.[3] Is there a free lunch? It appears as though it might exist, but finding it might be quite difficult.

Investors should be skeptical of claims that certain strategies "have proven track records of outperforming over the long term" because such claims rarely, if ever, include explanations of the risks associated with the strategies. As Figure 2.1 shows, 18 of the strategies do indeed outperform the S&P 500 during the time period studied. It takes remarkably little skill to find an outperforming strategy that incorporates taking more risk and more of them exist than you might think. The difficult part is finding a strategy that outperforms with less risk. Slightly less than half of the total number of strategies tested outperformed the market (18 of 39 strategies, or 46%), but only 2 of the 18 strategies that outperformed the market did so with less risk. Thus, if you randomly picked a stock selection strategy, you would have about a 46% probability of choosing one that outperformed the market. However, you would also only have slightly more than a 5% probability (2 of 39) of picking a strategy that would outperform with less risk.

At this point, you might question why stocks that outperform the market with less risk are so important. If stocks outperform, then why worry about risk? There are three reasons. First, we discuss in chapters 5, 6, and 7 how taking too much risk without realizing it can cause investors to make foolish or rash investment decisions that often hurt investment performance more than help it. As mentioned earlier, investors who follow volatile strategies tend to trade more frequently because of the difficulty of separating noise from true investment information.

Second, if you look closely at the chart, you will see that some of the strategies incurred 50 to 100% more risk than did the S&P 500. If you have ever had trouble sleeping at night because of the stock market's swings, it may be because you are not comfortable with such higher risk levels. Later on, in Chapter 6, we discuss investor risk tolerance, the difficulty in measuring it, and why it might be impossible for you to assess your own risk tolerance.

Third, if you had wanted to take more risk to achieve higher returns, then borrowing money at relatively low short-term interest rates and investing in an S&P 500 Index fund (i.e., buying index funds or stock index futures on margin) would have probably outperformed many of these strategies. Imagine how many day traders could have kept their regular jobs and still invested aggressively if they had only realized they might have been more successful by buying S&P 500 futures than by margining individual stocks? It probably would have been much cheaper as well because there would have been no need to pay high transaction costs, subscribe to new services, and so forth.

DATA MINING: EUREKA! OR FOOL'S GOLD?

Studies highlighting strategies that outperform over the long term often rely on data mining. The term *data mining* refers to the process of sifting through tremendous amounts of data until you find an acceptable result. Rather than proving an existing hypothesis, data miners typically search until they find a relationship in the data and worry about a hypothesis only as a secondary consideration. Today's computers are very powerful and data is plentiful. Investors can process huge amounts of information in a relatively short period of time and can typically find a strategy that seems to always outperform. Keep in mind that the previous study showed that nearly 50% of the strategies tested outperformed the S&P 500. Even a poor data miner has a reasonable probability of finding an outperforming strategy. A good miner is sure to find one.

When data mining, you never quite know the reasons why a particular strategy worked; it simply did. Typically, no economic or financial theory frames the exercise. Rather, a theory is constructed to fit the data. Some investors have actually told me they care only if a strategy works and not why it might work. Imagine if similar methods were used when the FDA tested new drugs or when engineers designed airplanes? Without proper testing, performance results are relatively meaningless.

Data miners often do not realize they are data miners. Take the example of a very large, very well known and, for a while, very successful hedge fund that mined data relating to the fixed-income and currency markets. Under the guise of being "purely quantitative" and despite having world-renowned economists on its staff, it developed strategies without fully investigating the economic rationale behind its strategies' successes. The strategies simply worked in the past and would work in the future. Of course, the strategies eventually blew up as do all data-mining strategies. Interestingly, the managers of the hedge fund blamed its exceptionally poor returns and its failing business on the markets' inability to adhere to the rules (of course it was their genius that provided the very good returns, but the market's fault when the strategy exploded[4]).

Data miners frequently lay claim to finding the Holy Grail of investing, or *the* strategy that will make its followers wealthy. Eureka!! However, before believing that you have found the mother lode, check to make sure the strategy is not simply fool's gold. Remember that anyone eventually might find an outperforming strategy given enough iterations through the data and the results presented in Figure 2.1. The question is whether an investor can find a strategy that consistently outperforms the market with less risk.

One commentator has raised an interesting issue regarding claims by data miners to have found the Holy Grail of investing. He wonders how many times data miners have failed at their goal before they claim to have found an outperforming strategy. The author insightfully states, "to determine whether an apparently successful strategy is worth a bet, we first need to know how many other strategies were also back-tested. An advisor might have tested 99 strategies that failed before coming across one that succeeded."[5] Similarly, he suggests that investors should be wary of strategies that are constantly changed or "tweaked" in order to improve performance.

Let's look at two popular strategies highlighted in two recent investment books. One author suggested that low price-to-sales ratios was the best strategy to follow,[6] whereas the other suggested a low price/earnings-to-growth rate strategy might be the best.[7]

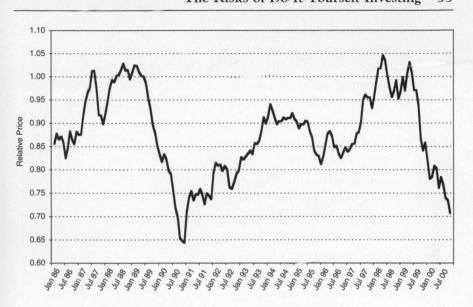

Figure 2.2   Relative Performance of Low Price/Sales Strategy

Figure 2.2 shows the performance of the 50 stocks within the S&P 500 with the lowest price/sales ratios. The portfolios in Figure 2.2 are equal-weighted, rebalanced monthly, and measured versus the performance of the Equal-Weighted S&P 500.[8] In this chart, the strategy was outperforming the broader market during periods in which the line was rising, and under-performed when the line was falling. A flat line indicates the strategy was performing similarly to the overall market.

According to the Library of Congress Online Catalog, 1997 was the copyright year of the book that advocated low price/sales as the preferred strategy. The generic low price/sales strategy outlined in the chart outper-formed the overall market from late 1991 until mid-1998. It subsequently underperformed so significantly that the cumulative outperformance fell to 1991 levels. Thus, the strategy has significantly underperformed in the roughly three years since the book's copyright.

Figure 2.3 shows a similar chart for the 50 stocks in the S&P 500 with the lowest P/E-to-growth rate ratios. According to the Library of Congress Online Catalog, the copyright year of this book is 1996. This example is similar to the first one in that the particular strategy highlighted in the

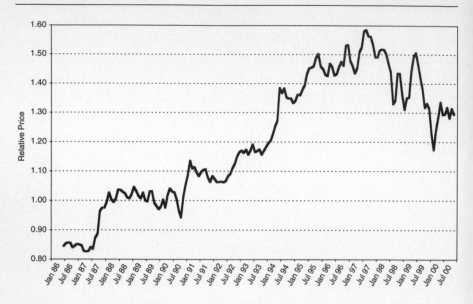

Figure 2.3   Relative Performance of Low Price/Earnings-to-Growth Strategy

book outperformed before publication and underperformed after publication. This particular book suggested that investors do not need professionals for advice because nonprofessionals can easily follow simple strategies such as low P/E-to-growth. The authors suggest that any "fool" can invest. That might indeed be true, but I certainly hope they did not use low P/E-to-growth as a basis for picking stocks after reading the book.

These examples are not intended to embarrass or discredit the authors of the two books cited. They are intended to demonstrate the reality that authors tend to champion strategies that *have* worked and not strategies that *will* work. Investment how-to books tend to look backward rather than forward. Nobody who hopes to sell copies of a book is going to write a book about a strategy that has performed miserably. Thus, investors should be skeptical of claims of finding a superior strategy, especially when there is no economic theory presented to support why and when the strategy outperformed and will outperform. Few strategies outperform all the time, and you should thoroughly understand why and when underperformance is most likely to occur. We examine some of these traits in chapters 8, 9, and 10.

Some investors might argue that these strategies ceased to outperform because the books' popularity caused too many investors to subscribe to the theory, and the effects were ruined by overinvestment. First, if that reasoning is correct, then you should question why the authors wrote the books in the first place. Did they intend to write unpopular books that would be read by only an insightful few? Although we cannot say for sure, it is more likely that the strategies were uncovered by data mining. Eventually, reality and risk catch up and ruin (at least temporarily) most data-mined strategies.

Table 2.1 shows the probability of a strategy outperforming the market during a three-year period subsequent to a three-year period in which it outperformed. In other words, if a strategy outperformed the S&P 500 during a three-year period, what was the probability that it would have repeated its outperformance during the next three years? This is an important consideration given that most researchers tend to mine data. If an outperforming strategy is uncovered and presented to others (remember, who is going to advocate investing in a poorly performing strategy?), then what is the chance that investors will be successful during the three years after the strategy is presented?

To conduct this study, my group examined three-year relative performance versus the S&P 500 of the roughly 40 stock selection strategies discussed earlier. The first three-year period was 1987 to 1989 with 1990 to 1992 used as the subsequent comparison period. Thus, 1988 to 1990 was compared to 1991 to 1993, and so forth. Among all the various strategies and time periods, more than 300 comparisons were included.

Table 2.1 is divided into a matrix containing four sections. The left side of the matrix shows whether a strategy outperformed or underperformed the overall market during the first three-year period. The top of the matrix shows whether a strategy outperformed during the subsequent three-year period. Thus, strategies that outperformed during both the first and

Table 2.1   **Probability of a Strategy's Sustained Outperformance (Based on Data from 1987 to 1999)**

	Outperformed During Second 3 Years (%)	Underperformed During Second 3 Years (%)
Outperformed during first 3 years	47	53
Underperformed during first 3 years	62	38

Source: Based on data from Merrill Lynch Quantitative Strategy.

second three-year periods would be included in the top left column. These are potentially worthwhile strategies, but keep in mind that the risk of the strategies has not been assessed. Strategies that outperformed during the first three-year period but underperformed during the second would be in the top right column. These are often the strategies advocated by those who look only at recent short-term performance as a guide for the future. Strategies that underperformed in the first three-year period, but outperformed in the second would be in the bottom left. These strategies are sometimes ignored by most investors because of their poor short-term performance. Sometimes these strategies gain popularity when they begin to outperform. Strategies that underperformed during both periods would be in the bottom right. It is probably wise to stay away from these.

The results of this table might be somewhat shocking. Strategies that underperformed during the first three-year period actually had a higher probability of outperforming the market during the subsequent three-year period than did strategies that initially outperformed. In fact, strategies that outperformed during a three-year period at any point in time had only a 47% chance of outperforming during the subsequent three-year period. An investor would probably have achieved better performance by randomly choosing a strategy that underperformed during a three-year period because 62% of the strategies that underperformed the market during a three-year period outperformed the market during the subsequent three years. Table 2.1 clearly shows that past performance is not necessarily indicative of future returns.

As a historical example supporting this table's results, think of the famous "Dogs of the Dow" strategy. You follow the "Dogs of the Dow" strategy by purchasing the 10 stocks in the Dow Jones Industrial Average with the highest dividend yields as of December 31st of each year, and then holding those stocks for one year. The historical performance of this strategy is quite good, but few investigated why it worked. They simply assumed that it would continue to work. It turns out that the "Dogs of the Dow" strategy is a contrarian, value-oriented strategy that outperformed historically when other value-oriented investments outperformed. Value investments performed extremely well in the United States from late 1990/early 1991 until late 1994/early 1995, depending on the particular strategy. Given the strategy's terrific outperformance during the early 1990s, it was being heavily marketed by the end of 1994. Value strategies, the "Dogs of the Dow" included, then proceeded to underperform for most of the next five years.

Thus, it is *extremely* important that investors realize that how to invest books or seminars that advocate particular strategies because of the recent outperformance of those strategies might provide little or no benefit. In fact, we could argue that it might actually be wiser to avoid strategies that have outperformed during the last three years and instead examine strategies that have actually underperformed.

Investors, whether professional or nonprofessional, should realize there is no all-encompassing, sure-to-outperform, risk-averse method of investing that has been somehow overlooked by millions of investors.

AN EXAMPLE OF TRUE "FOOL'S GOLD"

Data mining is more insidious than most might imagine. For example, consider the statistics of the following strategy. The strategy has outperformed the S&P 500 for 10 of the 13 years from 1987 to 1999. The annual average return was 33.3% compared to 15.6% for the S&P 500. In addition, the strategy's volatility was 30.6% versus the S&P 500's 15%. In other words, the strategy might be considered to be about twice as risky as was the overall market, but the returns were more than twice as high. The strategy had very low turnover. The average holding period was 12 months, and only one trade was made per year.

Table 2.2 shows the annual returns of what we call Strategy X versus the returns of the S&P 500. You have to admit that the returns are very impressive. If I were a marketer, I might call this strategy Rich's Autoregressive Nonlinear Dynamic Optimization Model, and I would tell you that the formula is proprietary. We put the stocks into the model and out come these tremendous results.

I hope you caught on to the model's name, Rich's Autoregressive Nonlinear Dynamic Optimization Model: R-A-N-D-O-M.

The stocks in this strategy were chosen completely randomly, despite the fancy name I attached to it (which by the way is simply nonsensical jargon). We used a random number generator to pick a stock from the S&P 500 at the end of each year and held the stock for one year. The random number generator gave us a random number between 1 and 500, and we matched the number to the ranks of the companies in the S&P 500 by

Table 2.2   Performance of Strategy X versus S&P 500

	Strategy X (%)	S&P 500 (%)
1987	22.0	2.0
1988	36.1	12.4
1989	−32.9	27.3
1990	−10.3	−6.6
1991	58.2	26.3
1992	23.1	4.5
1993	114.0	7.1
1994	−27.5	−1.5
1995	44.8	34.1
1996	27.2	20.3
1997	73.4	31.0
1998	61.8	26.7
1999	42.7	19.5
Compound return	1,775.2	526.7
Average annual return	33.3	15.6

Note: Compound returns include data through August 2000 not shown.

market capitalization. If the random number generator gave us 366, then we hypothetically bought the 366th largest stock in the S&P 500. If it gave us 147, then we included the 147th largest company. There is no economic rationale for this strategy. It is simply a random selection. Yet, it performed superbly in our back-test.

Lest you get too excited about our strategy and believe it could be run successfully in the future, look at Figure 2.4 in which we show the compound performance of our RANDOM model. However, we also show the results of nine other simulations of the RANDOM model. A large proportion of the strategies underperformed. Thus, our strategy's outperformance was clearly luck. However, if I had changed the story slightly, I probably could have convinced you that by using the performance figures shown in Table 2.2 that I had an excellent stock selection strategy.

Although the RANDOM model might seem like an extreme example, it does clearly show how luck and not skill might be more important in determining the performance of a strategy. Rather than blindly assuming a strategy that performs astoundingly well is one on which to build a portfolio, you should scrutinize the results extremely carefully.

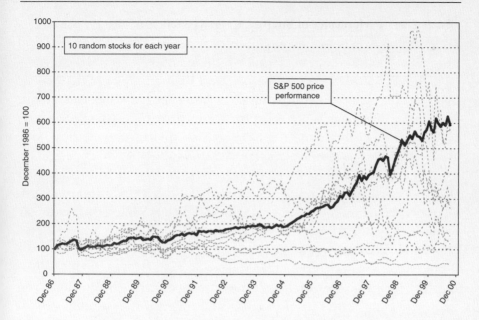

Figure 2.4   **Random Stocks Price Performance 1987 through September 2000**
Based on data from Merrill Lynch Quantitative Strategy.

TESTING STRATEGIES

There are many factors you should consider before choosing an investment strategy to follow or when purchasing a mutual fund. Most investors read a book or a newsletter or see a single presentation and decide the strategy being presented is worth following. Given the relatively high probability that a recently outperforming strategy will soon underperform, investors should more fully understand the strategy they want to follow.

A colleague of mine at Merrill Lynch has developed a system that quite effectively diagnoses a strategy's strengths and shortcomings. Believe it or not, he examines 17 different statistics divided into 4 categories: return, risk, turnover, and size/style.[9] Let's discuss return, risk, and turnover. Size and style are more fully discussed in Chapter 10.

Testing Strategies: Returns and Risk

Investors should obviously consider first the strategies' returns. When doing so, however, you must again remember that past performance does not necessarily reflect the future return of a strategy. As was just discussed, strategies that outperform for a three-year period have less than a 50% chance of out-performing during the subsequent three-year period. Thus, investors should fully understand the best, worst, and typical returns.

A good start is to look at the average 12-month return of the strategy over the time period studied, as well as the minimum and maximum returns. In addition, you might want to calculate the median (middle return) and the mode (most frequent return) if the periodic return data are available.

Using average returns alone can be very misleading. Often an average return can be skewed by a single exceptionally good or bad return, and therefore might not be indicative of the strategy's or fund's typical return. Consider the returns of two investments outlined in Table 2.3. The invest-ments had identical returns in each period except period 2, when #2 pro-duced a 100% return versus #1's 4%. Because of that one unique period, #2's average return per period is almost seven times #1's. However, the median (center) return is identical for the two strategies. In such situations, you must investigate why #2 performed so well (or #1 performed so poorly in comparison) during that single period. Was the disparity between the two investments meaningful or was it a fluke?

Also, you should hesitate to consider #2's 21.8% average return its *typical* return because only one period's return was as high as 6%. The median of the two strategies is identical perhaps indicating that the one period was indeed a fluke, and that investors' expectations for #2's returns might be too high (or those for #1 too low) if they used the average returns.

The stability or consistency of the returns should also be considered. Looking again at our two sets of returns, the second period's return makes

Table 2.3   **Simple Summary Statistics of Hypothetical Returns**

Period	Strategy #1 (%)	Strategy #2 (%)
1	2	2
2	4	100
3	6	6
4	–2	–2
5	3	3
Average (mean)	2.6	21.8
Median	3.0	3.0

the stability of the returns of #1 greater than are those of #2. As mentioned before and which we discuss in great detail in Chapter 6, you should consider whether you want higher returns or you want to sleep at night. As in many cases, there is a tradeoff here between the two, and investors should be skeptical of claims that a strategy can achieve both.

One method to use to determine if you will be able to sleep at night is to examine a strategy's worst 3-month and 12-month return. This examination is important for two reasons. First, if the worst return looks too risky then obviously the strategy should be avoided regardless of how often that result might occur. Sometimes investors rationalize that a bad outcome rarely occurs, but investors sometimes have no reason to believe a worst case outcome has any lower probability of occurring than does the best one.[10]

Investors might also want to consider their personal minimum acceptable return for a period, and examine how often the strategy underperforms that hurdle. For example, suppose you are deciding whether to invest in the stock market or whether to invest in Treasury bills. Perhaps a suitable test for an investor faced with this decision is how often a strategy's returns are higher than T-bill returns. Similarly, you might be extremely risk averse and focus on the preservation of capital. Then it might be wise to examine how often the strategy loses money. The strategy might outperform over the long term, but what if the long-term performance is comprised of one very positive year and four negative ones for each five-year period. The investor interested in capital preservation might ultimately feel such a strategy is inappropriate despite its long-term returns.

Testing Strategies: Turnover

Turnover, or how often an investor must trade, is often ignored when examining strategies. Some strategies might appear to provide significant returns, but the trading costs associated with the strategy eat up the profits. As mentioned in Chapter 1, transaction costs tend to rise with turnover, and turnover frequently rises because of noise. Also, as many investors are just beginning to realize, high turnover leads not only to transaction costs, but also to tax liabilities.

Investors seem to be finally realizing that turnover is important. Many invested in mutual funds that had very high returns, but found that those returns were predicated on very aggressive trading strategies. The result was that investors received their higher-than-average returns, but a significant proportion of those gains was then given to the government in tax payments. In some cases, investors bought near the peak of the bull market mutual funds that had significant unrealized capital gains. When the stock market started retreating in mid-2000 and some investors sold their mutual funds, some of those funds sold stock positions and realized gains in order to meet their outflow of funds. Investors who bought these funds late received a double whammy: a lower net asset value for the fund and a significant tax liability.

The recent increased awareness of tax liability has caused the formation of both tax-advantaged funds and exchange-traded funds (ETF). Similar to a closed-end mutual fund, ETFs are portfolios based on sectors, industries, countries, and so forth that trade on an exchange. When investing in an ETF, an investor's tax liability is solely a function of when the investor buys and sells the ETF. In a traditional mutual fund, the investor's tax liability is primarily a function of the turnover of the fund and when the fund was purchased. You can control the latter, but not the former.

Three simple turnover statistics that can be very helpful are average holding period, average number of stocks held per period, and average number of transactions per year as a percent of total holdings. The first, average holding period, is typically measured in months, and longer holding periods are better for two reasons. First, the longer a stock is held in a portfolio the less the possibility that trading costs will negate returns. Also, returns on stocks that are held longer tend to qualify as capital gains rather than as income, and capital gains taxes are usually lower than are income taxes (although there have been times when there was no such distinction).

It is hard to say what is the best average number of stocks held per period. However, you should remember that diversification requires a relatively large number of companies. Most academic studies suggest portfolios with more than 15 randomly chosen securities are well diversified. The key words are "randomly chosen." A portfolio of 15 stocks all in one industry is not considered well diversified. Wide fluctuations in the average number of stocks held can reflect both higher turnover and inconsistent management (if looking at a fund rather than a strategy). Neither are attractive characteristics.

Average number of purchases per year should be low. Again, when stocks are traded less frequently, transaction costs and tax liability tend to be lower.

BENCHMARKS TO MEASURE A STRATEGY

The performance of many strategies or funds is arbitrarily measured against the S&P 500 or other broad market index. However, investors should carefully define the correct benchmark on which to measure their strategies and funds. For example, should a technology fund be measured against the S&P 500, the NASDAQ Composite, or the S&P Technology sector? Should a value-oriented strategy or fund be compared to the S&P 500 or to the S&P/Barra Value Index?

With the increasing number of indexes being created and, more important, the number of tradable index or sector products being created, investors are increasingly comparing return and risk to a tailored index rather than to a broad one.

Comparing to the correct benchmark is important. Consider the performance of the following four technology funds in 1999 shown in Table 2.4. When compared to the S&P 500, all four significantly outperform. You might surmise that these are good investments because they outperformed the S&P 500 by so much. However, when compared to the performance of the NASDAQ Composite Index, we see a different story. Only two of the four funds outperformed the technology-laden NASDAQ Index. Given that you can now invest in sector-oriented products or sector index funds, why would you invest in a fund that did not outperform the sector? It is important to realize that the strategies used by the managers of Technology Funds #1 and #2 actually detracted from the value of investing in the sector. Some investors in these funds might not have noticed this fact because the funds outperformed the broader market. A bad manager might have gotten credit because the technology sector outperformed.

Table 2.4   Selected Technology Fund 1999 Performance

Fund/Index	1999 Total Return (%)
Technology fund #1	89.4
Technology fund #2	30.9
Technology fund #3	158.0
Technology fund #4	144.9
NASDAQ Composite	102.1
S&P 500	21.0

Source: Based on data from Bloomberg.

Incorrect benchmarking can lead to poor investment decisions. In this case, you might have continued to invest in Technology Fund #1 or #2, paid the expenses and fees associated with the fund, and then your fund potentially continued to underperform the technology sector and technology-index investments. You should look for strategies or funds that have risk/return characteristics that are superior to a benchmark that matches the strategy's or fund's goals and objectives.

LOOKING AT A STRATEGY? CHECK FOR "OUT-OF-SAMPLE" TESTING

Most data miners violate a primal rule for testing strategies. They do not do any out-of-sample testing. Out-of-sample testing is a very simple concept despite its sounding sophisticated. It is used to determine whether a strategy's outperformance is consistent. As said repeatedly, it is easy to find a stock selection strategy that outperforms, but it is difficult to find one that does so consistently. Out-of-sample testing is an easy way to begin to test for that consistency. Table 2.1 was a simple out-of-sample test.

Suppose data for testing stock selection strategies is available from 1970 to 2000. Typically, researchers would simulate strategies' buy/hold/sell decisions over the entire time period. Data miners would do that for hundreds of strategies. A typical conclusion would be to use the strategy that gave the best results over the entire time period. After all, you would have tested about 30 years of data. Sounds quite rigorous, right? Wrong.

It is much more meaningful if strategies can outperform consistently during nonoverlapping time periods. Instead of testing over the entire time period, as is usually done, it is more rigorous to break the full data set into smaller time periods. For example, find the best performing strategy from 1970 to 1975, and then see how that particular strategy would have performed from 1975 to 1980. Or, perhaps study the period from 1970 to 1980, and then test the conclusions using data from 1990 to 2000. This method is called out-of-sample testing, and most studies of stock selection strategies neglect it completely.

Out-of-sample testing is important because without it most performance studies contain something called look-ahead bias. Look-ahead bias means you have incorporated information into the study that you would not have had at a point in time had you actually been using the strategy to manage a portfolio. For example, I would not have known in 1975 that a particular strategy was the best-performing strategy from 1970 to 2000 simply because I would have only had data from 1970 to 1975 in 1975. If I had started investing in 1975, I would not have had the knowledge of what was going to happen in the future, and thus my study has look-ahead bias. Why didn't investors realize in 1975 that strategy XYZ was such a good strategy? Simply because they did not have the luxury of looking at 25 additional years of data as we do today. To the folks in 1975, strategy XYZ might have looked like a losing strategy.

So, whenever anyone advocates a certain stock selection strategy and presents you with performance charts, ask about out-of-sample testing. You might sound like a statistics nerd, but your portfolio performance might improve.

THE KISS OF DEATH IS TO BE CALLED A "CORE LONG-TERM HOLDING"

Some investors advocate a portfolio of core long-term holdings. Anecdotal evidence (there is no historical compilation of stocks that received the designation core long-term holdings) suggests that investors probably do not want to have their stocks coined *core long-term holdings*. It seems to be somewhat of a kiss of death.

The term seems to apply to stocks whose prices investors believe will consistently go up over the long term. Thus, historical stock price charts are often used to determine which stocks will receive the designation. The stock's past performance, and not the company's fundamentals, are used as the measuring device. However, this is where the look-ahead bias mentioned before comes into play. Investors look at the historical chart and have the benefit of knowing how the stock performed. Investors 5 or 10 years earlier did not. So, the question should be why the investors did not know these stocks were core long-term holdings. The answer generally is that the stock was not a favorite stock as it is today, but rather was an out-of-favor one, and many investors who now consider the stock a core long-term holding would not even have considered investing in the stock.

For example, a beverage company was considered a core long-term holding during the late 1990s. The company's stock had risen substantially in the prior 10 years, and it was considered a safe, conservative holding that consistently outperformed the market. However, few investors remembered the checkered history of the company, and why investors shunned the stock in the mid-1980s. A remarkably unsuccessful launch of a reformulated drink, and the odd, and ultimately unsuccessful, decision to purchase a movie studio hurt earnings growth and left investors questioning the future growth prospects for the company. Thus, an out-of-favor, contrarian investment in the late 1980s became a core long-term holding during the late 1990s. Once it received the dubious title of core long-term holding, the stock subsequently underperformed for completely different reasons than it had during the 1980s. Today, it is again a contrarian investment.

Core long-term holdings are usually those that simply have outperformed. Often the historical stock performance is what drives the designation, and not the designation that drives future performance. In Chapter 3, we discuss how noise influences investors' perception of a company.

I'M A DISCIPLINED INVESTOR, BUT MY STRATEGY ISN'T WORKING!

Some investors claim to be *disciplined* investors who follow a strategy that has a long-term history of outperformance regardless of how it performs in the short term. I believe this is a superior method of investing, but it can get nerve-racking. Take the following examples as evidence.

An analyst I know offered a stock selection model to clients of his firm. The model was back-tested during the late 1980s, and was used real-time beginning in 1991. Combining the back-tested period and the live performance, the model had outperformed the S&P 500 for 10 of 12 years. In addition, it did so while incurring less risk than the S&P 500. In 1998 and 1999, the model performed miserably. Although the model's followers were supposed to be disciplined investors who followed the model for the long-term performance it offered, the analyst actually received hate mail from some of the investors who followed the model. By mid-2000, the assets under management that followed the model's recommendations dropped significantly because *disciplined* investors decided to follow another strategy. My guess is that they switched to a strategy that might have had a poor long-term track record, but outperformed during 1998 and 1999. The analyst's firm asked him whether he thought it might no longer be appropriate to offer the model's recommendations to investors. Investors began to ignore the model, and the analyst actually began to pay less attention to it. Needless to say, the model outperformed the market during 2000 and looked to be back on track.

The moral of this story is many of us say we are disciplined investors, but how many of us really are? Short-term performance tends to alter our definition of "discipline."

If you have done the appropriate homework regarding a particular stock strategy, then periods of underperformance, although upsetting and unwanted, should not be surprising. If an investor has a very good understanding of a strategy's pitfalls, then the first step when a strategy fails is to compare the economic environments in which the strategy failed in the past, and to determine if the current environment is similar. For example, as we discuss in Chapter 10, value-oriented strategies that concentrate underappreciated fundamentals (as opposed to growth-oriented ones that focus on potential earnings growth) tend to perform poorly during economic recessions. If you were investing using a value-oriented strategy and the economy slipped into recession, it should not be surprising if the particular strategy underperformed.

When historical economic precedent can indeed explain the performance of a strategy, then the investor should probably continue using the strategy despite the poor short-term performance because attempting to time different strategies can be a very difficult task. Not only do you have to pick another good strategy, but you must do so at an opportune time. As pointed out, short-term performance is typically very misleading. So, the probability is reasonably high that you might give up on a strategy just before it begins to work again. The result would be a series of underperforming strategies as you bounce from one strategy to another (the grass is always greener on the other side).

If the economic environment is not one in which the strategy has historically fared poorly, then the next step is to be somewhat introspective. Is it I, the investor, or the strategy that is failing? It is entirely possible that the overall strategy is working, but the investor has poorly chosen individual stocks from the strategy's list of preferred stocks. Unless you buy the full basket of stocks highlighted by a strategy, there is a sizeable chance that poor stock selection, rather than a strategy's failure, is causing underperformance.

It is easy to test whether poor stock selection rather than the strategy's failure is the culprit. Simply monitor the performance of the strategy's entire portfolio versus that of the selected stocks. If the stocks outperform the portfolio, then the investor has actually picked good stocks and improved performance beyond what the basic strategy could offer. However, if the performance of the stocks is inferior to that of the entire portfolio, then the investor detracted from the strategy's basic performance. In the latter case, the investor was at fault.

Abandoning a strategy or a fund is always tempting, and today's investment noise is always ready to point out a strategy that is outperforming (at least for today). However, if you carefully study a strategy or a fund prior to investing, the temptation to frequently switch strategies or funds should rarely occur.

This chapter was a waste. I don't use a strategy.
I am simply a "stock picker."

If these statements describe your thoughts, I wish you luck. Out of the hundreds of portfolio managers that I meet every month, I have yet to meet an investor who has a successful long-term performance track record by simply picking stocks according to intuition. All successful professional stock pickers have certain characteristics that they look for in a company before investing, and they often must do significant research on the company in order to uncover that information.

One of the surest ways to filter noise from investment information is to follow a well-understood investment discipline. By following Wall Street's noise without some order or discipline to the investment process, investors are merely mimicking my RANDOM strategy mentioned earlier. Such a strategy might outperform for a while as mine did, but the outperformance will be purely luck. I suggest saving luck for Atlantic City or Las Vegas and applying well-thought-out discipline to Wall Street.

Chapter 3

Noise and Expectations: What Goes Around, Comes Around

We have discussed how noise is insidious, and how it can negatively influence portfolio performance. In addition, we examined how claims to have found the Holy Grail of investing should be viewed skeptically. In this chapter, we look at a theory of how noise influences the Street's opinions of stocks. We could simply describe this theory as "what goes around, comes around."

In Chapter 2, we briefly described a company that was extremely out of favor for a variety of reasons, then gained investors' attention. It subsequently became such a favorite of investors that it was called a core long-term holding. Unfortunately, it then underperformed for several years, and again became a contrarian investment. Was this a unique case, or do investors fall into and out of love with stocks all the time? The answer is that this happens all the time. Perhaps more important is that this happens to *all* stocks. Perhaps most important is that noise contributes greatly to the process and helps lead investors both to fall in love with stocks and to fall out of love with stocks later than they should.

51

PERCEPTION VERSUS REALITY

It is often said by experienced investors that the equity market discounts future events. Investors who support that contention believe that if you wait for an event to occur before investing, then you would probably be too late because the investment implications would already have been priced into the particular investment.

The notion that the equity market discounts future events necessarily leads us to the conclusion that the equity market prices stocks based on perception rather than on reality. Future events that are supposedly being discounted have not yet occurred. Therefore, stock price movements reflect investors' changing perceptions of what will occur, but not what will *certainly* occur. If the market were able to discount an event with complete certainty, then we would not worry about volatility or risk.

THE EARNINGS EXPECTATIONS LIFE CYCLE

The Earnings Expectations Life Cycle[1] is the theory I developed to describe the dynamic process with which investors view stocks. It is a metamorphosis of investor perceptions and expectations. Despite what we might think about a favorite stock, the expectations for *all* stocks follow this cycle, although those for individual stocks may not pass through every point on the cycle and expectations may go around the cycle at different speeds. In addition, stocks may go through minicycles in which they repeat portions of the larger cycle before passing to the next stage. This theory was presented in my earlier book that focused on style investing.[2] In this book, I adapt the theory to relate to investment noise.

The Earnings Expectations Life Cycle is depicted in Figure 3.1 and has the following points on it:

- *Contrarians.* Investors who are commonly known as contrarians invest in stocks with low earnings expectations. Most investors find these stocks unattractive or overly risky.
- *Positive Earnings Surprises.* Eventually a low-expectations company begins to disseminate more optimistic information; the stock regains investor attention. Research of such stocks may begin to increase.
- *Positive Earnings Surprise Models.* Stock-picking models that search for significant variations between analysts' earnings expectations

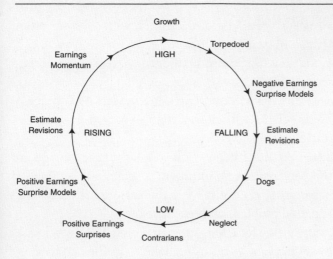

Figure 3.1   **The Earnings Expectations Life Cycle**
Based on data from Merrill Lynch Quantitative Analysis.

and actual reported earnings highlight stocks that enjoy positive earnings surprises. Traditional earnings surprise models wait for actual earnings to be reported, hence the models reside in Stage 3 while the event itself may be Stage 2.

- *Estimate Revisions.* Analysts begin to raise earnings estimates in response to rising earnings expectations following the earning surprise. Some analysts' estimate revisions may lag the initial surprise significantly because these analysts may be reluctant to believe that the surprise is a sign that the company's fundamental statistics are improving.

- *Earnings Momentum.* Investors who follow earnings momentum themes begin to buy the stock as estimates and reported earnings continue to rise and as year-to-year earnings comparisons begin to improve.

- *Growth.* When strong earnings momentum continues for a long enough period, a stock is termed a *growth* stock. These stocks are neither newly identified growth stocks, which are probably uncovered by superior growth-stock investors during Stages 4 and 5, nor are they true growth companies that completely alter the business environment. Rather, most investors now agree that these stocks are indisputably superior. In Chapter 2, I mentioned that the term *core long-term holding* was a kiss of death. These stocks are often thought of as core long-term holdings.

- *Torpedoed.* An earnings disappointment occurs. The stock is torpedoed. Its earnings expectations and price sink.
- *Negative Earnings Surprise Models.* The same models from Stage 3 begin to highlight stocks with lower than expected earnings as potential sell candidates.
- *Estimate Revisions.* Analysts begin to lower earnings estimates in response to the earnings disappointment. Again, some analysts tend to lag because they do not believe the earnings shortfall is a sign of a fundamental problem with the company.
- *Dogs.* After disappointing for a long enough period, these stocks are shunned by investors. Rumors regarding takeover, restructuring, or bankruptcy may affect the stock price temporarily, but investors generally avoid these stocks.
- *Neglect.* Investors have become so disinterested in the stocks or group that brokerage firms begin to believe that research coverage of the group may not be profitable, hence coverage begins to dissipate. The lack of available research information may set the stage for a renewed cycle.

When viewing the life cycle, we can think of many examples of companies that have toured the cycle's points. The most recent example is the Internet stocks. Consider the following points in the life cycle of the Internet industry. The stages are not meant to comply exactly with the life cycle's points, but the evolution nonetheless parallels the life cycle theory.

Stage 1   In the early to mid-1990s, venture capitalists invested in start-up Internet companies that they thought might have great potential. A majority of the investing public, both professional and nonprofessional, had probably never heard of most of the companies. Many of the eventual leaders of the 1990s technology sector, such as Cisco and Dell, issued stock. Most investors paid little attention.

Stage 2   Some Internet companies came public. Their stock performance began to attract attention. Professional investors viewed the companies as not being serious investments and considered their performance to be a short-term fad.

Stage 3   The outperformance of some of the stocks and their sizeable increases in market capitalization led them to be included in some of the generally accepted performance benchmarks. Professional managers began to buy the stocks, claiming that they must do so because of the stocks' inclusions in the benchmarks against which their portfolios' performance would be measured. They still generally believed the companies were jokes.

Stage 4   The continued outperformance of the Internet stocks began to attract broader attention. As the nonprofessional investor became more attuned to the Internet stocks' outperformance, mutual fund companies began to form an increasing number of Internet and technology funds. Day trading by individuals gained popularity. More companies came public.

Stage 5   The mania began. Many investors completely shunned other sectors of the stock market claiming that the Internet/technology sector was the only growth sector. The effect spilled over into the broader technology sector as investors believed that there would be a terrific need for the infrastructure to support all the Internet companies. Companies that produce every type of computer hardware and software remotely linked to the Internet were bid up. The spillover into telecommunications and media is reminiscent of how the Dutch tulip bubble of the 1600s was so powerful that it began to inflate the price of other flowers. Still more companies came public. With the valuations of Internet stocks extraordinarily high, companies that previously issued stock had secondary and tertiary offerings, and had little incentive to use cash wisely because they believed additional cash could easily be provided by yet another issuance. Wall Street began to bid up the pay of analysts who followed technology companies. As with many historical financial bubbles, this bubble began to spread to other countries.

Stage 6   Craziness. Venture capitalists fought with each other over deals. Television and radio reports commented on the NASDAQ as a measure of the stock market rather than the Dow Jones Industrials or the S&P 500 despite that NASDAQ essentially is comprised of only technology stocks and does not represent the broad stock market or the overall economy. Somehow, investors managed to overlook that the technology sector is more than 30% of the S&P 500's market capitalization and more than 75% of NASDAQ's market capitalization, but it is only about 5% to 6% of the economy. Despite that the average company in the S&P 500 was growing earnings 25% to 30%, the thought prevailed that technology was the only growth industry. Business periodicals fought to see which of them could be the most technology-oriented. There were rumors that start-ups in Silicon Valley were paying for everything (rent, office furniture, and even coffee machines) with stock options, as U.S. dollars became a secondary currency to stock options. Individuals left their jobs to become day traders. One telecommunications analyst was rumored to have been awarded a contract for $25 million per year. Bidding wars for technology analysts and investment bankers became common.

Stage 7 The bubble began to deflate. Weaker Internet companies were derided as being retail stocks instead of technology stocks. "Storage" stocks took the lead replacing "infrastructure" stocks, which had taken the lead from "B2B" (business to business), which took the lead from "B2C" (business to consumer), and leadership appeared increasingly short-lived as investors seemed to lose confidence more quickly with each passing trend. Some Internet-related shares on the Tokyo exchange remained "locked limit-down" (could not trade during the day because the first trade of the day was made at the maximum daily loss allowed on the exchange) for days or weeks at a time and virtually stopped trading.

Stage 8 The bottom began to fall out. So-called business models began to fail at a more rapid rate.[3] Larger companies whose stocks started underperforming were termed core long-term holdings (again, the kiss of death), and their underperformance was considered temporary. Personally, I began to receive résumés from failed day traders and Internet entrepreneurs.

Stage 9 The NASDAQ was down about 30% during 2000. Meanwhile, very boring stocks, such as utilities, were up more than 30% for the year. Portfolio managers were resiliently bullish on the sector, and were waiting for the next rally to begin soon. Investors were somewhat worried about the high-yield bond market (sometimes called the junk bond market) because about 25% of the market is comprised of telecommunications stocks. Ironically, some of the same business commentators who were championing the new economy only six months before were now among the biggest critics of technology companies. Regardless, the sector still dominated investor attention. It was clearly not yet five o'clock on the life cycle.

Stage 10? After the 1983 technology bubble (which was merely a "bubblette" compared to the 1999–2000 version), it took nearly eight years for the technology sector to gain investor acceptance.[4] Who knows this time?

Although this recent example of how expectations change for a sector, industry, or stock may be somewhat extreme, there are many examples of such attitudinal changes. Investors viewed the energy sector very differently during the 1970s than they did during the 1980s or 1990s. The energy sector was a star that became a dog for more than 15 years. Consumer staples stocks were viewed as dogs during the 1970s, became stars during the 1980s and 1990s, and then fell out of favor during the late 1990s. Financial stocks were certainly considered dogs subsequent to the financial crisis of the late 1980s but became stars during the 1990s. And, as mentioned earlier, while everyone was myopically focused on technology stocks during 2000, up sneaked the utilities sector when no one was looking.

The same changes in expectations apply to entire asset classes as well. Typically, when the popular press emphasizes the high returns in money market funds, it is sometimes time to look at equities or bonds. More recently, some articles written to encourage further equity investment claimed bonds were riskier than stocks. They were published just in time for bonds to outperform stocks.[5]

POPULARITY VERSUS PERFORMANCE

Is there something meaningful to the fact that CNBC's ratings surpassed CNN's ratings for the first time in history during 2000 at the same time that bonds and cash began to outperform stocks? One of the most dangerous aspects to the new age of media and hype is that noise is directly proportional to the popularity of an investment and has nothing to do with potential future performance. An increasing proportion of television, radio, and print media time will be spent on an investment as the investment's popularity increases. Therefore, if we consider the Earnings Expectations Life Cycle, noise will increase regarding a particular investment as the investment creeps up the left side of the life cycle. Conversely, noise will decrease as the investment slips down the right side.

This is particularly dangerous because noise will potentially continue to encourage investment until it is too late. Even subsequent to the peak in the NASDAQ index in March 2000, Wall Street and the media spent a disproportionate amount of time covering the technology sector despite its underperformance and relatively ignored other sectors. Despite the stocks' outstanding relative performance, financial reporters spent relatively little time covering real estate investment trusts (REITs) and utilities in 2000

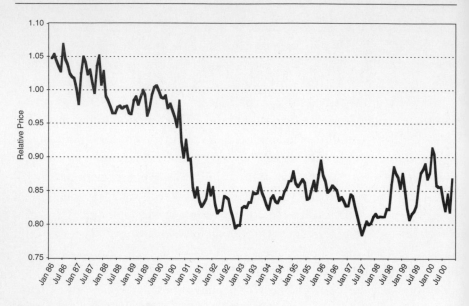

Figure 3.2   **Relative Performance of Stocks Predominantly Held by Individual Investors**

compared to the amount of time they spent covering technology stocks. Despite that bonds and cash were outperforming stocks during much of 2000, the financial media spent very little time discussing municipal bonds or CDs.

It is important to realize that popular investments are not the same as the best performing investments. As demonstrated in Chapter 2, the most popular investments are often on the list of investments that subsequently underperform. Figure 3.2 shows the relative performance of the 50 stocks in the S&P 500 with the highest percentage of individual investors (or the lowest institutional ownership),[6] or those that you might consider the most popular investments among individual investors relative to those that are popular among professional investors. As in the earlier charts, the line in the chart represents the relative performance of the portfolios against the broader market. The portfolios outperformed during periods in which the line rose, and underperformed during periods in which the line fell.

Figure 3.2 clearly shows that a stock's popularity among individual investors does not necessarily mean the stock will outperform. In fact, these

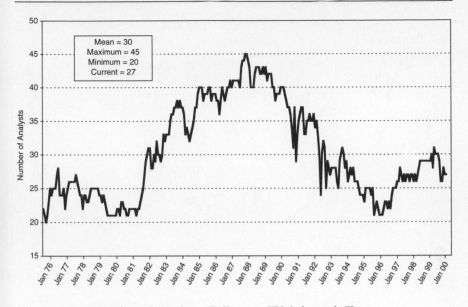

Figure 3.3   Number of Analysts Following IBM through Time
Based on data from I/B/E/S.

stocks generally underperformed the broader market during the 15-year period shown in the chart, that is, the line is at a lower point in the graph in 2000 than in 1986. Even during the last decade, the stocks have only performed in line with the broader market. That might suggest that popular investments are not as bad as I might lead you to believe, but they still were no better than unpopular ones.

Perhaps a better analysis of the inverse relationship between popularity and performance is shown beginning in Figure 3.3. This chart shows the number of analysts on Wall Street who were responsible for covering IBM through time. You might think that IBM as a stock market bellwether is always widely covered by the Street, but this chart shows otherwise.

Let's go one step further and compare the number of analysts following IBM to the stock's performance. Table 3.1 does just that. The number of analysts who follow IBM seems to increase in response to the stock's price appreciation (1992 to 1998 for example). However, their enthusiasm for the stock is hardly long lasting, as the number of analysts following the stock decreases as the performance decreases (1993 versus 1988).[7]

Table 3.1   Number of Analysts Covering IBM and
IBM Performance

Year	Number of Analysts	IBM Total Return (%)
1976	28	25.1
1977	26	−2.0
1978	25	13.9
1979	21	−9.6
1980	22	11.3
1981	23	−11.1
1982	32	77.9
1983	36	30.9
1984	32	4.5
1985	39	30.6
1986	40	−20.3
1987	41	−0.8
1988	42	9.6
1989	42	−19.4
1990	37	25.7
1991	33	−17.6
1992	24	−40.0
1993	26	15.8
1994	28	32.3
1995	25	25.7
1996	23	67.7
1997	26	39.3
1998	28	77.5
1999	31	17.6

Source: Based on data from I/B/E/S, Bloomberg.

WHAT MAKES A HOT STOCK NOT SO HOT?

More often than not, investors are disappointed by the returns from investing in a "hot" stock. They hear about the company from someone or something (e.g., television), invest in the stock, and the stock goes down. I don't know how many times I have heard someone say, "If you want a sure sign when a stock will go down, just look at what I am buying."

Why does this happen? Why do investors sometimes feel that they never participate when everyone else reaps the benefits of investing in riskier stocks? There are several reasons. First, psychological studies show that people tend to overstate their successes, but are relatively mute about failure. Thus, your friends might be telling you about all the great gains they have made in the stock market, but they omit telling you about the losses. In addition, studies show that because investors generally cannot admit that they have made a poor investment, they tend to sell their winners too soon and hold their losers too long. So, your friends might be telling you about their gains because their losses, although potentially quite large, are still unrealized within their portfolios. To make a long story short, cocktail party performance statistics are notoriously unreliable.

Second, my group recently did a study that showed the probability is low that a hot stock will actually provide hot returns over a five-year period.[8] In other words, if I find a hot stock today, what is the probability of it outperforming during the next five years? We used stocks' price/earnings (P/E) ratios as a proxy for the stocks' temperatures. Stocks with low P/Es at year-end were considered quite cold, while those with very high P/Es were considered quite hot. We examined whether the P/E and temperature were good predictors of future performance by examining whether stocks with higher P/Es did indeed produce both superior earnings growth and superior performance during the subsequent five-year period to when the P/E was calculated.

Table 3.2 shows a matrix of the probability of a hot stock staying hot, a cold stock staying cold, a hot stock becoming cold, and a cold stock becoming hot. The rows in the matrix measure the P/E ratio at the beginning of a five-year period. The columns show the average return five years

Table 3.2   **P/E Ratios versus Subsequent Earnings per Share (EPS) Growth: Relative Five-Year Performance (1986 to 1999)**

P/E Ratio at Beginning of Period	<5 (%)	5.0 to 9.9 (%)	Subsequent 5-Year EPS Growth Rate 10.0 to 14.9 (%)	15.0 to 19.9 (%)	20 (%)
<10	−10	29	38	62	93
10 to 15	−44	−8	30	75	111
15 to 20	−69	−36	6	67	90
20 to 30	−89	−55	−24	7	90
30+	−81	−54	−46	4	39

Source: Based on data from Merrill Lynch Quantitative Strategy.

after the P/E was calculated relative to the return of the S&P 500. For example, the P/E of a stock might have been measured at year-end 1986. We then measured the actual earnings growth rate during the subsequent five years (i.e., 1987 to 1991) and the return relative to the S&P 500 during the five-year period. Each cell in the matrix shows the average five-year return for the stocks in that particular category.

Surprisingly, many low P/E or cold stocks performed considerably better than did many high P/E or hot stocks. Stocks that had a P/E ratio of less than 10 at the beginning of a five-year period tended to significantly outperform the market so long as their actual earnings growth rate was higher than 5%. In other words, expectations for these stocks were so low that it was hard for them to disappoint and severely underperform.

However, stocks that were viewed optimistically and had high P/E ratios tended to perform poorly unless they produced significant earnings growth. Stocks that had P/E ratios higher than 30 during the time period measured tended to significantly outperform the overall market only when their earnings growth proved to be extremely high (i.e., greater than 20% per year). Expectations for these stocks were so high that the expectations were difficult to meet or surpass.

If a stock's P/E ratio is a viable proxy for its popularity, then Table 3.2 clearly shows that hot stocks should generally be avoided in favor of cold stocks. For any given eventual earnings growth rate, returns go down as the initial multiple rises. For example, a hot stock that eventually grew earnings 20% or more underperformed cold stocks that had the same earnings growth.

Perhaps more important than the average performance depicted in Table 3.2 is the probability of picking a winning stock in each cell of the table. Averages are just that, averages, and although the returns of cold stocks might be better, Table 3.2 gives no indication of how often such instances occur. Table 3.3 shows the percentage of stocks within each cell in the matrix that outperformed the S&P 500 during the five-year period after taking a stock's temperature. About 40% of the stocks with P/Es greater than 30 subsequently underperformed the market, whereas about 40% of the stocks with P/Es less than 10 subsequently outperformed the overall market.

Thus, the probability of outperforming was actually higher in hot stocks. However, if we were to combine Table 3.2 and Table 3.3 to form a weighted long-term expected return, the results would clearly favor cold

Table 3.3 P/E Ratios versus Subsequent EPS Growth: Distribution of Companies (1986 to 1999)

P/E Ratio at Beginning of Period	<5 (%)	5.0 to 9.9 (%)	Subsequent 5-Year EPS Growth Rate 10.0 to 14.9 (%)	15.0 to 19.9 (%)	20+ (%)
<10	61	16	10	4	8
10 to 15	47	20	16	7	9
15 to 20	33	19	22	13	13
20 to 30	27	11	23	17	22
30+	25	5	10	12	49

Source: Based on data from Merrill Lynch Quantitative Strategy.
Note: Rows may not add to 100% because of rounding.

stocks. Table 3.4 was constructed by combining the historical probability distribution in Table 3.3 with the return distribution in Table 3.2. Each cell's return is multiplied by its probability of occurring. This is not necessarily the most rigorous derivation (or admittedly, not even the most accurate) of expected returns, but it does demonstrate the potentially unperceived risks of investing in hot, high P/E stocks.

There appears to be somewhat of an inverse relationship between popularity and performance. The potential or expected return from the coldest stocks (i.e., the stocks with the lowest P/Es) does seem to be higher than that of the hottest stocks (i.e., the stocks with the highest P/Es). Because noise focuses on hot stocks and ignores cold ones, then why would an investor listen to noise for investment ideas given the results of Table 3.4?

Table 3.4 Weighted Average Five-Year Expected Return (1986 to 1999)

P/E Ratio	Weighted Average Expected Return (%)
<10	12.2
10.0 to 14.9	−2.2
15.0 to 19.9	−7.9
20.0 to 29.9	−17.0
>30	−3.7

Source: Based on data from Merrill Lynch Quantitative Strategy.

"GOOD" AND "BAD" INVESTORS AND THE EARNINGS EXPECTATIONS LIFE CYCLE

Using the life cycle theory, it becomes relatively easy to define "good" and "bad" investors. A good investor will buy or hold stocks with rising expectations, whereas a bad investor will buy or hold stocks with falling expectations. The data presented seem to suggest that hot stocks, very high P/E stocks, and the like appear to be very near midnight on the Earnings Expectations Life Cycle (if we use a clock analogy). Cold stocks, out-of-favor stocks, and very low P/E stocks tend to be closer to six o'clock.

As Figure 3.4 and Figure 3.5 show, good investors buy or hold stocks that are between six o'clock and midnight on the cycle or those with rising expectations. Bad investors buy or hold stocks between midnight and six o'clock or those with falling expectations.

GROWTH AND VALUE AND THE EARNINGS EXPECTATIONS LIFE CYCLE

We discuss the issues surrounding growth and value investing in detail in Chapter 10, but the subject is worth touching on briefly here. Noise can lead both growth and value investors to make mistakes that have the potential to significantly hurt portfolio performance.

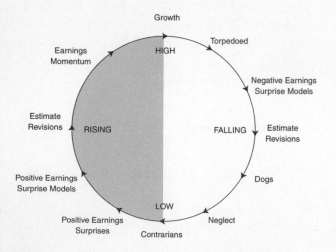

Figure 3.4   **Earnings Expectations Life Showing When Good Investors Buy or Hold Stocks**
Based on data from Merrill Lynch Quantitative Analysis.

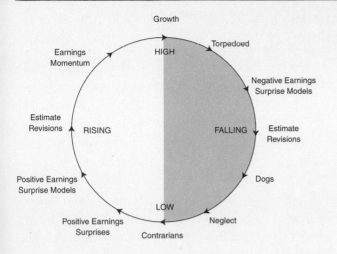

Figure 3.5   **Earnings Expectations Life Cycle Showing When Bad Investors Buy or Hold Stocks**
Based on data from Merrill Lynch Quantitative Analysis.

Figure 3.6 shows that growth investors tend to be high-expectation investors. They tend to purchase or hold stocks in the top half of the Earnings Expectations Life Cycle. Typically, the data needed to analyze growth stocks are readily available or are "visible." For example, momentum invest-

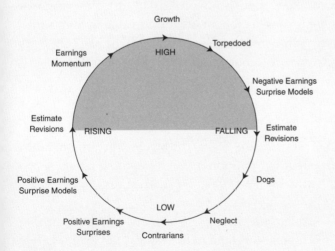

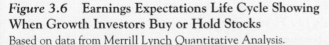

Figure 3.6   **Earnings Expectations Life Cycle Showing When Growth Investors Buy or Hold Stocks**
Based on data from Merrill Lynch Quantitative Analysis.

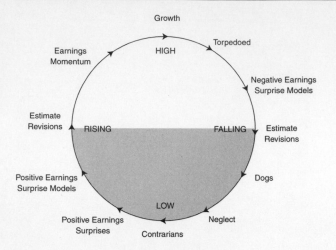

Figure 3.7   **Earnings Expectations Life Cycle Showing When Value Investors Buy or Hold Stocks**
Based on data from Merrill Lynch Quantitative Analysis.

ing, a subset of growth stock investing, has gained popularity during the last several years. These strategies rely heavily on readily and quickly available investment information.

However, as Figure 3.7 points out, value investors tend to be low-expectation investors. Whereas growth investors tend to look for popular stocks about which there is considerable information, value investors look for out-of-favor stocks. In some cases, value investors might have difficulty finding data necessary to analyze a company under consideration for investment.

A Simple Description of How Noise Causes Investment Errors

Let's overlay Figures 3.4, 3.5, 3.6, and 3.7 to get Figure 3.8. By doing this, we have divided the Earnings Expectations Life Cycle into quarters: Good Growth, Bad Growth, Bad Value, and Good Value when reading clockwise from nine o'clock.

Figure 3.8 helps to explain why investors make investment errors that are related to noise. Growth investors tend to hold stocks too long, whereas value investors tend to buy stocks too early. The silly phrase "buy low, sell high" is difficult advice to follow. Value investors have trouble buying low, whereas growth investors have trouble selling high.

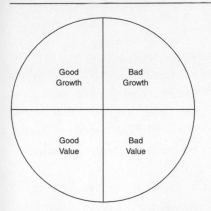

| Good Growth | Bad Growth |
| Good Value | Bad Value |

Figure 3.8   Good and Bad Growth and Value
Based on data from Merrill Lynch Quantitative Analysis.

Noise and Growth Investors

Growth investors often worry about finding a good growth stock, but the Earnings Expectations Life Cycle suggests finding such stocks is relatively easy. Analysts are upgrading earnings estimates and relative strength and momentum are building by the time a stock reaches nine o'clock on the cycle. Forecasts for earnings growth, sales growth, profit margins, and market share are reasonably readily available. Buying a growth stock may actually be relatively simple.

However, the Earnings Expectations Life Cycle suggests that the difference between good and bad growth stock investors is based not on what stocks they buy, but rather on what stocks they sell. Who was the investor who sold the hot stock at the stock's top tick? Most growth investors will admit that finding a growth stock is not necessarily difficult. However, it is very difficult to determine when the stock's story is going to blow up.

Why is selling so difficult for growth investors? One possible reason is that stocks probably receive the most attention and the news about the company is probably the most positive at midnight on the life cycle. When growth investors listen to noise and fall in love with a stock because it has performed (note the past tense) so well rather than doing sound fundamental research and predicting future returns, then the odds of being blindsided by bad news increase.

Thus, some growth investors' portfolio performance might be poor because they do not know how to ignore noise and sell stocks.

Noise and Value Investors

Value investors often worry about holding on to stocks too long. They cull their portfolios for stocks that are potentially overvalued, and ironically are more afraid of holding stocks too long than are most growth managers. However, the Earnings Expectations Life Cycle suggests that value investors' worries are somewhat unnecessary. Although holding value stocks for too long might turn an investor's portfolio into a growth-oriented portfolio, it probably will not hurt performance.[9]

The Earnings Expectations Life Cycle does suggest that value investors' performances typically suffer because they buy stocks prematurely. A value investor might think that all the bad news about a company is already reflected in the stock's price, but the stock might still underperform for some time. Value investors sometimes say they like to buy stocks early, but that they will at least own the stock at the bottom. That sounds good, but buying stocks too early means significant underperformance that might last longer than the outperformance incurred while holding the stock.

It is interesting that the phrase "buy early, but be there at the bottom" sounds so much more conservative than buying a hot stock and holding it too long. However, the life cycle aptly points out that neither strategy is the sign of a good investor. If you buy a stock and it goes down 20% then subsequently rises 40%, it is ultimately no different than buying a stock that goes up 40% and then drops 20%. Either way, the return is 12%.

Why do value managers buy too early? One potential reason is noise or rather the abundance of negative noise. Growth managers hold stocks too long because they are encouraged to do so by all the good news regarding companies' prospects. Value managers may buy stocks too early because of the abundance of bad news about the company. They may feel that the news is so negative that any improvement in a company's fundamentals would produce positive surprises. They forget, however, that the time to buy stocks as a contrarian is not when the news is overwhelmingly negative but rather when there is no news at all. Consensus is that the company is so bad there is no need to report, comment, or research the company.

Noise can effect investment decisions regardless of whether the news flow is positive or negative. Value investors need to realize that overwhelming negative news should be ignored as much as growth investors need to ignore overwhelming positive news.

THE NOISE LIFE CYCLE

We now know expectations for stocks change through time, and the noise surrounding a stock is probably more proportional to its past performance than to its future performance. Voiced popularity does not necessarily mean outperformance. Actually, neither does voiced unpopularity. Rather, it is the lack of attention at all that probably is the key to outperformance.

We can construct a Noise Life Cycle, Figure 3.9, based on the Earnings Expectations Life Cycle. At six o'clock there is no noise whatsoever. A stock would be completely ignored. At midnight, we would probably find the maximum amount of news flow and noise. In between, noise gets louder from six o'clock to midnight, and it gets softer from midnight to six o'clock.

The maximum temptation to invest will occur close to midnight. There will be abundant good news about a company, a company's managers will be lauded for their skill (they might even write their own management books), or a company might be considered a core long-term holding. At six o'clock, stocks will be dropped from the S&P 500, managers will be fired, and everyone will forget the company even exists (are they still around?).

Perhaps the most important point of this chapter is good investors buy when there is no noise, and sell when there is a lot of noise.

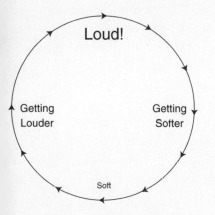

Figure 3.9   Noise Life Cycle

Chapter 4

Noise and Long-Term Investment Planning

Twenty-three years ago, I was in college and had long hair. Jimmy Carter was president; the Iranian hostage incident was in the future. I drove a Datsun with a 1.4-liter engine, and Japanese cars were quickly gaining market share in the United States because of the 1970s oil scares. Energy was a growth industry, and *Dallas*, the lurid stories of a back-stabbing Texas oil family, was becoming a very popular television show. There were no personal computers, fax machines, or 800 numbers. Disco was still growing in popularity thanks to *Saturday Night Fever*. Because of rising inflation, the stock market's return for the prior 10 years was about 47%. That's not 47% per year as many speculative investors now expect from an investment. That's 47%, a mere 3.9% per year, for the full 10 years. Stocks comprised a very small proportion of individuals' investment portfolios.

In 23 years, I will be 65. Given how dramatically life has changed in the past 23 years, do I really know with any certainty what will happen during the next 23 years? Should I extrapolate recent events into the future, or should I anticipate changes as extreme as those that have occurred during the last 23 years? The return on stocks has been nearly 400% during the last 10 years. Although it might sound reasonable to expect equity returns to be as high or nearly as high for the foreseeable future, if I had extrapolated asset returns 23 years ago, I would probably have been significantly

71

underinvested in equities relative to an asset mix that might have proved more successful. Technology has been the hot sector during much of the 1990s. Perhaps I should concentrate a long-term portfolio in that growth sector? If I had concentrated in the hot sector 23 years ago, I would have invested in the energy sector. Energy subsequently performed miserably compared to other sectors of the equity market. Even risk-averse investors would have been seriously misled by the past performance. Bonds under-performed cash during the 1970s by a compounded 1.8 percentage points per year. Yet bonds outperformed cash by 2.3 percentage points per year during the 1980s.

Undoubtedly, things today will seem as silly or as amazing 23 years from now as those of 23 years ago appear today. As mentioned earlier in this book, the phrase "past performance is not necessarily indicative of future returns" is usually dismissed as legal mumbo-jumbo, but it is more true than most investors believe. However, if the statement is generally true how should you plan a long-term investment strategy?

I NEVER SUSPECTED THAT THINGS WERE CHANGING

During the summer of 1980, I remember the father of a friend literally danc-ing around the kitchen table one morning because his money market fund had yielded 25% for the previous week. Short-term money market funds were a hot investment because inflation had caused short-term interest rates to be very high. The funds were relatively risk free and offered very high returns when compared to the paltry returns of the stock market at that time. As noted before, investors like less risk with higher returns, and money market funds seemed to offer both. It was easy to monitor your investment because the newspapers had special weekly tables that showed the yields on every money market fund available. Bank deposit returns were printed only quarterly, and you had to physically go to the bank to get them. Money market funds seemed to be the best of everything.

When I got my first job that summer and began to save and invest, I only looked at money market funds. Everyone else was investing in them, and it was easy to find information on the funds because the newspapers were filled with advertisements for them. Stocks were considered by many individual investors to be too risky given the poor returns of the 1970s and the 1980 recession. I sent away for five or six prospectuses and read each one thoroughly. I was intent on researching each fund carefully before making my investment. After my thorough research, I invested in the one with the second highest yield. The highest yielding fund seemed somewhat extreme to me, but the second highest seemed fine.

The 1980s bull market in stocks began in August 1982. I continued to invest in money market funds and ignored the stock market entirely until after the 1983–1984 correction. In fact, I probably had too much invested in money market funds and not enough in stocks for most of the early to mid-1980s.

Why did I invest in money markets? I saw my friend's father jumping for joy at his returns, inflation was a common fear, and newspaper advertisements made obtaining information about the funds very easy. I thoroughly researched the funds, although realistically I did not know very much about the characteristics of the short-term fixed-income markets. Ultimately, I simply chose the second highest yielding fund based on past performance. I did no analysis of future potential returns.[1] Despite the bull market in stocks, I remained in my money market fund. Why? Past performance was etched in my mind. I never suspected that things were changing.

This story will sound similar to many investors' recent experiences if we change a few words.

Why did I invest in technology stocks? I saw my friend's father jumping for joy at his returns, the new economy was forming, and newspaper and television advertisements made obtaining information about technology funds very easy. I thoroughly researched the funds, although realistically I did not know very much about the characteristics of the NASDAQ or IPO markets. Ultimately, I simply chose the second highest returning fund. Despite the bull market in other sectors, I remained in my technology fund. Why? Past performance was etched in my mind. I never suspected that things were changing.

NOISE AND LONG-TERM INVESTING DON'T GO TOGETHER

The moral of the preceding story is that noise and long-term investing don't go together. As mentioned many times so far in this book, the providers of information often do not have the investor's best interest in mind. Providers of information are hardly altruistic despite the claims of some to the contrary. Thus, we would have to ask whether information flow is geared to long-term or short-term investing. We have already concluded most information flow is geared to short-term trading in order to make the user of the information return for yet more information. Not unlike a pusher and drug addict relationship.

Sometimes purveyors of information resort to the core long-term holding moniker mentioned in Chapter 2 and Chapter 3 in order to persuade investors that a stock or sector is still a hot investment despite underperformance. For example, an investment newsletter that focuses on technology stocks might start concentrating on longer-term investment ideas when the sector underperforms in order to keep investors interested in the sector and, of more importance, interested in the newsletter. A technology sector newsletter that encourages investors to avoid the technology sector probably will soon be out of business. Thus, investors might want to be wary of investment information that claims to focus on the long-term prospects of a previously hot sector.

Rather than relying on the pat claim that stocks outperform over the long term, this chapter focuses on how noise disrupts true long-term planning. I frequently meet people who "manage" their IRAs on a daily basis, but have no idea how much money they will need to retire to the lifestyle they desire. They merely assume that the necessary funds will be amassed because of superior investment returns historically provided by stocks.

In addition, we discuss how often to review a long-term investment plan. Daily review allows noise to play too large a role in one's long-term strategy. However, if you had invested in energy stocks in 1977, you might have had good performance for a few years but would have suffered during the next 20 or so. When is it appropriate to review your long-term strategy? How do you avoid letting noise influence the process? One good rule to follow: disciplined investors invest according to time, not according to event.

HOT TODAY; GONE TOMORROW

I mentioned in the previous paragraph that you probably would have been severely disappointed by the long-term returns associated with investing in the hot stocks of the late 1970s. In fact, we could choose many periods and we would find that investors were ultimately disappointed by the long-term returns provided by investing in hot stocks. Will investors be disappointed by the returns from investing in today's hot stocks such as technology, telecom, and media during the next 10 to 15 years? My guess is they will.

Different events can ruin hot stories within the stock markets. In the case of energy, slowing global growth cut the demand for energy combined with tremendous amounts of exploration and overproduction. In the case of the 1980s technology companies, overcapacity and rapidly changing technologies quickly made products obsolete. Interestingly, in the 1980s technology case, everything that economists predicted might come true because of the personal computer did indeed come true. However, many of the companies that were hot stocks during that period no longer exist. They were never profitable despite the strong trends toward the greater use of technology within the economy.

As Chapter 3's Earnings Expectations Life Cycle highlighted, hot investments at one point in time become the next period's cold ones. In addition, remember that the phrase *core long-term holding* is often merely a euphemism for an underperforming investment that is many investors' favorite because of superior past performance. Investors looking for long-term performance might look at stocks about which no one cares rather than at those that are considered hot. When making long-term plans, therefore, it is important to remember the lesson of the Earnings Expectations Life Cycle.

Rather than following the latest investment fad and attempting to invest for the long term by listening to short-term noise, long-term strategies should be based on understanding liabilities, goal setting, diversification, risk tolerance, time horizon, and discipline (see Table 4.1).

Table 4.1   How Noise Affects Long-Term Strategic Planning

Factor for Long-Term Strategy	*Effect of Noise*
Diversification	Reduces desire for diversification and risk reduction
Goal setting; understanding asset/liability matching	Reduces tendency to pay attention to asset/liability matching because of high past performance
Risk tolerance	Tendency to take too much risk.
Time horizon	Tendency to think short term instead of long term
Discipline	Tendency to abandon set strategy because of event

Diversification. We fully discuss the importance of diversification in Chapter 5. Nonetheless, a brief comment is warranted here. Diversification is perhaps the simplest tool for reducing the risk of a portfolio. By combining assets that have positive long-term returns, but whose returns move in somewhat opposite directions in shorter time periods, overall portfolio volatility goes down, and an investor can sleep more easily at night.

Noise can distort the propensity to diversify a portfolio in two ways. First, because noise tends to accentuate a hot sector, investors tend to concentrate portfolios in that particular sector. In extreme cases, such as energy in the 1970s, small caps in the early 1980s, junk bonds in the late 1980s, or technology during 1999–2000, investors do so to extreme proportions; they specifically do not diversify in order to obtain higher returns. Investors shun diversification's simple risk-reduction potential in order to take more risk. Of course, such strategies are not perceived to be risky, but rather are perceived to be safe because it is inconceivable to investors that they would actually lose money in the particular hot sector.

Second, noise makers often ridicule those who suggest diversification might be appropriate as not being attuned to the opportunities of a hot investment. Many analysts have been criticized for taking contrary views. Such criticism not only occurs in the media. Sell-side analysts (those who work for brokerage firms, as opposed to buy-side analysts who work for money management firms) are often criticized by their clients for taking contrary views. Thus, there often is little incentive for analysts to be contrary and buck the noise.

Portfolio managers face the same pressures and tend to ignore basic diversification in order to take excessive risk. For example, the performance of many portfolio managers' portfolios is measured relative to that of a peer group. If the peer group's portfolios are not diversified and have significantly overweighted a hot sector, then the contrarian portfolio manager might be viewed as a poor manager if the hot sector performs well despite the manager's concerns regarding risk and diversification. Pension consultants and individual investors might begin to avoid the contrarian manager because the manager's portfolio performance significantly lags that of other managers. As the contrarian manager's business begins to erode, the tendency often is to conform, to stop diversifying, and to take more risk.

Goal Setting. Noise reduces the propensity to set goals and understand asset/liability management because investors believe that long-term returns of the particular hot sector or investment will more than satisfy any future liabilities. For example, a goal for many investors these days is to find the "next Microsoft." Instead of defining future liabilities and devising a long-term strategy to meet those liabilities, investors looking for the next Microsoft are speculating. Whether they strike gold or not, their future liabilities are not going away.

More important, they have no idea whether finding the next Microsoft will actually satisfy those future obligations. An investor might actually be lucky enough (appropriate words, I think) to find the next Microsoft. The stock might actually appreciate 10- or 20-fold in the next 15 years. However, the investor might not have invested enough in the stock to make the investment's value large enough to offset future liabilities.

Risk Tolerance. Assessing risk tolerance is one of the most difficult aspects to investing, and we discuss it fully in Chapter 6. Noise tends to entice investors to take more risk than they truly want to. Risk tolerance and diversification are obviously somewhat related. If you are more risk adverse, then it is generally wise to diversify your portfolio more. To do this, you could either hold a larger proportion of truly safe assets (e.g., T-bills) or increase the proportion of inversely correlated securities (i.e., when your asset's returns go up, another's returns go down).

Noise makes risky assets appear safer than they truly are, and thus encourages investors to take more risk in their portfolios than they think they are. Again taking a recent example, many investors probably thought technology stocks were safer than the stocks were during 2000 because of the noise surrounding the sector. Most investors probably could not conceive at the beginning of the year that the returns of many of the stocks in the sector would be so disastrous, thus they concentrated their portfolios in technology stocks.

Whenever the market becomes highly volatile, I remind investors that if they are disconcerted by the volatility, then they should reassess their risk tolerance and diversification. The day-to-day, week-to-week, and month-to-month volatility of the markets should have no bearing on your ability to sleep at night, providing that your risk tolerance is assessed correctly and your portfolio is diversified properly.

A good rule of thumb is that, if you ever have trouble sleeping at night because of your portfolio's volatility, you are probably taking too much risk. My personal portfolio is often positioned less aggressively than are the strategies that I suggest to some investors because I know my own risk tolerance. If I have trouble sleeping at night, it might be because of a publisher's deadline, but it will not be attributable to the volatility of my personal portfolio.

Time Horizon. Noise tends to shorten investors' time horizons. Investors may claim they are investing for the long term, but noise tends to make them act like traders, rather than like long-term investors. Perhaps the most extreme cases I have ever seen are today's day traders. To these folks, investing is measured in minutes rather than months, quarters, or years. My guess is that they are not aware that the probability of outperforming goes down as one makes an increasing number of investment decisions; a topic that we discuss at length in Chapter 7 on time horizon. Consider the following question. If you are a long-term investor, then why do you look at the stock tables in the newspaper or log on to an investment website every day to check stock prices? Will the day-to-day movements of a stock really affect your long-term strategy? The answer is simple: no.

UNDERSTANDING SIMPLE ASSET/LIABILITY MANAGEMENT

Perhaps the most important aspect of long-term planning is the understanding of your future liabilities. Most investors have no idea whatsoever what their future financial obligations will be. A single person with no children clearly has a very different future liability stream than does a parent of five children, but how much different? Just as you budget your income to allow for shorter-term liabilities such as mortgage payments, insurance payments, auto payments, and so forth, you should have a long-term budget as well.

Let's assume that you want to save for your child's education and you have 10 years before the child goes to college. Looking for the next Microsoft might help you to achieve this goal, but it probably is not the smartest method for achieving the goal of being able to pay for college in 10 years.

There are several things that you should consider in framing the above-stated goal. First, how much do the costs of a college education rise every year, and what is a reasonable approximation of the cost of college in 10 years? Second, what is the probability that your investment will actually achieve the goal? Third, if your investment does not achieve the goal, how far off can you afford to be? Fourth, and always important, do you want to sleep at night?

Today's noise probably only tells you college is getting more expensive, you must save for it, and you should take a lot of risk when saving to pay for college education because you are saving for something well into the future, and stocks outperform over the long run. Some noise makers may further emphasize riskier stocks because those who take risk are compensated for it over the long run. However, here is how I would approach the problem.

Reasonably Estimating a Liability

The first question was how much do the costs of a college education rise every year, and what is a reasonable approximation of the cost in 10 years? The point to this question is to reasonably estimate a future liability. College might cost $25,000 per year today, but we all know that the odds of it costing the same or less in 10 years are rather low. We need to approximate the cost 10 years hence.

Figure 4.1 shows the year-to-year rate of change in the Consumer Price Index (CPI) for Education since its inception in 1994. Since 1994, the slowest increase in education costs was 4.5% and the highest was 6.7%. Approximating the cost using the lowest rate of change would probably lead you to invest too little. Using the highest rate might be more conservative, but saving so much might constrain your family's current standard of living.

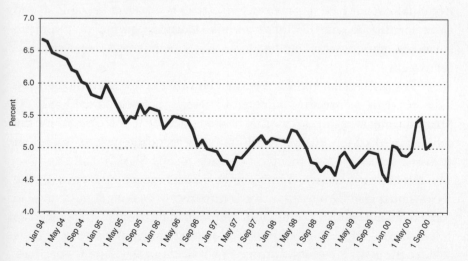

Figure 4.1 Consumer Price Index for Education (Year to Year Percent Change)
Based on data from the Bureau of Labor Statistics.

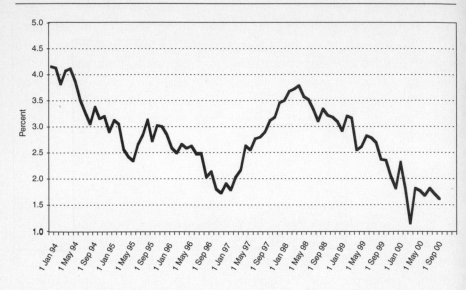

Figure 4.2   **Difference between Consumer Price Index for Education and Overall Consumer Price Index**
Based on data from the Bureau of Labor Statistics.

It may be more accurate to consider college costs within the context of price increases in the overall economy. Figure 4.2 compares the CPI for Education with the overall CPI. The CPI for Education typically rises more than the overall CPI. That means investments aimed at keeping up with overall inflation, such as inflation-linked bonds, will probably not provide enough return to keep up with the price increases associated with education.

Figure 4.3 estimates the potential best-case and worst-case scenarios. The best-case scenario is computed by taking today's $100,000 ($25,000 times four years of college) cost and assuming that the increases in the cost of higher education increase by 4.5% per year for the next 10 years. The worst-case scenario is computed by taking today's $100,000 and assuming the cost of higher education increases by 6.7% per year for the next 10 years.

The spread between the two is rather wide, making long-term planning quite uncertain. You might, therefore, assume the worst-case scenario because you certainly would not mind having budgeted for the worst-case scenario to have the costs ultimately be less. However, as we soon discuss, although it is obviously very conservative to assume the worst-case scenario, the costs of such safety can be prohibitively high.

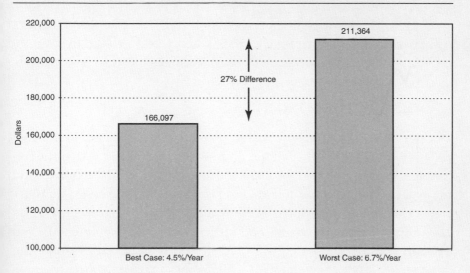

Figure 4.3   Potential Best- and Worst-Case Scenarios for Education Costs 10 Years Hence

This analysis does, however, give us some general idea of how much we must eventually save in order to pay for college. Table 4.2 outlines the potential eventual cost of a four-year college education beginning in 10 years. It is important to remember that only the freshman year begins in 10 years. Senior year is three years later, meaning that you must anticipate 13 years of cost increases for that year rather than simply 10. The table includes three scenarios: one in which the cost of college increases 4% per year, one in which the cost increases 6% per year, and one in which the cost increases 8% per year.

Table 4.2   Potential Cost of 4-Year Education Beginning in 10 Years

Year	Cost in 10 Years Present Cost ($)	4%/Year Inc ($)	6%/Year Inc ($)	8%/Year Inc ($)
Freshman	25,000.00	37,006.11	44,771.19	53,973.12
Sophomore	25,000.00	38,486.35	47,457.46	58,290.97
Junior	25,000.00	40,025.81	50,304.91	62,954.25
Senior	25,000.00	41,626.84	53,323.21	67,990.59
Total	100,000.00	157,145.10	195,856.77	243,208.95

The table clearly points out that you should anticipate that the cost of college will nearly double if the cost increases by 6% per year. Even at 4% per year, you should expect more than a 50% increase in the cost of college.

STOCKS FOR THE LONG TERM?

The next step is to attempt to match the anticipated liability, in this case college education, with a portfolio of investments that best match the risk preference of the investor, the funds that are anticipated to be needed, and the expected return of the investment. Figure 4.4 takes the best- and worst-case scenarios and compares those annualized inflation rates with average 10-year rates of return on the S&P 500, long-term Treasury bonds, and Treasury bills during the postwar period.[2] During the best of times, the safest assets, T-bills, might provide a high enough return to cover the costs of college education, but only stocks provide returns high enough to offset the costs during the worst of times. So far our analysis seems to be pointing toward riskier assets, however, our analysis has so far assumed a one-time investment.

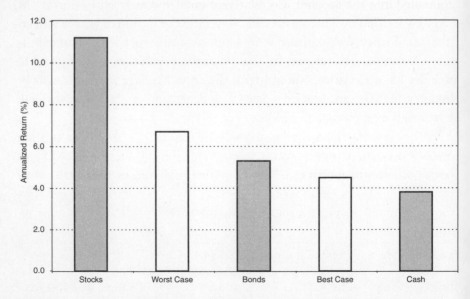

Figure 4.4   **Potential Best- and Worst-Case Scenarios and Asset Returns**

Table 4.3   An Obvious Point: More Invested Means More Returned

Amount Saved	Annual Return ($)				
	3%	5%	7%	9%	11%
5,000.00	59,038.98	66,033.94	73,918.00	82,801.47	92,807.15
10,000.00	118,077.96	132,067.87	147,835.99	165,602.93	185,614.30
15,000.00	177,116.94	198,101.81	221,753.99	248,404.40	278,421.45
20,000.00	236,155.91	264,135.74	295,671.99	331,205.87	371,228.60
25,000.00	295,194.89	330,169.68	369,589.98	414,007.33	464,035.75

THE MODERN DAY "CHRISTMAS CLUB"

When I was young, banks used to have plans to help people to save for Christmas gift spending. They were called Christmas Clubs, and members would each week pay an installment into their Christmas Club account. The money could be withdrawn prior to Christmas to support gift buying. Although somewhat hokey by today's standards, such clubs did get savers to plan for eventual liabilities and to calculate how much they would need to save in order to buy some dollar amount of gifts. Of course, because the time horizon was so short (i.e., generally less than one year), the interest that was computed into the account was relatively small and meaningless.

Unlike with a Christmas Club, when attempting to budget for longer-term liabilities you should not ignore the compounding effects of an investment. You might think that you have to save $5,000 per year in order to save for college, but you should remember that the initial $5,000 will be invested for 10 years, the second for 9, and so forth. Each investment will compound over its time horizon.

In addition, again similar to the Christmas Club, the more you put into the account, the more you will eventually have. If I invest $10,000 per year, I will eventually have more than if I invest $5,000 per year in the same investments. Table 4.3 supports this rather obvious point. (Keep reading, there is a reason to present such an obvious fact.)

MATCHING ASSETS AND LIABILITIES

By combining Tables 4.2 and 4.3, in order to pay for college, we must save between $10,000 and $15,000 per year when anticipating a return of about

9% or about $20,000 per year when anticipating a return of about 3% when assuming a relatively conservative 6% increase in costs during the next 13 years. If we assume that college costs will rise by 8% per year, then Table 4.2 demonstrated that we would need slightly more than $243,000. Thus, only the combinations in Table 4.3 that produce figures greater than $243,000 are worth considering if we assumed that 8% per year increase in college costs was more appropriate. It is impossible to reach the goal at all if we saved only $5,000 per year. Similarly, we must assume a return of at least 9% per year if saving $10,000 per year even if college costs increase by only 3% per year. If we received 11% return per year and invested $5,000 per year, we would still fall short about $150,000 of the target amount needed.

A QUICK COMMENT ON RISK AND RETURN

The combination of Table 4.2 and Table 4.3 also shows that there is no free lunch when investing. If you want ultimately to have more money in the future, you must do one of two things (or both if you are very aggressive). If you want to invest only small amounts so as to have more funds for current consumption, then you must take more risk in order to attempt to attain higher returns. If you want to take less risk so as to sleep better at night, then you must save more and potentially limit your current standard of living.

DEBT AND THE STANDARD OF LIVING

Maintaining their standard of living may be why so many people find it difficult to save for future liabilities. A typical family might not be able to save so much per year (and per child) without scrimping their standard of living. Household debt, and the management of it, is well beyond the scope of this book. However, noise does encourage individuals to take on more debt than they probably should. Given the preceding simple example and the easy availability of debt, it is easy to see why many Americans have high debt levels.

Many people might believe they are saving for the future, but if their current debt levels are high, they might not be saving at all. They are essentially borrowing money to invest. This does not mean that they are directly using their credit cards to buy stocks. Rather, it means they are saving and using debt to maintain current consumption. This is a very bad practice in my opinion. The return on investment under these conditions must not only be high enough to pay for college, but also must be high enough to pay off the debt. This may be a daunting task. For example, if debt used to maintain current consumption must be paid at 15% per year and college costs are rising 5% per year, then investments must return 20% per year to break even. Despite noise to the contrary, we cannot save *and* spend. A choice must be made.

By this point, you might be wondering what noise and hype have to do with this process. Noise encourages poor decision making with respect to long-term planning and measuring potential liabilities in a number of ways. Although there might be many, we focus on three. The first has to do with searching for the next Microsoft. The second might be termed "get rich quick." The third might be called "have your cake and eat it too."

ATTEMPTING TO FIND THE NEXT MICROSOFT

I believe the attempt to find the next Microsoft is a futile effort. For a stock to appreciate 10-fold during a 10-year period, it would have to appreciate about 26% per year or roughly triple the long-term return on the S&P 500. That's not 26% for one year, that is 26% for each of 10 years. Despite what most investors believe regarding their stock selection prowess, the only way most will find such a stock is by luck.

Even if you were lucky enough to find a stock that appreciated 10-fold during the next 10 years, you might have to have a substantial initial investment in order to pay for college in 10 years. A $5,000 investment would only appreciate to $50,400 during the 10-year period, and that would not be nearly enough to pay for college in our example. Simple math shows that an initial investment of about $16,000, an amount many households could not afford to incrementally save in any one year, would have to be invested in the one stock to meet the liabilities that would occur when aggressively assuming that college costs increase by only 4% per year. Investing in only one company also implies no diversification. Would you be able to sleep at night knowing that your child's future college education relies on the success of only one company?[3]

Another thing to consider when looking for the next Microsoft is that if you had a stock that appreciated 10-fold and paid for the anticipated college costs after only 5 years instead of 10, would you sell the stock and lock in your gains?[4]

GET RICH QUICK

A character in a television commercial for an online broker says that he wants to retire rich, and he is going to do so based on trades that cost him $8.95 per trade. Although investors certainly should seek to limit transaction costs whenever and however possible, the commercial leads us to believe that this person will make a lot of trades on his way to becoming rich.

Another commercial for an online broker showed a teenage son being reprimanded by his parents for coming home after his curfew. He claims that he had to drop off his friends and got caught in traffic. It turns out that the teenager flies a helicopter and was dropping off his friends in different cities in the United States. The implication is that he can afford his helicopter because of his successful online trading.

I believe such advertisements do unknowing investors a disservice. If investors are led to believe that they can easily get filthy rich by frequently and actively trading in the stock market, then there is little incentive to actually plan for the future or to consider risk/return preferences. Perhaps supporting my point, I strongly doubt that many day traders have well-thought-out financial plans or have even considered long-term asset/liability matching.

A Wall Street senior executive was once vilified for making a statement to the effect that online trading would ruin investors' financial futures. Although I certainly have no idea what the executive truly meant, I think there was an element of truth in his statement. I do not think the ability to trade online should be criticized. However, I do believe we should criticize brokers (whether online or traditional) who do not encourage their customers to plan. I think many of the online brokers' advertisements are quite clear: Wealth is achieved by trading, not by planning. At $8.95 per trade, it may be easy to understand why they advertise as they do. Fewer trades from structured and disciplined long-term investing might mean lower profits.

HAVE YOUR CAKE AND EAT IT TOO

Noise can lead investors to believe that risk and return are not opposites. As mentioned, we discuss the notion of risk more fully in Chapter 6, but it is important to realize that noise encourages risk taking without ever outlining the risks. Think of all the hype that surrounded Internet stocks during 1999, but few ever suggested that the stocks might lose 50%, 75%, or 90% of their values during 2000.

We have all heard that stocks outperform over the long term, but few discuss the risks that come with that long-term view. Because most investors have not experienced a bear market, few have any concept of the risk surrounding equities. As mentioned earlier, some articles advocating equity investment have suggested that bonds are riskier than stocks. Sounds great doesn't it? High returns with no risk.[5] I don't believe it for a second. There are no free lunches in the financial markets. There are no superior returns in the financial markets without perceived risks. Not to be a party pooper, but you can't have your cake and eat it, too.

TAXES TAKE THEIR BITE

Our college expense example left out one important factor: taxes. Short-term gains are taxed as income, whereas long-term gains (the definition of which seems to change every several years) are generally taxed at a lower rate to encourage long-term saving and investment. Thus, if you are in one of the higher income tax brackets, frequent trading has yet another draw-back in that a larger proportion of your gain goes to the government. Some have suggested that the combination of a bull market in stocks and investors' increasing propensity to trade more frequently has generated so much revenue for the government that it has helped to contribute to the current federal budget surplus. I don't know if that is true, but I do know that long-term capital gains are generally taxed at lower rates than are short-term gains. Thus, if you want to trade frequently, your short-term investment returns must be incrementally high enough to compensate for the incremental costs of higher short-term tax rates.

DISCIPLINE IS REVIEWING STRATEGIES BY TIME AND NOT BY EVENT

One of the best investors I know rebalances his portfolio only twice per year. He can tell you today the dates of his rebalances going out into the future. I think one of the things that makes his track record so terrific and so consistent is he revisits his strategy according to time, not according to event.

Reviewing a long-term strategy according to time creates discipline and helps to prevent three things. First, it helps to cut down on the propensity to trade because of noise. Noise and hype encourage trading, but rebalancing according to time helps to control the urge to trade. Second, it helps an investor keep sight of the eventual goal. Noise tends to obscure the goal by highlighting events that seem important but will probably be forgotten in several weeks. Third, noise tends to lead investors away from a stated strategy. For example, investors are increasingly investing by following a program of a stated disciplined strategy. If the disciplined strategy does not work for a period of time, noise will encourage the investors to switch to a *better* strategy. Remember that the Holy Grail of investing has yet to be found. Strategies will always have periods of underperformance. Constantly switching strategies defeats the purpose of attempting to be disciplined in the first place. There are cries for more discipline when investing, but the oddity is that many of those who claim discipline is helpful actually encourage the opposite by constantly searching for, and claiming to have found, the Holy Grail.

Sometimes there are what appear to be major events in the financial markets, and investors tend to alter or abandon strategies when those events occur. However, it is only well after the event occurs when we realize whether the event was truly important for long-term investors or not. Perhaps a great example was the so-called mini-crash. My guess is that most readers of this book have never heard of it or know when it occurred (October 1989). At the time, it was considered a major event in the financial markets. Roughly 11 years later, most investors have not even heard of what was considered a major financial event. This shows how we must be careful to avoid letting noise affect our long-term planning. We might have been tempted to significantly alter a sound long-term plan in October 1989. Although important at the time, history has shown that the mini-crash was not a significant event for long-term investors.

Thus, I suggest that investors review true long-term strategies by time rather than by event. One of the simplest methods for screening out noise is to review strategies by the calendar. For many investors, once per year is probably satisfactory. Realistically, once every two or three years is probably even better for true long-term investors (i.e., time horizons of more than 15 years), but asking an investor to ignore that much noise might be too much to ask. Thus, I typically suggest that strategies and plans be reviewed once per year.

Rather than worrying about whether a strategy is outperforming and considering switching to another one if it is not, I think it is critically important to review the portfolio's diversification and risk characteristics if one is not pleased with shorter-term results. These topics are discussed in the next two chapters.

Chapter 5

Noise and Diversification

The popular perception is that diversification will help your portfolio perform better over the long term. That perception is actually incorrect. Diversification is a risk-reduction tool and not a return-enhancement tool. It will not necessarily improve a portfolio's returns through time, but it will probably help the owner of the portfolio sleep better at night.

As stated several times before in this book, there are no free lunches in the financial markets. The noise that surrounds the financial markets today might lead you to believe that higher returns and lower risk are readily available, but there are very few investments that truly offer higher returns with lower risk. In Chapter 4, I stated that it was impossible to save and consume, and one of the reasons to plan for the long term was to make the choice between current consumption and paying for future liabilities. Similar choices exist with respect to diversification. Noise makers will argue otherwise, but investors must choose between high returns and lower risk.

This chapter is intended to do several things: (1) define exactly what diversification is; (2) explain how investors should consider many layers of diversification; and (3) show how noise attempts to counter attempts by investors to diversify their portfolios.

I think it is worthwhile to repeat a theme of the book that was mentioned in the Introduction. This book is not a how-to book. This chapter is not intended to teach you how to diversify your portfolio. Rather, the chapter's purpose is to dispel certain misconceptions, and to point out important issues regarding diversification that get buried by noise.

WHAT IS DIVERSIFICATION?

As mentioned, the popular perception is that diversification is something that will help your portfolio perform better than if you had not diversified. All too often, riskier assets are sold to investors by showing them how adding a risky investment to a portfolio will enhance their portfolio's returns. The combination of assets might reduce the overall risk of the portfolio, but few would invest if the proposed investment was shown to reduce the portfolio's overall return. A risky asset that outperforms for one period might underperform during the next. The diversification effects might remain within the portfolio despite that the superior returns of the additional asset might be fleeting.

First, let's define diversification, then we can investigate how the term is sometimes misused. To diversify your portfolio means to add assets to an existing portfolio so that the overall portfolio's returns are less volatile or are more predictable than are those of either asset alone. Perhaps the following three charts will make the purpose of diversification clear. Figure 5.1 shows the value of a hypothetical asset for 10 periods. Although the asset performs well over the entire 10 periods, there are periods during which it performs well and periods in which it does not. I have classified those periods in which the asset performs well as "happy" ones, and those periods in which it performs poorly as "sad" ones.

For this investment, the investor would be happy, then sad, then happy again, then sad again, and so on. The investor might sleep well when happy, but worry at night when sad. In the example as I have drawn it, the periods of happiness and sadness are roughly of equal intensity and equal lengths of time. However, suppose that the periods of sadness last longer than the periods of happiness. In other words, the happy periods are very short, but the sad periods are very long despite that the long-term returns of the asset are quite good. The investor might consider getting rid of this asset either because of the manic-depressive nature of the returns, or because a

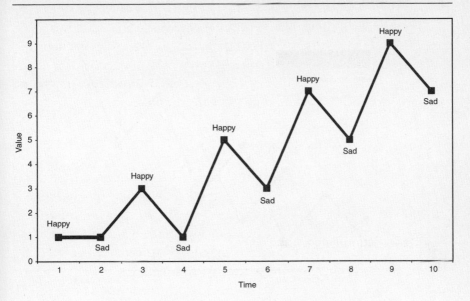

Figure 5.1   **Single Asset's Value and Volatility through Time with Investor Reaction**

sad period might last quite long. During extended periods of sadness, the investor might think that the asset might no longer appreciate and be tempted to sell it during sad periods.

Suppose we add a second asset to the single-asset portfolio. The second asset is somewhat special in that its returns are the inverse of those of our first asset. A statistician would say that Asset #2's returns are inversely correlated with Asset #1's. Inversely correlated means that the returns of Asset #2 go up when those of Asset #1 go down, and vice versa. In no period are their returns similar despite that both appreciate through time.[1] Figure 5.2 shows the values of two hypothetical assets that are inversely correlated. Notice that one asset's returns rise as the other asset's falls.

Further, suppose that Asset #1 and Asset #2 are in a portfolio so that they both comprise 50% of the portfolio. We can now easily see the effects of diversifying. Figure 5.3 shows the value of Asset #1, the value of Asset #2, and the value of the overall portfolio through time. Notice that despite the volatility in Asset #1 and in Asset #2, the overall portfolio has very little volatility. If we had held either asset by itself, we might have had trouble sleeping at night. By combining risky assets, the returns of which have very low correlation, we are able to sleep better at night.

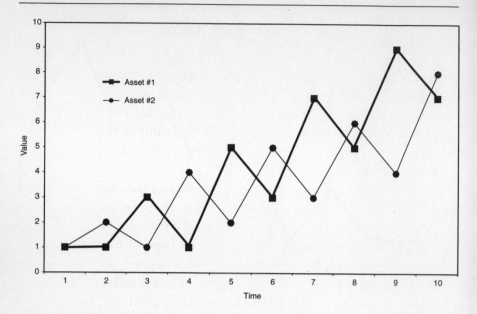

Figure 5.2 Value of Two Inversely Correlated Assets

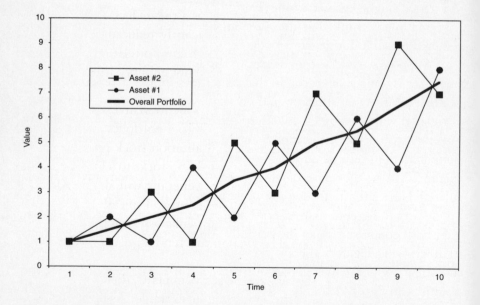

Figure 5.3 Effect of Diversification on Portfolio Value and Volatility

RISK REDUCTION, NOT NECESSARILY
RETURN ENHANCEMENT

It is very important to point out that we reduced the overall return of the portfolio by adding Asset #1 to Asset #2 to form a two-asset portfolio. The value of Asset #2 by itself was higher at the end of the 10 periods than was the total portfolio's value. We reduced the volatility of the portfolio substantially (actually, we removed about 90% of the volatility!), but there was a price to pay in doing so.

You might argue that Asset #1's return over the entire time period was lower than that of the total portfolio, but that may only have been a function of arbitrarily stopping the study at 10 periods. If history was any guide (perhaps a foolish thought given the comments of the previous chapters), then Asset #1 might have outperformed Asset #2 in the eleventh period. It also turns out that Asset #2 was slightly more risky than Asset #1. Therefore, we added riskier assets to the portfolio, but the returns decreased. Fortunately, in our example, the risky assets were inversely correlated to our existing one-asset portfolio so the overall portfolio risk decreased as well.

Diversification should be thought of as a risk-reduction tool and not as a return-enhancement tool. We significantly reduced the portfolio's volatility by combining two risky assets with low correlation (in this case they were negatively correlated), but we did not enhance the return of the portfolio.

Advertisements and the like sometimes mention diversification in the context of adding a new asset or asset class to a portfolio, such as adding small capitalization stocks to a large capitalization stock portfolio, bonds and cash to a 100% stock portfolio, or non-U.S. stocks to a U.S.-only portfolio. Such advertisements and comments generally will also demonstrate how adding the asset enhances portfolio returns. Typically, these advertisements and comments come after the particular asset has performed quite well. Thus, the diversification benefits shown tend to suggest both reduced risk *and* enhanced returns.

When reviewing such advertising and comments, there are two things you should keep in mind. First, in our simple example, Asset #1 and Asset #2 flipped back and forth as to which asset was the best performer. The enhanced performance of the asset being offered might reverse so that the returns of your portfolio might be hurt despite the portfolio's reduced risk.

Second, diversification studies are often done using many years of data. For example, many studies that show the diversification benefits of adding smaller capitalization stocks to a large capitalization stock portfolio use data that begin in 1926. Although the dual benefits of reduced risk and enhanced returns might occur, you should remember that there were many shorter periods within that very long time span during which smaller capitalization stocks performed miserably. Data from a 75- or 80-year period might lead you to the wrong conclusion if your time frame is even slightly shorter. For example, small cap stocks underperformed for several 5- to 10-year periods.

MANY LAYERS OF DIVERSIFICATION

You might think that diversification applies only within your stock portfolio, but there are many layers of risk that you might want to attempt to diversify away. Few people diversify their total capital. By total capital, I do not mean simply financial capital, but also human capital. Secondarily, few people seriously diversify their financial assets. Only after these layers of diversification should you worry about diversifying your stock portfolio. Contrary to what most investors do, I would argue that the diversification of your stock portfolio is the least important level of diversification of the three. Most investors worry a great deal about their stock portfolios with no consideration for their total capital.

Investment noise focuses on the least important level of diversification and spends no time whatsoever on the most important. Whether drug stocks diversify a technology-laden portfolio or whether non-U.S. stocks diversify a U.S. portfolio are hardly as important as diversifying your total capital. As previously mentioned, the media spends little time on truly risk-averse assets because they are longer term in nature and do not appear very exciting. Although you might want to diversify a stock portfolio with bonds, it is quite difficult to find information on bonds relative to the wide availability of information on stocks. This lack of information is yet another example of how noise can lead astray the unsuspecting investor. Noise makers really don't encourage diversification at all, let alone address the various more crucial levels of diversification.

DIVERSIFYING TOTAL CAPITAL

Capital is not only that which is invested in the financial markets. When considering diversification, you should consider the location of your home, your human capital, and your financial capital. We tend to think of capital as only that which is invested, but serious mistakes can be made when making that assumption. Let's look at some examples of how important it is to diversify your total capital.

Local Stocks. Some investors like to buy stocks of the companies that are located physically close to where they live or work. My local newspaper prints a list of local companies' stock prices every day. If you own a house in the area, investing in stock of a local company may be a particularly foolish thing to do. Suppose the local economy goes into recession, that is, the local industry is very concentrated in one industry and very cyclical. If the growth in the businesses in the area starts to turn negative, workers probably will be laid off. If workers are laid off, then the value of local real estate will depreciate. Thus, you would not want your financial nest egg invested in local stocks if you are unfortunate enough to be laid off. The value of the nest egg would decline right at the time when it is most likely to be drawn on. In addition, the equity in your house might decline as local real estate values drop.

I once worked on a project for a state government that was similar to this example. The state government had a fund that was supposed to be used as a "rainy-day" fund for the state. The fund was designed to fund public works projects and retraining efforts if the state's economy went into a recession. The state's economy was not terribly well diversified at the time, and the state was disproportionately dependent on the vagaries of the energy markets. The board that oversaw the fund was particularly worried that the fund was not well positioned for a prolonged downturn in energy prices (pretty good foresight given that energy prices slumped during much of the 1990s). My first review of the fund's portfolio showed that it was very heavily concentrated in the stocks of local employers. Politicians wanted to show the electorate that the local government was supporting the voters' employers. However, this was a mistake. If the employers' businesses significantly slowed, then the odds were their stock prices would fall as well. The state would not only be faced with rising unemployment, but the value of their rainy-day fund would probably start falling. My suggestion was to restructure the fund to invest in assets that had the lowest correlation (or high negative correlation as did Asset #1 and Asset #2 in our earlier example). That way, if the energy business did turn down and the stocks of the local companies did fall, the probability might be high that the economic environment that caused trouble for the local economy might benefit other sectors of the overall U.S. economy. For example, the stocks of airlines and consumer product companies sometimes rise when energy prices fall. If the local economy was strong, then the fund would not be drawn on, and contributions might actually be made into the fund.

Employee Stock Ownership Plans or Investing a 401(k) in Your Own Company's Stock. Many people buy their employer's stock for shorter-term investment or for their 401(k)s and/or retirement accounts. Again, because of the lack of diversification, I think this is unwise. Your human capital is tied up in the company for which you work. Investing in the company's stock is essentially putting a lot of eggs in one basket. If the company falls on hard times and you are laid off, the odds are the value of your company stock will drop as well. So, as in the earlier example, the value of the nest egg would fall coincidental with the need to draw on it.

Some employees essentially have little choice but to invest in their company as they are sometimes paid in stocks and options, and there has been much written in the academic community supporting the need for stock and option-based pay incentives. I agree that such plans are very worthwhile from the corporate perspective in order to motivate and retain employees. However, I think it is important for employees to realize the risks such plans can present to them, and the significant need for employees to diversify the remainder of their assets.

Regarding 401(k)s and retirement accounts, it is very hard to predict the success of a company over a very long time period. Many of the companies that were growth companies or major leaders in the U.S. economy have fallen on hard times in the last 23 years. Many of today's leaders will undoubtedly fall on hard times during the next 23 years until I turn 65. I used to work for a firm that is no longer in business. On the day the company's stock sank to $6 per share, I vividly remember the blank looks on the faces of the people who had invested their many years of retirement savings in the company's stock. They thought the company was a leader in the industry, and would never fail. Sound familiar? You should diversify if it does.

THE SEESAW ANALOGY

Another project I once worked on is a good anecdote to explain this type of lack of diversification and the risks it can present. A corporate pension fund was severely underfunded. That means the value of the fund was below a level that actuaries deemed necessary to meet the company's future pension liabilities. For accounting purposes, an underfunded pension plan would reduce the reported earnings of the company. The company was a very mature and cyclical company whose earnings growth had been in steady decline for some time. Management did not want to further increase the cyclicality of an already cyclical company.

The company wanted to issue stock to the pension plan to fund it. However, I suggested that that was not a very good solution. If the company's cyclical problems continued, the fact that the pension fund was loaded with the company's stock would only exacerbate its funding problems. If the company's stock price went down, the pension fund would be increasingly underfunded. In addition, if the stock price correctly reflected the problems of the company, the company's earnings would already be under pressure. The last thing the company would want in that situation was to have to fund the pension and increase the pressure on earnings, when the company's earnings growth was negative.

I suggested that we restructure the pension fund to look for assets that would diversify the risk of the pension fund of a very mature and cyclical company. We looked for assets in which to invest that had a negative correlation (again, as our Asset #2 correlated to Asset #1 in our example) with the assets of the overall corporation. That way, if the overall economic environment was not conducive to the success of the company's business, it might be for the assets that had negative correlation. Because companies can add the amount overfunded to earnings, we even calculated the probability of the fund becoming overfunded by following this strategy, and whether it could possibly help support earnings.

Specifically, the company's earnings and cash flow depended heavily on commodity prices. If commodity prices rose, the company's earnings rose. If commodity prices fell, the company's earnings fell. The company's ability to fund the pension fund was ultimately directly related to commodity prices. Thus, we looked for assets that had a negative correlation to commodity prices. A simple answer was long-term Treasury bonds. When inflation rises, the value of long-term T-bonds falls. However, the cash flow of the company would rise. Funding might be less of a problem. When inflation falls, the value of long-term T-bonds rises, potentially raising the funding status of the pension plan, and therefore potentially offsetting the shortfall in cash flow. Our plan was simple. By using standard diversification principles, we attempted to create a seesaw between the funding status of the pension plan and the firm's ability to further fund the plan.

The seesaw analogy in the previous anecdote is an important one when discussing diversification. When anything must be concentrated in a particular asset, we should attempt to diversify as much as possible by finding assets that move in an opposite direction to the value of the concentrated asset. Our commodity company's pension fund and T-bonds are a perfect example.

DIVERSIFICATION AND TOTAL CAPITAL: A PERSONAL EXAMPLE

My human and financial capital is closely tied to the successes of the financial services industry, and in many ways directly tied to the stock market. Not only do I work in the financial services industry, but also I am partly paid by my company in stock and in options. This is a much more difficult issue for financial services employees than most of them realize because they lose some diversification simply by investing in the financial markets. Their human capital and financial capital are necessarily very closely linked.

There are several things I do to attempt to diversify my total capital. First, I do not live in a town known for being a "Wall Street community." The human capital of the people in my village is pretty well diversified relative to that of the people in a known Wall Street community. If everyone in a village worked on Wall Street and a prolonged bear market occurred, then the value of real estate in the village would be more likely to decline or fluctuate more than does that in a multi-industry village. An extreme example of this would be the ghost towns in the West. When the mining business ended, everyone left the town. I am not naive about this point. Certainly, by simply living in the New York metropolitan area my real estate's value is linked to Wall Street. However, employer or job diversification within a community is a risk-reduction tool even for real estate.

I do not invest in other financial companies. Not that I would necessarily consider it disloyal, but why would I want to put more eggs in the same basket? The last thing I need is more exposure to the financial services industry. I also keep a disproportionate amount of cash in my portfolio. I am not bearish on the financial markets, and I realize that being invested is a necessary part of successful long-term investing. However, my total capital is already so sensitive to the financial markets that cash is a diversifying investment.[2]

DIVERSIFICATION AND TOTAL CAPITAL: A SILICON VALLEY EXAMPLE

In March 2000, I spoke before about a thousand people who were employed in the financial services industry near Silicon Valley. I was not sure I had ever seen an audience whose clients' total capital was more poorly diversified. I suggested that nearly their entire livelihoods were wrapped up in Silicon Valley and the technology sector. The value of their real estate in the San Francisco Bay area had skyrocketed because of the success of many technology companies and their expanding workforces. Many of the audience's clients were getting paid an increasing proportion of stock options in the technology companies in which they worked. Many were also investing in the stocks of their suppliers and customers. To me, this was the epicenter of the 1999–2000 technology bubble, and their clients had amassed a great amount of wealth on paper. Their investment strategies should have aimed at maintaining that wealth.

Rather than give a set speech on the prospects for the stock market, I attempted to offer more value to the audience by demonstrating how poorly their clients' total capital was diversified. The topic of the speech was not how to get wealthy, but rather how to keep wealth. I thought it was easy: diversify.

However, the noise associated with the technology bubble (the so-called new economy) skewed their visions of the world. I mentioned before that I thought it might be fruitless to search for the next Microsoft. Their clients who worked for technology companies saw no need to search for the next Microsoft because they thought they *worked* for the next Microsoft. My guess is that very few people in the audience took my comments seriously.

I don't mean to say "I told you so." Rather, I want to demonstrate how most people do not consider their total capital. If you work in or have a business that depends on the chemical sector, you should look to diversify your total capital from the chemical sector. If you work in the auto sector or have a business that depends on the auto industry, you should look to diversify your total capital from the auto sector. If you work in or have a business that depends on the technology sector, you should look to diversify your total capital from the technology sector. Whether working in a mature industry or an emerging growth industry, the need for diversification of capital remains the same. Actually, given the uncertainty of emerging industries, the need for diversification of capital might actually be greater in start-up sectors, such as technology, than in more mature industries.

DIVERSIFICATION AND TOTAL CAPITAL: A TEXAS EXAMPLE

Another example of the importance of total capital diversification is Texas after the fall of energy prices during the 1980s. The stocks of oil companies fell, unemployment in Texas rose, Texas real estate prices fell, and capital was lost. The "see-through" office buildings of Dallas and Houston became famous because they had no tenants at all, and literally could be seen through because of their glass walls. Texas was effectively in a depression, but the people who maintained the most wealth were the ones whose total capital was diversified. Is it impossible that the same thing could happen in New York if the stock market had a multiyear bear market, or in San Francisco if profitability of technology companies takes much longer than most investors currently expect?

DIVERSIFYING FINANCIAL CAPITAL

The level of assets that you should consider after diversifying total capital is financial capital. A proper decision must be made for an allocation to stocks, bonds, cash, gold and commodities, and private equity and alternative investments. Perhaps you should consider an allocation to small capitalization stocks at this level as well because some consider small cap stocks to be a separate asset class.

Let's start with the simple stock/bond/cash decision. Figure 5.4 shows a traditional risk/return chart for combinations of stocks, bonds, and cash. As in the earlier charts in this book, the vertical axis measures the average annual return from the combination of assets, and the horizontal axis shows the risk of the combination measured as the volatility of the returns. Next to each point in the chart is a series of numbers representing the proportion

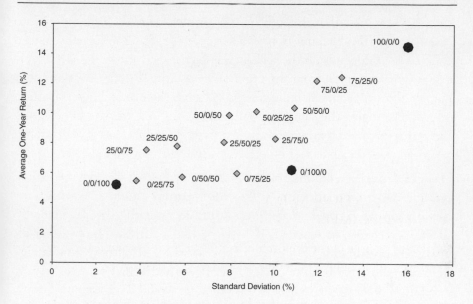

Figure 5.4   **Risk/Return for Selected Asset Allocations (Rolling One-Year Total Returns from 1950 through 1999)**
Figures represent weighting of stocks, bonds, and cash.
Based on data from Merrill Lynch Quantitative Strategy and Ibbotson Associates.

of the portfolio that was invested in stock, in bonds, and in cash. A figure of 75/25/0 would indicate that the particular portfolio had 75% of the assets invested in stocks, 25% in bonds, and 0% in cash. The S&P 500 is used as a proxy for the asset class stocks, while long-term T-bonds are used to represent bonds, and three-month T-bills are used to represent cash.

As with all risk/return charts, the goal is to invest in combinations that ultimately are as far northwest as you can find. A northwesterly portfolio is one that has had higher returns with less risk. Those that lie southeasterly are those that have had lower returns with more risk.

Combinations of stocks and cash generally lie northwest of combinations of stocks and bonds. That suggests, for given levels of risk, it might be more efficient for investors to use cash as a diversifying instrument rather than to use bonds.

Table 5.1 shows the correlation between stocks, bonds, and cash. Correlation coefficients such as those shown in Table 5.1 can range from 1.0 to –1.0. A correlation of 1.0 implies that the assets move in the same direction (although not necessarily by the same amount). A correlation of –1.0 shows

Table 5.1   Correlations of Stocks, Bonds, and
Cash Returns 1965 to 2000

	Stocks	*Bonds*	*Cash*
Stocks	1.00	—	—
Bonds	0.33	1.00	—
Cash	−0.07	0.09	1.00

a perfectly inverse relationship. Our Asset #1 and Asset #2 from the earlier example had a correlation of −0.77. Our portfolio's returns became quite stable when we added in equal proportion an asset that had a decidedly inverse correlation to Asset #1. If Asset #2 had a correlation of −1.0 (perfect inverse correlation), the graph of the overall portfolio's returns in Figure 5.3 would have been an exact line. If we had added an asset with a correlation of +1.0, the returns of our portfolio would have remained quite volatile.

Cash is a better diversifying asset to an all-stock portfolio than are bonds because the correlation between stocks and cash is lower than that between stocks and bonds. As we mentioned earlier, the lower the correlation among assets, the better the diversification benefit.

GOLD BUGS AND THE WRONG KIND OF DIVERSIFICATION

Diversification is important, but we must be careful not to diversify into assets that have low correlation with the existing portfolio because they are secularly depreciating while the portfolio appreciates. Gold has about the lowest correlation with stocks of any asset class. Some investors, called "gold bugs," still use it as a hedge or protective asset for all-stock portfolios despite that it has not worked well as such a hedge for nearly 20 years! Gold's correlation with stocks is virtually 0. Clearly, we want to diversify using assets that have low correlation with the assets in the existing portfolio, but gold's history is that it outperforms during periods of high and rising inflation. The U.S. economy has generally been in a period of disinflation rather than inflation during the last 20 years. Thus, even though gold has a low correlation with stocks, it can hardly be viewed these days as an effective diversifying investment. My guess is the returns from investing in companies that produce horse and buggy whips have a low correlation with the overall stock market, but they clearly are not going to provide any sort of positive long-term return. There may be no free lunch when diversifying, but we should try to limit the universe of potential diversifying assets to those that tend to appreciate through time.

Gold might be appropriate as a diversifying asset if we thought that the U.S. economy was going through a secular change. Instead of forecasting disinflation (or deflation in parts of the world), we would have to forecast secular inflation. There are and will be periods of inflation in the U.S. economy, but such periods currently appear to be only cyclical and short term within the context of secular disinflation. If that secular environment were to change, then gold might be a viable diversifying asset.

Some gold bugs see recent central banks' sales of gold as a potential contrary signal. Instead of selling gold when it was at $800/ounce in 1980, central banks have been selling gold at today's considerably lower prices. Some gold bugs have suggested the poor timing of the central banks' selling of gold is a good contrary signal, and that gold will soon appreciate. Without some serious inflation threat (perhaps energy prices?), it will probably be difficult to get an extended bull market in gold.

PRIVATE EQUITY AND ALTERNATIVE INVESTMENTS

Alternative investments are a relatively new breed of assets that are specifically marketed as having low correlation with other asset classes. Realistically, the jury is still out on these investments as to whether they truly do provide the diversification benefits their backers claim. However, the results so far do seem to support the claims. Some investors remain skeptical because alternative investments so far have produced both superior returns and diversification. As mentioned before, diversification and superior returns do not necessarily go hand in hand. Thus, some investors are drawn to these investments by only the diversification they offer. Those investors feel there is substantial risk that returns will significantly decrease from today's lofty levels.

Alternative investments include private equity, distressed securities, and timber and energy royalty rights to name a few categories. Private equity is exactly what its name implies. It is stock issued to investors that does not trade on an exchange. The stock is generally in smaller or start-up companies and investors can gain substantially when the company issues public equity. This is the category of alternative investments that concerns some investors today. A majority of private equity deals have been in the technology sector in recent years. A NASDAQ bull market allowed for quick, easy, and lucrative "exit" strategies for private equity investors because companies quickly issued public stock at very high valuations. If NASDAQ were to continue to correct through 2001 or longer, then some investors worry that the speed and ease of private equity exit strategies might change dramatically. Distressed securities investments invest in companies that are near bankruptcy. These investors attempt to uncover and extract hidden value in the assets of the companies that are in or near bankruptcy. Royalties allow the investor to share in the profits of a productive asset rather than in the profits of the company operating the productive asset.

Alternative investments theoretically provide higher returns because of their inherent risk. First, they are generally much more illiquid than are traditional investments, and investors are often locked in to the investment for a certain number of years. For example, an investor might be committed to invest $5 million for each of the next five years. If the returns of the investment turn negative, the investor could still be committed to investing the full amount.

There also is less information about alternative investments than there is about more public investments. A public stock investor can read research reports from Wall Street analysts, can visit a company's website, call a company's investor relations department, and can read about the company in the newspaper. None of these information sources are available to the investor in alternative assets. Rather than relying on other sources who do primary research, alternative asset investors must do their own primary research.

A colleague and I once tried to determine whether alternative investments, in this case private equity, did indeed provide investors with superior returns given the liquidity and information risks.[3] The interesting part of the study was that we could not find reliable data on private equity returns, therefore, we had to create a proxy for private equity performance using public equities that we felt had similar characteristics to the private equity market. We screened our database for stocks that were extremely illiquid (in terms of trading volume) and were very risky (in terms of the volatility of their returns), but had little stock market-related risk. Our results seemed to support the contention that private equity did indeed diversify all-stock portfolios. This has remained true during the time period since the original report was written.

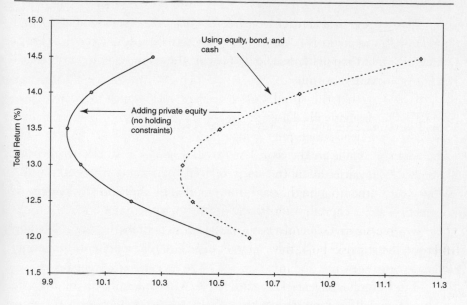

Figure 5.5   **Efficient Frontier with and without Private Equity (Using Private Equity Proxy; Returns from January 1980 to September 2000)**
Based on data from Merrill Lynch Quantitative and Equity Derivatives Strategy.

Figure 5.5 is a typical risk return chart that includes a set of combinations for a traditional stock/bond/cash portfolio as well as one for a stock/bond/cash/private equity portfolio. For every level of expected return, the portfolio that includes private equity incurred less risk. In other words, the combinations of stocks/bonds/cash/private equity lie west of the traditional stock/bond/cash combinations.

DIVERSIFYING STOCK AND BOND PORTFOLIOS

Finally, we should look at the diversification of just the stock and bond portion of our assets. Large capitalization stocks versus small capitalization stocks, U.S. stocks versus non-U.S. stocks, corporate bonds versus municipal bonds, and sector, industry, and quality concentrations should be considered last. In our noisy financial world, the latter is considered first and foremost. To reiterate, I think diversifying total capital is the most important step. Then you should look to diversify total financial assets. Only after these two levels have been diversified should you worry about the construction of equity or bond portfolios.

Many books and articles have been written on diversifying stock and bond portfolios, and this book is not designed to be a how-to book. Thus, I spend minimal time on this topic. However, there are several points that I feel most investors overlook.

Small versus Large and U.S. versus Non-U.S.

The issues of small stocks versus large stocks and U.S. stocks versus non-U.S. stocks are actually more closely related than many investors think.[4] Most equity investors have heard that small capitalization stocks help to diversify a large capitalization stock portfolio, and that non-U.S. stocks help to diversify a U.S.-only portfolio. The two strategies are related in that smaller stocks tend to have a larger exposure to the domestic economy than do larger ones.

The largest companies, regardless of where domiciled, tend to be multinationals. Their businesses are influenced not only by their domestic economies, but also by the economies of the countries in which they do business. Many large U.S. companies now get more than half of their total sales from outside the United States. Similarly, the largest companies in Japan may be more influenced by foreign economies than by the Japanese economy. The businesses of smaller companies, which are hardly multinationals in size or scope, are predominantly tied to the local economy.

When diversifying globally, it might make more sense to purchase smaller stocks because the returns of those stocks might be a more pure-play on non-U.S. economies. It might make sense to invest in small Japanese companies if a U.S. investor wanted to invest in Japan in order to diversify a U.S. stock portfolio. If the investor invested in large Japanese companies, the diversification effect might be somewhat muted because large Japanese companies often get a sizeable proportion of their sales from the United States. Small Japanese companies might be a purer play on the Japanese economy. A non-U.S. investor seeking to diversify a portfolio by investing in the United States might be better off investing in smaller U.S. stocks because the probability of those stocks' sales and earnings being tied to the investor's economy would be quite low.

Figure 5.6 shows the relative performance of the 50 stocks in the S&P 500 with the highest percentage of sales coming from outside the United States. The performance of these stocks is very closely tied to global economic events. The portfolio underperformed during 1997 and 1998 when

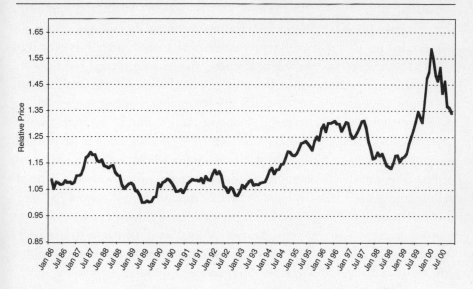

Figure 5.6   **Relative Performance of S&P Companies with the Highest Foreign Exposure**

the global economy slipped into recession despite the continued strength of the U.S. economy. In 1999, the portfolio's performance improved tremendously as the global economy strongly rebounded. The portfolio suffered again in 2000 as the global economy appeared to again be peaking.

Ironically, the media focuses only on large multinationals when discussing global diversification, and some observers have come up with indexes of global multinational companies. Again, this is noise. If you want to truly diversify internationally, then you should probably be looking at global small capitalization funds. Investing in the likes of Sony or Toyota probably will not give a U.S.-based investor the same diversification benefits as would investing in Japan's smaller capitalization companies.

Exchange-Traded Funds

A new and interesting tool that can be used to diversify portfolios is exchange-traded funds (ETFs). ETFs are essentially a basket of stocks that can be purchased and sold on an exchange similar to the way you trade an individual stock. ETFs are available for indexes, industries, sectors, countries, and capitalization ranges.

ETFs are becoming increasingly popular for several reasons. First, they represent a basket of stocks that are maintained by a custodian. The investor does not have to do any maintenance work. For example, suppose you bought an ETF for the energy sector. If the stocks in the basket had splits, reorganizations, merged, or the like, the investor would not have to do anything. The custodian takes care of all rebalancing. Second, as baskets, they offer immediate diversification benefits without having to do extensive fundamental research. Suppose you wanted exposure in the emerging markets. You could purchase an ETF that offered diversified emerging-market exposure. Third, there are tax advantages to buying and selling ETFs relative to buying and selling mutual funds. As when buying or selling individual stocks, the date of purchase and date of sale of the ETF dictate the investor's tax liability. With a mutual fund, other investors' buy and sell decisions can influence the tax liability for all investors in the fund.

ETFs are relatively new. The full advantages and disadvantages of the structure are not yet fully known. However, it appears that investors interested in diversification should investigate whether ETFs are an appropriate tool for them to use.

NOISE DETERS DIVERSIFICATION

Similar to our previous discussion on noise and long-term planning, noise tends to deter attempts to diversify. First, it skews investors' perceptions of traditional risk/return relationships so that they are led to believe there is a free lunch within the financial markets.

Second, noise ignores the various levels of diversification (total capital, financial capital, and securities portfolios) and focuses only on the third and least important level. Discussions regarding total capital and financial capital are not as exciting as is discussing individual securities because those issues do not change very frequently. Financial noise needs and wants change to fill airtime, page count, and so forth, and diversifying total capital will not serve that purpose well.

Third, noise tends to lead people to take more risk than they think they are taking. In Chapter 4 we noted that investors sometime abandon investment plans because of noise. Relevant to this chapter, investors sometimes underdiversify because of noise. My earlier Silicon Valley example is a perfect one. If the hubbub about the so-called new economy had not existed, some of the audience's clients would have been much better diversified.

Finally, and perhaps of most importance, noise ridicules those who diversify. The media and investors typically ridicule analysts and portfolio managers when the analysts and portfolio managers suggest diversifying and limiting the risks of a hot investment. The pressures to underdiversify can be great.

Of course, the probability exists that a ridiculed investor is indeed being overly cautious. In Chapter 6, we investigate how we can begin to understand what level of risk is appropriate.

Chapter 6

Noise, Risk,
and Risk Assessment

Let's begin this chapter with a series of simple quizzes. A couple of things are necessary in order for this chapter to be truly effective. First, you must take each quiz. Second, you must be honest with your answers. Third, you must not cheat by reading ahead. Fourth, you must not change earlier answers as you progress through the quizzes.

I teach a course in risk tolerance to the Financial Consultants in my firm, and we use these simple quizzes to teach them how difficult it is to assess risk tolerance. Experience suggests that if you play by the rules outlined in the previous paragraph, you will probably learn something about your own risk tolerance and preferences by the time you have finished this chapter.

Let's begin. I give you several pairs of assets. You must choose one of the two assets in each pair. You are not allowed to choose both or neither. You must choose one of the two in each pair. There is no specific duration of the investment. Simply consider which investment sounds better to you right now. Write them down as you choose. There are no correct or incorrect answers to this exercise.

Quiz #1: In which asset of each pair would you rather invest?

1. The United States or the emerging markets
2. Semiconductor stocks or food stocks
3. Treasury bonds or Treasury bills
4. Internet stocks or brick and mortar retailers
5. Biotechnology stocks or insurance stocks

Now let's try another quiz. This time, instead of choosing between two named investments, the choice will be between the characteristics of two investments. For each investment, I give you the average 12-month return, the best 12-month return, and the worst 12-month return for a reasonably representative period of time. As in the previous quiz, you must choose one from each pairing and write down your answers.

Quiz #2: In which would you rather invest?

1. Average: 16%; Best: 49%; Worst: –10%—or—Average: 8%; Best: 74%; Worst: –51%
2. Average: 50%; Best: 151%; Worst: –27%—or—Average: 8%; Best: 45%; Worst: –32%
3. Average: 10%; Best: 31%; Worst: –12%—or—Average: 5%; Best: 6%; Worst: 3%
4. Average: 60%; Best: 305%; Worst: –73%—or—Average: 25%; Best: 63%; Worst: –16%
5. Average: 40%; Best: 297%; Worst: –34%—or—Average: 18%; Best: 71%; Worst: –22%

Third quiz: Answer the following two questions. Again, you must pick one of the two choices, and there are no correct answers.

Quiz #3: Which is riskier?

1. $1,000 invested in a diversified mutual fund or $1,000 invested in lottery tickets
2. $1,000 invested in Treasury bills or $1,000 invested in lottery tickets

Fourth and fifth quizzes: Unlike the other quizzes, these will result in only one answer per quiz.

Quiz #4: How much risk do you want to take in your portfolio?

1. Very little risk
2. Less than average
3. An average amount
4. More than average
5. A lot of risk

Quiz #5: How much risk do you want to take in your portfolio?

1. Very little risk
2. Less than average
3. More than average
4. A lot of risk

Again, if you have answered the questions in these little quizzes truthfully, this chapter will probably end up teaching you about your own risk preferences. We will uncover the purpose behind the questions as we go through the chapter.

WHAT IS RISK?

One of the hardest things for an investor to do is to assess his or her own risk tolerance. Investors are commonly asked a series of questions on a form, and the answers to the questions can change dramatically, depending on how the questions are phrased, who is present while they are being answered, and even the investor's own mood on the day the questions are answered. The end result is that the investor ultimately decides how much risk he or she wants to take in the portfolio without even being asked to define risk.

There are two basic definitions of risk. The first, and the one that we have used in the book so far, is the academic definition. Academics define risk as the uncertainty of an investment's outcome typically measured as the standard deviation or volatility of the returns of the investment. A very volatile stock would be considered very risky when using this definition because the inherent volatility of the investment makes it very difficult to predict what the return will be for the upcoming period. However, a very stable investment, such as a one-year Treasury bill, is very safe under this definition. If you purchase a one-year T-bill, then you know with near certainty what the return will be for the next year.[1]

The second definition of risk is the probability of losing money. The theory behind this definition is that investors do not think of volatility symmetrically. Investors might not be concerned about risk if the volatility of an investment is high and the returns are unpredictable, but the returns are positive. Investors simply do not want to lose money.

Let's see how you define risk. There were two pairs of choices in Quiz #3 to answer the question, "Which is riskier?"

1. $1,000 invested in a diversified mutual fund or $1,000 invested in lottery tickets
2. $1,000 invested in Treasury bills or $1,000 invested in lottery tickets

If you chose the mutual fund for the answer to the first question comparing the mutual fund to the lottery tickets, then you defined risk using the traditional academic definition of risk. The answer might sound crazy, but the future returns of the mutual fund are relatively unknown. We know that if it is indeed a well-diversified mutual fund, its returns will probably track those of the overall equity market over the long term, but we really do not know the returns with any certainty. However, we know with near complete certainty that the return of the lottery tickets will be −100%. You will lose the full $1,000.[2] Thus, using the traditional definition of risk, the lottery tickets are actually safer than is the mutual fund.

If you said the lottery tickets were riskier than the mutual fund, then you probably define risk as the probability of losing money. If you chose the lottery tickets, do not feel as though you are alone. Nearly 100% of the people to whom I have asked this question choose the lottery tickets as the riskier investment. If this is a fair question to ask (and admittedly some people feel the question is biased because of people's negative feelings about lottery tickets), then it says that the academic studies of risk and its implications could be flawed. This should not be taken lightly. Most risk/return studies you have seen, including the ones shown so far in this book, use the academic definition of risk. It is entirely possible that investors act quite differently than many investment theories might suggest because they define risk as the probability of a loss rather than as the uncertainty of returns.

Table 6.1 shows the risk ranking of stocks, bonds, bills, and lottery tickets when using the two definitions of risk. Lottery tickets are the riskiest when using the probability of a loss as the measure of risk, but they are the safest when using the uncertainty of return. Again, their return is certain.

The meaning to the answer of the second question on risk is now obvious. If you defined T-bills as the safer asset then you are using the probability of a loss, but you would have been using uncertainty of return as the definition if you answered lottery tickets. My guess is that no one answering this question chose lottery tickets as a safer asset than T-bills.

Academics and traditionalists argue that those who choose lottery tickets as the riskier investment are confusing rationality with risk. The fact

Table 6.1 **Ranking Asset from Risky to Safe Using Two Definitions of Risk**

	Rank Using Uncertainty of Return	Rank Using Probability of a Loss
Stocks	1 (Riskiest)	2
Bonds	2	3
T-bills	3	4 (Safest)
Lottery tickets	4 (Safest)	1 (Riskiest)

that the return is typically –100% for lottery tickets makes us question the rationality of a person who buys lottery tickets. The traditional camp might argue that people confuse an irrational investment with a risky one. We can indeed question the rationality of investing in an asset that has a near certain return of –100%, but lottery tickets are indisputably very safe when their risk is defined by the traditional academic definition of risk. If nearly 100% of the people I poll perceive lottery tickets as risky, then correct or not, something seems to be wrong with the traditional definition of risk.

Figure 6.1 and Figure 6.2 show how assets might be perceived differently when their risk is defined as the probability of a loss rather than as the volatility of return. The vertical axis in each figure depicts the average 12-month return of the asset class. The horizontal axis in Figure 6.1 depicts risk defined as the volatility of returns. The horizontal axis in Figure 6.2 depicts risk defined as the probability of a loss. Note the distinct difference for lottery tickets. In Figure 6.1 lottery tickets are the safest asset. They have a decidedly negative return, but they are the safest asset. However, in Figure 6.2, lottery tickets are the riskiest asset. Because people who buy them generally lose their money, the probability of a loss is extremely high (100%).

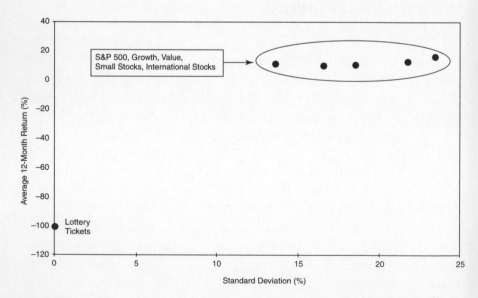

Figure 6.1   Twelve-Month Risk/Return Relationships When Risk Is Defined as Volatility of Returns (1970–1999)

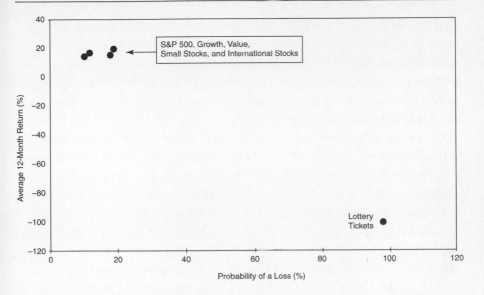

Figure 6.2   One-Year Risk/Return Combinations When Risk Is Defined as
Probability of a Loss (1970–1999)
Based on data from Merrill Lynch Quantitative Strategy.

NOISE AND PRICE CHARTS

Noise greatly influences risk assessment. It can make risky assets appear
safe, and safe assets appear risky. Noise can easily make risky assets appear safe
because, as stated, noise often concentrates on assets that have performed
the best. If you define risk as the probability of a loss, then a hyped sector
might appear quite safe because the probability of a loss appears quite low.
Frequently, sectors that have underperformed are hyped as out-of-favor sectors. Their stock price charts are obviously downward trending because they
have underperformed. When shown such charts, investors who define risk
as the probability of a loss will automatically consider such investments to
be very risky.

One thing that I have noticed is that television and magazine stock
price charts are generally constructed to make the most dramatic impact.
Some charts might show the last two weeks, some might show the last two
months, while others might show the last two years. If the writer or reporter
wants to make a bullish case for the stock, he or she will show a chart of the
stock's price that might best support his or her argument. If a bearish case

is to be made, the stock price chart that best supports that case is used. I have even seen varying time frames used in the same article in order to show that the market was punishing one stock and rewarding another. The consistency of the magazine's or television station's reporting seems to become immaterial.

If the media were truly acting in investors' best interests, they would keep their charts to a consistent time frame, that is, the data in every stock price chart would span one year. Such consistency would present more fair and balanced reporting and would be an easy method for filtering noise. Price changes that appear large today might be actually quite small when scaled properly and objectively. The obvious argument against keeping a standard time frame is that important news happens in shorter time periods. Realistically, everything can be hyped as meaningful when we do not know if it is noise or not, which means that viewership and readership will be higher. Daily reports about stock price changes are rarely put in proper perspective. Even though we know that a $1 move in a $50 stock is not as meaningful as a $1 move in a $40 stock, daily news reports continue to highlight the day's biggest point movers.[3]

DON'T USE PRICE CHARTS TO ESTIMATE RISK

We have already demonstrated that strategies that outperformed during one three-year period have a lower probability of outperforming during the next three-year period than do strategies that underperformed. Thus, if you define risk as the probability of a future loss, using price charts to estimate risk might actually lead you to construct a much riskier portfolio than you want. You might consider the asset that has appreciated the most during the past three years to be extremely safe because it rarely had a negative return. Conversely, you might consider the asset that performed the worst to be the riskiest asset because it typically had a negative return.

Table 6.2 (Table 2.1 reprinted here) shows that the probability of finding an outperforming strategy is higher among strategies that have underperformed during the past three years than among strategies that have outperformed. A strategy that outperformed during the past three years might have only a 47% chance of outperforming during the next three years. Thus, there might be a 53% chance that an investor might construct a riskier portfolio than was intended assuming that the investor defines risk as the probability of loss. However, there might be a 62% chance of con-

Table 6.2   **Probability of a Strategy's Sustained Outperformance (Based on Data from 1987 to 1999)**

	Outperformed During Second 3 Years (%)	Underperformed During Second 3 Years (%)
Outperformed during first 3 years	47	53
Underperformed during first 3 years	62	38

Source: Based on data from Merrill Lynch Quantitative Strategy.

structing a safer portfolio than was intended by looking at strategies that have previously underperformed. Of course, this table looks at strategies' performances relative to the S&P 500, so the above implications are not completely true. If risk were defined as the probability of underperforming the S&P 500 rather than the probability of a loss, then this discussion would be somewhat more accurate.[4]

If you have not completed Quiz #4 and Quiz #5, please do so before reading further.

HOW MUCH RISK DO YOU WANT TO TAKE IN YOUR PORTFOLIO?

This is actually a ridiculous question, but it gets asked all too often on brokerage firm questionnaires. In Quiz #4, you were asked this question and given five choices. Psychological studies show that people answer questions with an odd number of choices close to the center answer. My guess is that most of you answered "an average amount" of risk, with slightly more answering "less than average" or "more than average." Probably few readers answered "very little risk" or "a lot of risk."

In Quiz #5 you were not given a center choice, and were forced to answer "more than average" or "less than average." By having only four choices, you were forced to make a decision and show a more clear opinion regarding the acceptable level of risk within a portfolio.

Thus, the construction of the survey can give very different insights about an investor's preferences regarding a rather nebulous concept. The four-choice question seems more informative and helpful to the reviewer of the quiz because the quiz clearly demonstrates whether the investor wants to err on the side of safety or aggression. The five-choice question can leave an investor's risk preference in doubt.

This arbitrary point about the construction of a risk tolerance survey is that "average" could mean some conservative and some aggressive investments that sum to an average amount of risk, or it could mean a portfolio comprised of solely average-risk investments. There is no way for the interviewer to determine this if the five-choice quiz is used.

Quiz #4 in combination with Quiz #5 leaves nothing in doubt. If you chose the middle choice in Quiz #4 you were nonetheless forced to make a decision in Quiz #5. Look to see how you answered Quiz #4 and Quiz #5. Would an interviewer have been able to determine how you would have answered Quiz #5 by your answer in Quiz #4?

If you are ever asked the question of how much risk you would like to take in your portfolio, and assuming you know your questioner's definition of risk, you should next consider the following issues: What types of assets does the questioner consider risky and what types do you consider risky? More important, to whom are you being compared when your willingness to take risk is measured and to whom are you comparing yourself? Let's examine each of these issues.

If you did not complete Quiz #1 and Quiz #2, please do so before reading any further.

It is now time to review the first quiz you completed. Did you choose the United States or the emerging markets? Did you choose semiconductor stocks or food stocks? Did you choose T-bonds or T-bills? Did you choose dot-com retailers or brick and mortar retailers? Did you choose biotechnology stocks or insurance stocks?

Let's review the second quiz you completed. Did you choose the first or the second asset in each case? In each group, one asset provided higher returns than did the other, but it probably seemed riskier to you as well because the range of returns was higher, or perhaps you felt the probability of a loss was greater.

Although there were no correct answers to either quiz, I played a trick on you. Quiz #1 and Quiz #2 compared the exact same assets. In Quiz #1, you chose assets by name. In Quiz #2, you chose assets by the probability of future returns distributions. In other words, 1 through 5 in both quizzes were the exact same assets. In the first quiz you saw names, whereas in the second you saw returns. You were comparing the United States to the emerging markets, semiconductors to foods, bonds to bills, dot-com to brick and mortar, and biotech to insurance in both quizzes.

If you did not pick the same assets in each combination (i.e., the first asset in Quiz #1 is the same as the first asset in Quiz 2), then you have some thinking to do. Most people who have taken quizzes similar to these have had some thinking to do. It is rare that the two quizzes results are identical.

The first quiz tests to see how much you are influenced by the name of the investment. Investment noise generally helps us to form preconceived notions about the risk/return potential of an investment. The second test is to see your true risk preferences. By combining the two, you can see how you might have been misled by noise into thinking you were taking more or less risk within your portfolio than you actually might be taking.

For example, depending on when you are reading this book, you might have chosen the United States instead of the emerging markets because you believe the United States might be safer or have higher return potential. If you did not choose the first of the two assets in example 1 of the second quiz, then you can see how noise might be keeping you from taking the risk (and gaining the potential return that accompanies risk over the long term) that you might be prepared to take.

The best anecdotal example I can give regarding these quizzes and their power in uncovering poor assessments of risk were the results in one particular class I taught. There were three people from Hong Kong in the class. A large proportion of this particular class was from Asia, and the Asian markets were performing quite well, so I used an example in which I compared Hong Kong to the United States. As in the quiz you took, the people in the class had no idea that the returns were directly related to the names of the investments at which they were looking. All three people from Hong Kong chose Hong Kong as a superior investment to the United States when choosing by name, but all three chose the United States when choosing by returns. When we removed the hype that the Hong Kong market was getting at the time, we uncovered that the Hong Kong stock market was probably too risky for these three people. Needless to say, they were shocked.

Quiz #1 and Quiz #2 should have demonstrated two things to you. First, you should now realize that it is very difficult to assess your own risk tolerance. Second, it should have shown you how noise has potentially influenced your own investment decisions. Most people find that they have responded to the first quiz according to intuition and image. The second quiz is the more important one because it is objective, but most people surprisingly believe the first is more important. That most people believe the first is more important than the second again shows how influential noise can be. The influence of investment noise is so powerful that people do not even believe their own answers to the quizzes.

It is not uncommon, by the way, for people to argue with me about these quizzes. They suggest they are rigged or that I did not explain them fully, or they would have answered the questions differently if they had known more about it. One class got openly hostile with me. I had to explain that their emotional response is how investors feel when their risk tolerance is assessed improperly. ("You told me it was a safe investment, and look what happened!!")[5]

FRAME OF REFERENCE: DEFINING RISK PEER GROUPS

When discussing risk and risk preferences, it is important to define a risk peer group. To whom are you being compared when your risk tolerance is assessed, and to whom do you compare yourself when you are asked about risk?

You should realize that you might respond differently to the question, "Do you like to take risk in your portfolio?" depending on who is asking the question. You might not want to appear as a wimp to the questioner, thus leading him or her to believe a riskier portfolio is appropriate, or you might not want to appear too bold, providing an answer that leads him or her to believe a conservative portfolio is more appropriate.

It is also important to gain some profile of the people the questioner considers risk takers and the people the questioner considers risk adverse. The questioner's definition of a risk taker might be completely different from yours. If the questioner deals mainly with retirees, then even a moderately aggressive investor will appear to be a wild risk taker to the questioner. In that case, the questioner might eventually recommend a portfolio that is too aggressive. On the other hand, the questioner's base might be very aggressive risk takers, and then the moderately aggressive investor will seem very conservative. The result might be the construction of an overly conservative portfolio.

Similarly, to whom are you comparing yourself? If the people you most frequently discuss investing with are retirees, then you might think you are an aggressive investor. If you discuss investing with day traders and high rollers at Atlantic City, then you might consider yourself quite conservative.

Now imagine the potential mismatch that could occur given the previous two paragraphs. It turns out that you are actually a normal risk taker. You are neither particularly aggressive nor conservative. However, you discuss investments most often with your retired parents and their friends and, as a result, you consider yourself a risk taker. You meet a broker with whom you can sit down to discuss your goals, objectives, and risk preferences. The brokers' clients are mainly very aggressive investors. The broker asks you if you like to take risks, if you are aggressive, and so forth, and you answer based on your personal experiences and tell the broker you are an aggressive investor. The broker, however, classifies you according to his or her personal experiences and hears a set of answers that correspond to those of most of his existing clients.

The odds seem pretty high in this example that the portfolio will probably be too aggressive, and it will be nobody's fault. The broker is acting in good faith and is hearing answers to the questions asked that correspond to his or her existing client base. The client is answering in good faith according to life experience. My guess is this relationship will not be long-lived because the broker's and client's frames of reference were completely different.

We could construct a similar example regarding the construction of a portfolio that is too conservative for the investor. The broker's clients are retirees, the client is nearing retirement and claims to be conservative. The problem is the client's family is full of very aggressive investors, and relative to most investors, the client actually prefers an aggressive portfolio as well. My guess is this relationship does not work well either because the client will think the broker kept her out of too many potential winning stocks or did not get the higher yields of the junk bond market.

It is of paramount importance to understand fully your frame of reference when discussing risk, as well as the frame of reference of the person with whom you are discussing it.

HOW DO I KNOW IF I'M TAKING TOO MUCH RISK?

An easy way to tell if you're taking too much risk is if you can't sleep at night because of your investment portfolio. I write this both figuratively and literally. There are days when the market goes down sharply in the morning, and I can tell which of my colleagues are taking too much risk in their portfolios because of how they stare at their quote machines and how they lose their appetite for lunch. When the market goes down extremely sharply, I can tell among my friends who is taking too much risk because he or she calls me and asks me for my view on the markets. The longer the time period in which I have not spoken to the person prior to the call tells me how much risk he or she is taking relative to the amount he or she should be taking. Those to whom I have not spoken in months or years, are probably taking extreme amounts of risk relative to the amount they should be taking. They finally call me (admittedly, I am not always a social butterfly myself) not to relate family stories, but rather to find my views on the markets. They are so worried about what to do with their portfolios that they call.

THE FINANCIAL MARKETS' GYRATIONS SHOULD HAVE NO IMPACT ON YOUR SLEEP

A simple rule of thumb is that if you have correctly assessed your own risk tolerance, then the day-to-day, week-to-week, and month-to-month gyrations of the financial markets should have no impact on your ability to eat or sleep (although I hope my friends will call to say hello). If those gyrations are disturbing, even for a day, it signals that you are probably taking too much risk in your portfolio. Market volatility sometimes does not last long. Instead of wiping your brow and sighing with relief, you should investigate why your brow was sweaty in the first place.

When there is extreme market volatility, I always suggest the same thing to the Financial Consultants at my firm. If their clients are disturbed by the volatility, that is a signal that their clients' risk tolerance has been improperly determined. They should sit down with their clients and review the asset allocation of the portfolio in order to construct a more conservative combination of assets. Of course, the clients will want to do so, but they will probably be upset that the changes were made the next time the market races upward. As the noise changes from being overwhelmingly pessimistic to being overwhelmingly optimistic, the clients will forget their earlier consternation. Unfortunately, there is no remedy for a short memory and an ear that listens to investment noise.

APPENDIX: ARE BONDS REALLY RISKIER THAN STOCKS?

I have tried very hard in this book to avoid commenting on specific strategies relating to current market conditions and trends. As said, this is not a how-to book. However, the noise surrounding the issues of stock and bond risk seem so strong and so silly that a comment cannot be avoided. I have inserted it into an appendix to separate it from the main text and purpose of this book.

The long-standing rule has been that stocks are riskier than bonds, and that the inherent risk of stocks helps to explain why they outperform bonds over the long term. Their extra return is considered a "risk premium" or compensation given to investors for investing in a riskier asset.

Some researchers have recently argued that stocks are decidedly undervalued relative to bonds because bonds are actually riskier than stocks. The implication is that stocks will outperform bonds as investors realize that the risk premium currently imbedded in the stock market is too rich, and that the risk premium in bonds is too small. In short, this group asserts that everyone believes stocks are riskier than bonds, but they are not riskier. As a result, stocks will rally as investors appreciate that fact.

Personally, I believe this view is poppycock. First, let's take the simple definition of stocks and bonds, which this group seems to have forgotten. Stocks are a partial ownership in the assets of a company. Bonds are loans in which the assets of the borrowing company are used as collateral. If the company goes out of business, it is the bond holders who have claim to the assets of the company. The stockholders have claim only to the residual assets of the firm. Thus, stocks are subordinated to debt, and are, therefore, more risky by definition. Regardless of what these observers may claim, I have yet to see bond covenants that suggest bonds are subordinated to equity.

Second, as mentioned in an earlier note, these studies have confused *ex ante* expectations of returns with *ex post* results. Stocks outperform over the long term because expectations of their returns (*ex ante*) are typically lower than the actual returns (*ex post*). That difference is the risk premium previously mentioned. If investors begin to accept that the returns of stocks are typically higher than the returns on bonds, and their expectations for future stock returns accordingly go up, then the risk premium has been bid away. Simply put, stocks would be overvalued relative to bonds.

The crux of the arguments suggesting that bonds are riskier than stocks is based on the volatility of the two asset classes during the past couple of years. The equity market's bubblelike run during the second half of 1998 and all of 1999 has caused the volatility of the overall asset class to fall if it is measured for short periods. Because the equity market went straight up without interruption during this year-and-a-half period, the volatility by definition went down. The same thing would happen if the market went straight down without interruption. The predictability of returns gets greater as the variation of those returns goes down. The researchers then came to the conclusion that the risk premium between stocks and bonds was too high given that the predictability of the stock market's returns was now greater than the predictability of the bond market's returns.

Let's look at a few things relevant to this discussion. The volatility of bonds and stocks using two-year returns, the volatility of bonds and stocks using more traditional five-year returns, the risk premium as I measure it, and a measure of Wall Street's bullishness.

Figure 6.3 shows the volatility of stocks and bonds based on two-year rolling periods of monthly returns. The volatility is the standard deviation

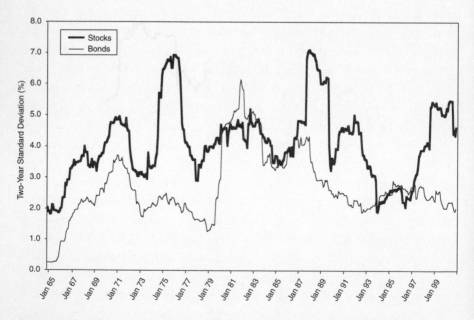

Figure 6.3   **Stock and Bond Risk Based on Two-Year Rolling Periods of Monthly Returns**

(or the variation) of the monthly returns during a two-year period. A higher standard deviation implies that the variability among the monthly returns was higher, and the asset was riskier. You can see that the variability of bond returns did not rise above the variability of stock returns during the past couple of years despite some researchers' claims.

Figure 6.4 shows the same type of calculation based on five-year rolling returns instead of two-year rolling returns. This is the more traditional calculation because most statisticians believe that two years of data is not long enough to make a definitive statement regarding the volatility of the asset class. Five years typically include the majority of a business cycle and, therefore, give a better indication of how the investment behaves in a variety of economic settings than does a two-year measure. The five-year calculation did not yield the same conclusion regarding the relative risk of stocks and bonds as did the two-year calculation. Stocks were increasingly riskier than bonds during the past several years using this more traditional measure.

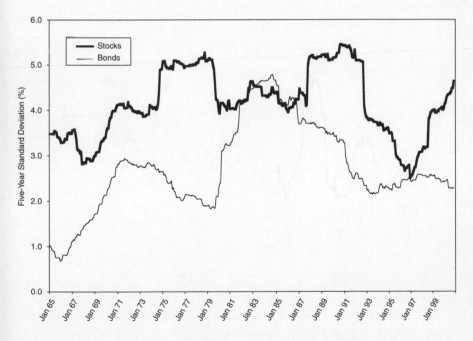

Figure 6.4   **Stock and Bond Risk Based on Five-Year Rolling Periods of Yearly Returns**

The risk premium can be measured in a variety of ways, and there is no general consensus regarding the appropriate definition to use. I measure the risk premium by taking the expected return on the S&P 500 and subtracting the AAA Corporate Bond Rate. I use a model called a Dividend Discount Model (DDM) to estimate the expected return for the S&P 500.[6] The DDM's expected return is compared to the AAA Corporate Bond Rate rather than to T-bonds for two reasons. First, some people believe that the normal relationship between stocks and T-bonds has been skewed because of the Treasury Department's decision during 2000 to repurchase bonds to reduce the government debt. Second, we potentially get a better comparison between assets of like credit risk. When comparing stocks to T-bonds, there is a question whether we are comparing the private sector to the public sector. Figure 6.5 shows the risk premium through time as I measure it. The risk premium hardly seemed overly generous during 2000 when the reports advocating the safety of stocks relative to bonds were written. Rather, the opposite could be said. The risk premium during 2000 was well below average.

Finally, let's examine how bullish Wall Street was toward stocks when these articles were written. You might assume that investors were terribly

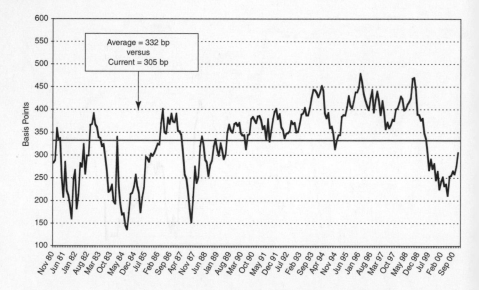

Figure 6.5 **S&P 500 Dividend Discount Model Expected Return Less AAA Long-Term Corporate Bond Rates (Basis Points)**
Based on data from Merrill Lynch Quantitative Strategy.

bearish regarding the overall equity market, and the overwhelming bearish sentiment made the risk premium for equities unusually high. In other words, investors were so fearful of equities that the compensation for risk was unusually high in order to reward investors for overcoming their fears. However, the risk premium was lower than average, and Wall Street was not overly bearish. In fact, by my measure, they appeared overly bullish.

Figure 6.6 shows an indicator that I developed many years ago to keep track of exactly how bullish or bearish Wall Street is toward the equity market. The indicator is called the Sell-Side Indicator because it tracks the recommended asset allocation of the strategists at most of Wall Street's largest brokerage houses (thus the name Sell-Side Indicator). I have found when adding a little math, the consensus asset allocation among Wall Street strategists is a reliable contrary indicator for a 12-month investment horizon. It has historically been a bearish signal when Wall Street was overly bullish, and vice versa.

Contrary to what you might conclude when reading the articles suggesting that the equity risk premium was much too high and bonds were riskier than stocks, Wall Street was not even close to being overly bearish on the equity market during 2000. In fact, the indicator hit a new all-time

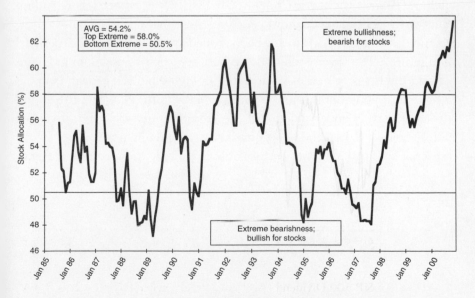

Figure 6.6   **Sell-Side Consensus Indicator (as of November 30, 2000)**
Based on data from Merrill Lynch Quantitative Strategy.

level of optimism during late 2000. At that point, Wall Street was suggesting that late 2000 was the best time in the last 16 years to buy stocks. This situation certainly does not support the notion that the risk premium on stocks is too high, and that stocks are a safer asset class than bonds.

Thus, the authors of the articles suggesting that bonds are riskier than stocks not only ignore that bonds are safer than stocks by definition (i.e., stocks are subordinated to bonds), but they might not be looking at the data either. Traditional risk measures do not support the notion that bonds are riskier than stocks. A historical analysis of the risk premium itself does not support that notion either. Finally, if the risk premium were extraordinarily high, you would expect Wall Street to be extremely bearish on the equity market. They were extremely bullish rather than extremely bearish.

The fact that these articles have even been written seems to me to be a very significant factor in favor of presently overweighting bonds to stocks in a multiasset portfolio. The articles seem to me merely to be an attempt by the authors to justify the extreme bullishness demonstrated by the Sell-Side Indicator.

As mentioned before, noise tends to build for an asset as it becomes more popular, and Figures 6.5 and 6.6 certainly support that contention. Notice how large the risk premium was during 1995, 1996, 1997, and 1998, but how bearish (or at least how not bullish) Wall Street was regarding equities. In 1999 and 2000, however, Wall Street became extremely bullish, but the risk premium had already been eroded away by the previous periods' high returns. The inverse relationship between the risk premium in Figure 6.5 and the investor sentiment depicted in Figure 6.6 is a perfect example of how detrimental noise can be to investment returns. When the equity market was truly undervalued and the risk premium was high, investors hated equities. When the equity market's risk premium was gone, it was fashionable to be bullish and fashionable to ridicule those who were not.

Chapter 7

Investment Losses, Time Horizon, and Risk

"Investors should think long term." How many times do we hear that? However, most investors ignore this simple advice, and allow investment noise to creep into their decision making. Investors often lose sight of longer-term investment results, especially during short-term periods of extreme volatility. It is during these periods of extreme volatility that the volume of noise increases. Planning and managing portfolios for the long term is one of the simplest methods for screening out such noise.

DON'T QUIT YOUR DAY JOB

Investors' time horizons seem to be getting shorter and shorter despite the supposed acceptance of long-term investing. The increased popularity of day trading during the past few years seems to support my contention. If we know that long-term investing is superior to short-term investing (and

Special thanks to Kari Bayer and Lisa Kirschner for the historical analyses presented in this chapter. See Kari E. Bayer and Richard Bernstein, "Equity Asset Allocation Update: Year-End 1999," *Merrill Lynch Quantitative Viewpoint*, 31 January 2000.

quite a bit easier as well), then why would investors want to focus on holding stocks for minutes or hours instead of quarters and years?

A startling experience for me occurred one day at the National Association of Securities Dealers (NASD) testing center in New York. As a registered principal of my firm, I am required to take the NASD's continuing education programs. The programs are given at the same center as are the exams to become a registered representative, equity trader, and so forth.

The waiting room at the testing center was packed full the last time I took my continuing education program. There were not enough chairs in the waiting room. The staff at the center seemed quite taxed as well and was having difficulty keeping up with the flow of test takers.

I asked one person why he thought the center was so crowded. He looked at me in a rather perplexed manner and said that everyone was taking the exams to become a professional day trader. He was surprised to find out that I was not attempting to become a day trader. His personal story was that he was giving up a 13-year career in the recording industry because a friend had made a "lot of money" the previous year as a day trader.

A standing-room only crowd, giving up their careers to trade stocks for minutes and hours? I could not believe what I was hearing. These people clearly did not realize that if they extended the time horizon of their investments they would probably be more successful investors and they would be able to keep their professional careers. I wished my new acquaintance luck on his exam, while secretly hoping he would fail and return to the recording industry.

The conclusions of this chapter may be somewhat surprising to those who think they invest for the long term, but yet allow the daily noise of the financial markets to influence their decisions and keep them awake at night. If you read the financial newspapers every day, watch financial television shows every day, and keep track of your portfolio's value daily, the odds are you are not investing for the long term despite what you might think. The daily newspapers, financial television shows, and your portfolio's daily value are relatively unimportant if your time horizon is truly long term. A positive quarterly earnings surprise and all the analysis that follows it will probably have relatively little impact on the stock's price 5 or 10 years from now. Therefore, true long term investors have little need for daily updates.

DEFINING RISK ONCE MORE

As we previously discussed, traditional risk/return analyses usually consider risk to be the historical volatility (the standard deviation) of the returns of an asset. However, judging by the results of the quizzes in Chapter 6, a more appropriate measure of risk might be the probability of a loss for a given time period. Investors usually do not mind risk so long as performance is positive. In this chapter, we change the definition of risk to match how most investors define risk, namely, as the proportion of the returns that were negative (i.e., the probability of losing money). If an asset in the following figures and tables had a negative return during 5 of 25 periods, then the risk measure would be 20% (5/25 = 20%). Conversely, the asset would have provided positive returns 75% of the time.[1]

It is extremely important to understand that measuring risk as the percent of the periods' returns that were negative does not give any insight as to the magnitude of the positive or the negative returns. It is entirely possible that the negative returns of what appears to be a very conservative asset class might be much larger than those of what appears to be a very risky asset class. For example, an asset might provide a negative return once every 10 years, but the negative return could be –90%. Another asset might provide a negative return rather frequently, say once every five years, but the negative return might be only slightly negative.

WHY USE ONE-YEAR TIME PERIODS?

Time horizon plays a more significant role in determining an efficient asset allocation than most investors think. Results of an asset allocation study or analysis can change dramatically by simply using 10-year, 5-year, or even 3-year time horizons instead of the 1-year horizon that is used in most studies. It seems as though the early asset allocation studies used 1-year time horizons rather arbitrarily, and most investors now accept it as standard. Few have thought to consider whether one year is the appropriate analytical time horizon if an actual investment time horizon is much longer. Investors whose time horizons are indeed 10 or 15 years might make poor decisions by using data based on 1-year time horizons because the volatility or losses that might occur during the shorter time period might be filtered out during the longer time period. An investment that historically might have looked quite risky for 1-year time periods might look quite safe when viewed in the context of 5-year or 10-year periods.

Let's examine the risk/return relationships of five types of equity investments, and how the relationships change as we change the time horizon. First, let's define the data we are going to use. All the returns begin in January 1971 and go through December 2000. The series are as follows:

1. *S&P 500*. The total return of the S&P 500 with dividends reinvested monthly.
2. *Growth*. The Merrill Lynch Quantitative Strategy Growth Fund Index, which is a measure of the total return of nine large and well-known growth mutual funds. The index is equal-weighted, meaning that the returns of all nine funds are averaged to get the total return for the group as a whole. The index was constructed using only nine funds in an attempt to limit cheating among the managers. We mentioned before the possibility of growth funds buying value stocks and vice versa. By using a small sample of well-known funds, the probability of such cheating is reduced.
3. *Value*. The Merrill Lynch Quantitative Strategy Value Fund Index, which is similar to the growth fund index, except growth and income funds are used instead of growth funds.
4. *Small Stocks*. The returns of the Ibbotson Small Stock Index as calculated by Ibbotson Associates in Chicago. They define small stocks as the 9th and 10th deciles of the New York Stock Exchange when sorted by market capitalization and any AMEX and NASDAQ stocks that fit under that market capitalization ceiling.
5. *International Stocks*. The total return of the Morgan Stanley Capital International Europe/Australia/Far East (EAFE®) Index based in U.S. dollars.

Figure 7.1 is a scatter diagram of the historical risk/return relationships between these five equity asset classes. The vertical axis measures the average 12-month return from the particular equity asset class over the past 29 years, and the horizontal axis represents the percent of those 12-month returns that were negative.

In this figure, the returns were calculated on a trailing 12-month basis beginning in January 1971 in order to simulate random buying events. It is

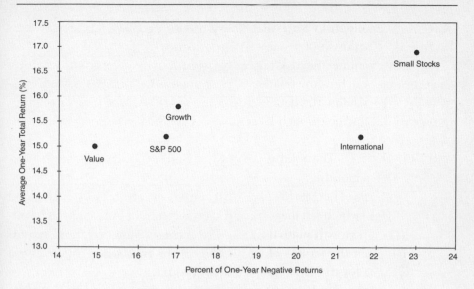

Figure 7.1 **One-Year Equity Risk/Return Relationships (1970–2000)**
Based on data from Merrill Lynch Quantitative Strategy.

unclear whether forming portfolios every December 31 imparts a bias into risk/return results, so returns are computed January to January, February to February, March to March, and so forth. We chose 1971 as the start date in this study because that is when the total return data for the EAFE® Index began within the database used.

As with all risk/return relationships, the goal is to attempt to invest in a portfolio that will end up northwest in the chart. Portfolios or assets lie northwest of others when they have experienced higher returns than those of the benchmark (north), but with less risk (west).

Table 7.1 shows the results from the graph in tabular format, and several facts are evident:

- The historical probability of a negative return is actually less for the value funds than for the overall S&P 500 despite the similarity of the returns. Value funds were actually safer investments than the other categories.
- The probability of losing money does vary significantly between the asset classes. For example, when investing in small stocks, you should be prepared for a positive return only about 77% of the time

Table 7.1   Equity Risk/Return Relationships Using a 12-Month Time
Horizon (1970 to 2000)

Equity Index	Average Annual Total Return (%)	Probability of Loss (%)
S&P 500	15.6	16.7
Value	15.5	14.9
Growth	16.5	17.0
International	15.7	21.6
Small stocks	17.5	23.0

(i.e., a loss occurs about 23% of the time). However, you should
expect a positive return about 85% of the time when investing in
value stocks.

- It is hard to find higher returns with less risk. Risk tends to increase
  in conjunction with higher returns.
- Currently, international stocks do not appear to provide the superior risk-adjusted returns that some might suggest. Several investments lie northwest of international stocks. This does not mean
  that international investing would not provide diversification for
  an all-U.S. portfolio, rather it means it might not be wise to hold a
  portfolio comprised solely of international stocks.

ACTIVE MANAGEMENT VERSUS S&P 500 INDEX FUND

The active manager indexes used suggest that both growth and value managers have been able to provide superior returns to those of the S&P 500
either on an absolute basis (growth), or on a risk-adjusted basis (both growth
and value). It is generally accepted that indexing outperforms actively managed mutual funds, but this study clearly questions that accepted axiom.

In Figure 7.1 the growth funds lie northeast of the S&P 500, indicating that their returns were higher, but investors would have had to take
some incremental risk to invest in them. However, it turns out that the
incremental return was actually higher than the incremental risk. Although
the value funds are southwest of the S&P 500 (lower return, but less
risk), the incremental reduction in risk versus the S&P 500 was greater
than the incremental reduction in return. Thus, both growth and value

ended up being more *efficient* investments (higher return for risk) than was the S&P 500.

These results in favor of active management may be surprising given the numerous articles that have suggested that active managers cannot outperform the market. The findings in those articles may be influenced by the time periods the authors have used (in most cases the 1980s and 1990s). The analysis in this book covers nearly 30 years, and contains both inflationary and disinflationary periods.

The breadth of the equity market (i.e., the number of stocks that are performing well within the overall market) may effect equity managers' abilities to outperform the overall market. In other words, as the breadth becomes more narrow and a smaller number of companies dominate the overall market's performance, equity managers will have a more difficult time outperforming simply because they may be hesitant to hold a less well-diversified portfolio with a smaller number of stocks. Market breadth generally narrowed during the latter half of both the 1980s and the 1990s, thus tending to restrict manager outperformance. However, market breadth generally widened during the late 1970s and early 1990s as evidenced by the outperformance of smaller stocks during those periods. Those changes in market breadth coupled with the use of data spanning a longer time span than in most studies may help explain our results that appear to conflict with the generally accepted notion that active managers cannot outperform the market.

A potential bias does exist with the growth and value manager data used in this study. The indexes were built on nine extremely large and well-known mutual funds in each category. The fact that the mutual funds used had those positive characteristics may have skewed the performance in favor of active managers. In other words, the funds' abilities to outperform might be why they are large and well known. Mutual fund data that are based on a broader group of funds (although less pure to style) might show performance results that better match those of the accepted studies on the benefits of indexing.

ANOTHER QUICK COMMENT ON GROWTH AND VALUE

Figure 7.1 also suggests that value investing may be more appropriate for risk-averse investors than growth investing. This is certainly counter to current popular wisdom. The growth index in Figure 7.1 does outperform the value index during the time period studied. However, even when including the tremendous outperformance of growth funds during the last several years, the long-term performance spread is only about 1.0% per year. However, the index of value managers had negative one-year returns only 14.9 % of the time, compared to 17.0% for the growth manager index. The question for some investors, therefore, is whether an additional 1.0% per year is worth losing about 2.1% more sleep at night (17.0% – 14.9% = 2.1%)

This is particularly interesting because of the past several years' interest in growth and aggressive growth funds. My guess is that many investors consider these types of funds to be the safest ways to invest for the long term in the equity market, but these data call that assumption into question. As previously mentioned, it can be dangerous to assume that what has outperformed during one three-year period will outperform during the next. If investors do define risk as the probability of a loss and they are using the last several years instead of some longer time period as their benchmark for determining risk, then the outperformance of growth and aggressive growth funds during the last several years probably explains individual investors' recent preference for such funds. They see both higher returns and safety in growth funds, but that view may be biased by the short time period used.

Also, value investors tend to buy stocks that have higher dividend yields than do growth stock investors. A larger proportion of total return of value stocks and value funds is, therefore, not related to the volatility of the overall stock market. The higher dividend yield dampens price returns so the probability of a loss is less.[2]

THREE-YEAR TIME HORIZONS

Let's repeat the analysis in Figure 7.1 and Table 7.1, but change the time horizon of the risk and return figures from one year to three years. Thus, instead of returns simply being measured from January to January, February to February, they are calculated as January to January three years later, February to February three years later, and so forth. Instead of counting the number of one-year returns that were negative, we now count the number of three-year returns that were negative.

Figure 7.2 graphically shows the results of the risk/return analysis when changing the time horizon from one year to three years, and Table 7.2 shows the actual data.

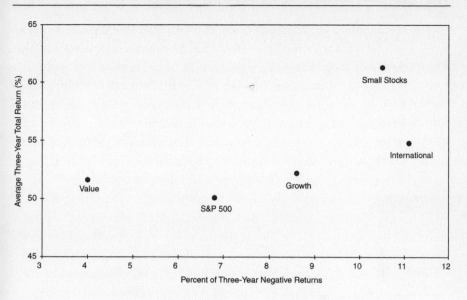

Figure 7.2   Three-Year Equity Risk/Return Relationships (1970–2000)
Based on data from Merrill Lynch Quantitative Strategy.

Several points emerge from Figure 7.2 and Table 7.2:

- Of most importance, the risk of all five investments decreases by simply extending the time horizon from one year to three years. The risk associated with the riskiest asset class, small stocks, fell significantly. Small stocks had positive returns about 77% of the time when using one-year time horizons (probability of a loss was about 23%). However, that proportion rose to about 89% when the time horizon was extended to three years.

Table 7.2   Equity Risk/Return Relationships Using a Three-Year Time Horizon (1970 to 2000)

Equity Index	Average Three-Year Total Return (%)	Probability of Loss (%)
S&P 500	50	6.8
Value	52	4.0
Growth	53	8.6
International	55	11.1
Small stocks	62	10.5

- Value funds again appear to be the most conservative of the five groups. Historically, when investing in value funds, investors lost money during three-year periods only about 4% of the time. Or, turning the data around, investors received a positive return about 96% of the time when investing with a three-year time horizon. Investors did not have to give up much return versus growth funds to gain that extra safety. Growth and value funds performed quite similarly for three-year time periods, but growth funds posted negative returns nearly twice as often as did value funds.

- Value was the only asset class that fell northwest of the S&P 500 when measured over three-year periods. Thus, it was the only asset class that provided higher returns and less risk than did the overall market.

- Both growth and value managers tended to outperform the overall market during three-year periods. With the biases noted regarding the growth and value fund indexes used, active management again seemed to outperform an S&P 500 index fund. The same could be said for small stock and international managers.

- Small stocks lie northwest of international stocks. Again, this does not comment on the diversification benefits of investing in international equities, but it does suggest that a small stock fund might be a better sole investment than would an international equity fund for a typical three-year period.

Again, some of these results might be surprising because of the outperformance of growth funds during the late 1990s. Value funds remained more conservative than growth funds, and only underperformed growth funds by about 1% per three-year period despite the tremendous outperformance of growth funds during the past several years.

FIVE-YEAR TIME HORIZONS

Now let's examine five-year time horizons. Returns will now be measured from January to January five years later, February to February five years later, and so forth. Instead of counting the number of one-year returns or three-year returns that were negative, we now count the number of five-year returns that were negative.

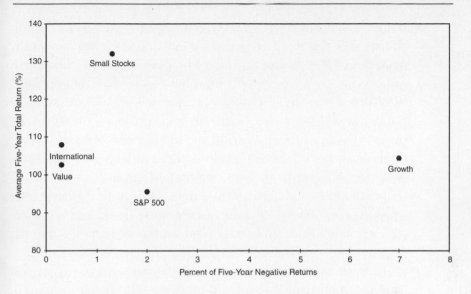

Figure 7.3   Five-Year Equity Risk/Return Relationships (1970–2000)
Based on data from Merrill Lynch Quantitative Strategy.

Figure 7.3 and Table 7.3 highlight the results.

As occurred when the time horizon was changed from one year to three years, there are some substantial differences in the data when we change the time horizon from three years to five years. They are summarized as follows:

- The overall risk of the investments when defining risk as the probability of a loss again significantly declines for most of the asset groups. In fact, the probability of a loss falls to under 1% for both value and international stocks.

Table 7.3   Equity Risk/Return Relationships Using a Five-Year Time Horizon (1970 to 2000)

Equity Index	Average Five-Year Total Return (%)	Probability of Loss (%)
S&P 500	96	2.0
Value	101	0.3
Growth	105	7.0
International	109	0.3
Small stocks	132	1.3

- Growth stocks now appear to be the riskiest asset class of the five included in this study. Whereas the other asset classes historically provided positive returns during at least 98% of the five-year periods included in the study, growth provided positive returns only about 93% of the time (the probability of a loss was 7%). Of most importance, they did not provide higher returns than some of the other asset categories despite their riskier nature. International and small stocks both outperformed growth stocks and did so with less risk. Value stocks provided nearly the same returns for considerably less risk.
- Extending the time horizon from three years to five years greatly changed the risk level of international stocks. It appears as though the stocks are susceptible to shorter-term poor performance that may get smoothed out by extending the time horizon.
- All four of the asset categories (growth, value, small stocks, and international) tended to outperform the S&P 500 for the typical five-year period.

Given most individual investors' current thoughts on the stock market, it is worth repeating a very important point. This study suggests that investors who believe that growth stocks and growth funds are the only way to invest for the long term should seriously consider altering their views. Figure 7.3 indicates that both international equities and small capitalization stocks outperform growth funds during the typical five-year period, and do so with less risk. In addition, value funds underperform growth funds but only by about 4% per five-year period, which is a very slight margin. They do so, however, while incurring much less risk.

TEN-YEAR TIME HORIZONS: THE TRUE LONG TERM

Finally, let's examine 10-year time horizons. Ten years are as close to the true long term as one can probably get while maintaining some semblance of a realistic investor expectation. There are obviously longer time horizons to consider (e.g., the 23 years that I used earlier in the book to plan for my retirement). However, factors in the economy and the financial markets can change very dramatically during such long time periods, and we could question whether the statistics are realistic or reliable.

The 10-year statistics used in this section were rolling 10-year statistics. The study does not simply use three 10-year periods in the analysis

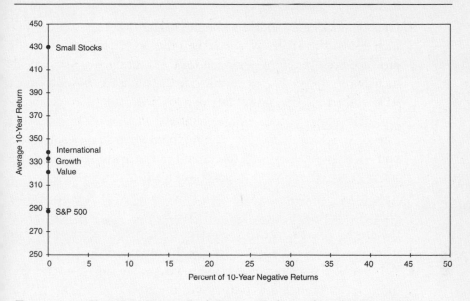

Figure 7.4   **Ten-Year Equity Risk Return Relationships (1970–2000)**
Based on data from Merrill Lynch Quantitative Strategy.

(i.e., 1970 to 1979, 1980 to 1989, and 1990 to 1999). Instead, the statistics were calculated from January to January 10 years later, February to February 10 years later, and so forth, so there were over 200 10-year periods included. The periods do overlap, but the intent was to simulate the random timing of a 10-year investment.

The results for a risk/return study based on 10-year time horizons are fascinating. Risk, as defined in this chapter, becomes immaterial. Investors should probably focus solely on return potential. Figure 7.4 and Table 7.4 summarize the results.

Table 7.4   **Equity Risk/Return Relationships Using a 10-Year Time Horizon (1970 to 2000)**

Equity Index	Average 10-Year Total Return (%)	Probability of Loss (%)
S&P 500	289	0
Value	322	0
Growth	331	0
International	339	0
Small stocks	430	0

Let's summarize the 10-year time horizon data:

- Since 1970, there has never been a rolling 10-year period in which any of the five equity asset classes lost money.
- Given the first statement, it appears as though true long-term investors should focus on the return potential of an investment, and pay little attention to an investment's shorter-term risk.
- The S&P 500 was the worst performing of the five asset classes during the average 10-year period. Actively managed growth and value funds outperformed the index, as did passive small stock and international stock investments. Recognizing again the biases in the growth and value indexes used, true long-term investors should not rule out investing in actively managed funds.

I don't want to sound overly repetitive, but the relationship between growth and value is worth looking at one more time. Growth funds outperformed value funds by only about 9% per 10-year period. That is less than 1% per year during these longer time horizons. You would probably never know that given the attention that growth stocks and growth funds have received during the past several years.

TIME REDUCES RISK

This analysis shows that extending your time horizon when investing can be an effective way to diversify risk. Risk was a very important consideration when considering 1-year time horizons, but was relatively unimportant when analyzing 10-year time horizons. There remain rational and irrational investments even when considering a longer time horizon (i.e., think of the lottery tickets from the previous chapter), but risk should probably be a secondary consideration for true long-term investors. The probability of actually losing money appears to decrease as the time horizon increases.

The key phrase of the preceding paragraph is "true long-term investors." As we shall discuss later in this chapter, investment noise tends to shorten investors' time horizons rather than lengthen them.

Figures 7.5 though 7.9 show how time can potentially reduce the risk of each of the five asset classes we discussed. In each figure, notice how the probability of a negative return decreases as the time horizon increases.

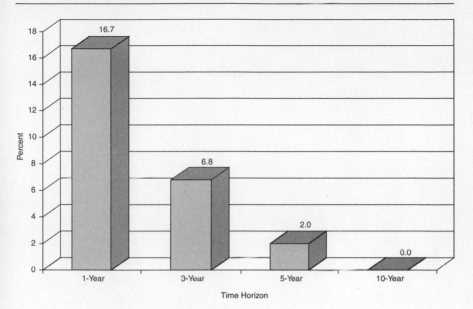

Figure 7.5   Percent of S&P 500 Negative Returns versus Time Horizon
(Rolling Total Returns, 1970–2000)
Based on data from Merrill Lynch Quantitative Strategy.

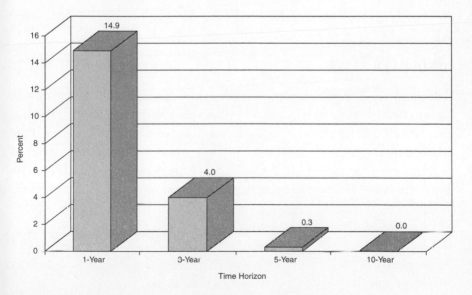

Figure 7.6   Percent of Value Fund Negative Returns versus Time Horizon
(Rolling Total Returns, 1970–2000)
Based on data from Merrill Lynch Quantitative Strategy.

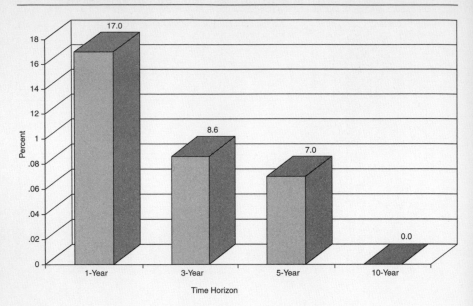

Figure 7.7   **Percent of Growth Fund Negative Returns versus Time Horizon (Rolling Total Returns, 1970–2000)**
Based on data from Merrill Lynch Quantitative Strategy.

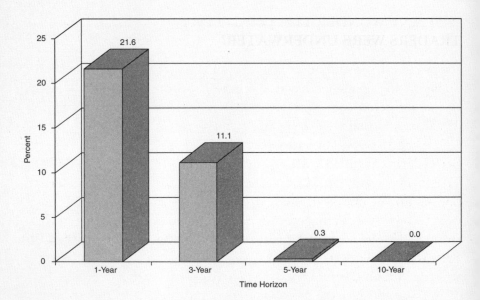

Figure 7.8   **Percent of International Equity Negative Returns versus Time Horizon (Rolling Total Returns, 1970–2000)**
Based on data from Merrill Lynch Quantitative Strategy.

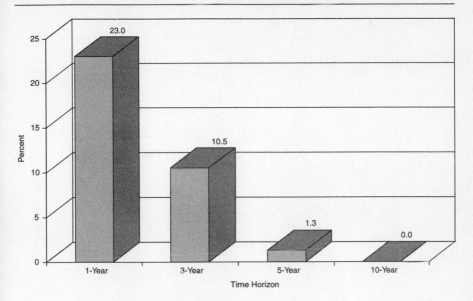

Figure 7.9   **Percent of Small Stock Negative Returns versus Time Horizon**
(Rolling Total Returns, 1970–2000)
Based on data from Merrill Lynch Quantitative Strategy.

IS IT ANY WONDER THAT MANY DAY TRADERS WERE UNDERWATER?

Suppose we go in the other direction. What is the probability of losing money during a one-month period? Figure 7.10 shows the percentage of the one-month returns for each of the above asset classes that were negative. The figures are quite high compared to the figures in the previous charts for 1, 3, 5, and 10 years. The probability of losing money when investing in the S&P 500 was about 38% during any random month, but it was only about 17% in any given year. Thus, by simply extending your time horizon from one month to one year, your probability of losing money historically decreased by 21%. Perhaps this conclusion is more powerful if thought of the opposite way. Your probability of gaining was 62% during a month but 83% in a year. The probability of a gain in the S&P 500 rose to 98% if you stretched your time horizon to only five years.

You can reduce the probability of a negative return by increasing your time horizon and increase it by decreasing your time horizon. Given these probabilities, is it any wonder that many day traders' portfolios did not perform well? Day traders are not looking at years of performance or even

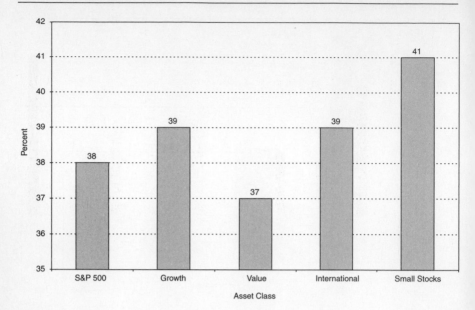

Figure 7.10   Percent of One-Month Negative Returns

months of performance. They are looking at minutes and hours. Their probability of success is extremely low.

ARE YOU SURE YOU WANT TO BE A DAY TRADER?

Extending your time horizon is good advice when investing in individual stocks as well. I mentioned earlier that I believe day traders are the ultimate junkies for investment noise. They concentrate on stock returns based on minutes and hours rather than on months, quarters, or years. Would day traders be more successful if they extended their time horizons for individual stocks? I think they would be, and they could probably keep their real jobs as well.

Figure 7.11 shows the performance of the average stock within a roughly 1,600-stock universe for one-month, three-month, and one-year time horizons as of each December 31 from 1990 to 1999. In 7 out of 10 years during the decade of the 1990s, investors would have benefited from investing with a 12-month time horizon instead of investing with a 1-month horizon.

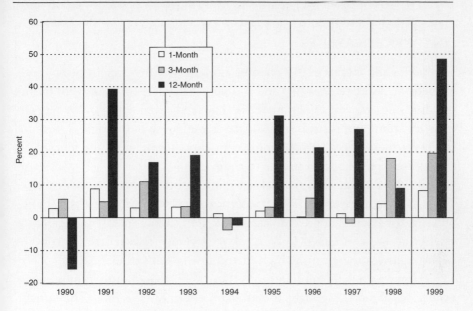

Figure 7.11   Individual Stock Returns for Varying Time Horizons

REMEMBER WELL THE FIVE-DAY WEATHER FORECAST

In the Introduction I used the five-day weather forecast as an example of noise. Despite that we know that the weather forecasters cannot accurately forecast the fifth day in the five-day weather forecast, each Monday evening we watch diligently for the upcoming weekend's forecasted weather. I also pointed out that simple and obvious forecasts have a greater probability of coming true than does the forecast for the fifth day. For example, it will be very cold in Minneapolis in January. I think we will all agree that stating it will be cold in Minneapolis in January will be true more often than will the five-day weather forecast.

The examples I have just presented about time horizons are exactly the same as the relationship between the five-day forecast and the January forecast for Minneapolis. The probability of being wrong in the financial markets goes up if we use a short-term forecast. However, the idea that we should invest for the long term seems as obvious as my forecast for cold in January in Minneapolis. Both are more likely to be more successful forecasts than what the stock market will do next month, or what the weather will be on Saturday, but both are more likely to be ignored as being silly and obvious.

NOISE FOCUSES ON RISKY ASSETS AND NOT ON RISKLESS ASSETS

The tables and graphs in this chapter explain why investment noise tends to focus on short-term events and is able to persuade investors that unimportant issues are very important. Risk tends to be higher for investments in the short term, but it tends to dissipate as we lengthen the time horizon of the investment. Because risk tends to be short term, and noise focuses on risk, noise tends to focus on short-term events.

Figure 7.12 shows a theoretical relationship between noise and risk. There is little noise about riskless assets or assets with very little risk. Noise picks up for assets that are of average risk, and then grows dramatically for assets that are considered to be of above average risk. There is no noise regarding investments of the highest risk levels. Let's examine why.

How much daily information is there about one-month T-bills? Television shows rarely highlight the rates on one-month T-bills. They might mention rates for three-month T-bills, but never do for one-month T-bills. How much daily information is there about six-month federally insured certificates of deposit (CDs)? Newspapers might give a listing every now and then, but rarely will you find a daily listing.

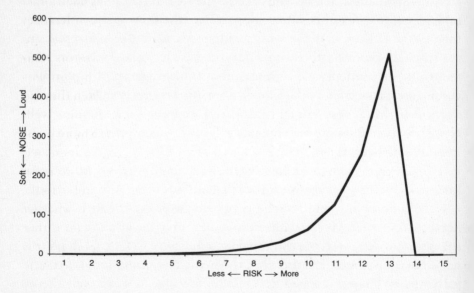

Figure 7.12   **Noise versus Risk**

Investors rarely hear in the media about these types of investments because they are nearly riskless. An investor's probability of losing money in a one-month T-bill is virtually zero. The same can nearly be said for the six-month federally insured CD. Investors have little to worry about when investing in these instruments.[3] There is little to report on these investments because things do not change very much for riskless assets. They basically remain riskless and do not have to be regularly monitored. Imagine a regular report on the nightly news highlighting that federally insured CDs remained federally insured today! There is nothing to report and little to worry about. Thus, there is little noise about riskless assets.

The relationship in Figure 7.12 suggests that riskier assets increasingly attract noise. Investments of average risk get some attention, but their risk is expected and many investors are already prepared for the periodic loss or volatility. This is akin to saying that some stocks go up and some stocks go down. There are reports to this effect (called advance/decline statistics). Such reports are included in the financial sections of most daily newspapers and are often updated hourly on financial news programs, but the print space and on-air time they receive are relatively minimal.

As we move toward still riskier assets a vortex forms, and noise begins to increase significantly. These are investments in which many people probably should not be investing because they are too risky. As mentioned in Chapter 6, investors often misperceive their own risk tolerance. Investors think they want to invest in an asset, but either do not appreciate the risk associated with the asset or think they are bolder investors than they truly are. Thus, these investors constantly worry about their portfolios and regularly monitor how their investments are performing. Often they are worried or cannot sleep at night if the investment is not performing well. Noise overdramatizes the investment's volatility, which leads to more monitoring of the investment, which leads to more nervous nights. Increased investor interest because of the tension leads to more noise. More noise leads to more monitoring, which leads to more nervous nights, and so forth.

An interesting question relating to this part of the chart is whether noise causes risk or whether risk causes noise. The discussion so far is that risk attracts noise, and thus causes increased noise. However, perhaps it is noise that causes risk. The theory of the Earnings Expectations Life Cycle presented in Chapter 3 argues that noise causes risk. The life cycle theory indicates that increased noise will cause investors to misperceive risk, but

Figure 7.12 suggests that risk might cause noise. I think the relationship between risk and noise is somewhat of an odd symbiotic one. Risk causes noise, which in turn causes more risk, which in turn causes more noise.

Little noise surrounds extremely risky assets for a couple of reasons. First, these assets are considered to be so risky that the general public does not typically invest in them. The purveyors of noise, therefore, see little return to any generation of noise focused on such assets. For example, commodities futures markets receive very little attention in the media. Second, these assets are so risky that general information is typically not available. It is difficult for the general public to learn about them or to find sources of noise on which to base stories. Thus, noise increases exponentially as assets become riskier than average, but then falls off completely with respect to the riskiest assets.

The technology bubble of 1999–2000 has altered this relationship slightly in that an unusual amount of investment noise is starting to be generated regarding the riskiest types of assets. For example, private equity funds are being offered to a broader range of investors, and some private equity general partners have begun to appear in the media discussing this asset class. The general acceptance of this asset class by a broader range of investors might be considered by some to be a warning sign that some investors are taking more risk than they understand they are.

THE UNCERTAINTY OF RISK IS MORE IMPORTANT THAN RISK

Two factors should be considered when discussing how noise can lead investors to alter their strategic time horizons. The first is the level of noise itself, and the other is the level of concern about the uncertainty of the risk of the investment. The media might generate a tremendous amount of noise about one-month T-bills, but it would probably have little effect on most investors. The term of the investment is one month, and the credit quality of the U.S. government is the best in the world. Thus, few T-bill investors would care if there were noise or not about their investment.

Noise can significantly alter your investment time horizon if the investment is supposed to be long term (i.e., a term measured in years rather than months), and if you do not feel certain about the risk characteristics of the investment. It may not be the risk of an investment that actually allows noise to disrupt a long-term strategic plan; it may be investors' uncertainty regarding the risk of the investment. If investors know an investment is definitely risky, then losses or volatility should not be surprising. If investors pay no attention to investments that are certainty safe, noise can again have no impact. However, noise can have a great impact on our decision making if we think a long-term investment is safe, but we are not very certain about the safety of that investment. The uncertain mind easily succumbs to noise.

It should now be clear why the preceding chapters on risk assessment and diversification were so important. If you have assessed your risk tolerance correctly and are well diversified as a result, then noise should minimally impact your investment decisions. Noise has its greatest influence over investors who are taking too much risk and are underdiversified.

Chapter 8

Don't Search for
Good Companies,
Search for Good Stocks

Do good companies make good stocks? Intuitively, you would think they must, but an intriguing question posed by two academic researchers is whether good stocks lead investors to the perception of what is a good company. In other words, do investors ferret out good companies about which no one knows, or do they see good stock performance and then surmise that it must be because the company is a good company?[1]

Surprising as it may seem, it appears that bad companies actually make better stocks than do good companies over the long term. Thus, while most investors attempt to find good companies, and invest in those companies when they are found, the time might be better spent searching for good stocks.

Parts of this chapter are adapted from a chapter on the investment implications of company quality from my earlier book. See Richard Bernstein, *Style Investing—Unique Insight into Equity Management* (New York: John Wiley & Sons, 1995).

DEFINING QUALITY

Quality, per se, is a relative term. What I consider to be a good company at one point in time may be completely different from a good company at a different point. In addition, quality may be defined relative to the goals of the particular investment. Guidelines or regulations placed on certain mutual funds, pension plans, or trust accounts may restrict quality-oriented strategies so much that the stocks one manager might consider to be low quality might be considered very high quality by another manager.

Investors define quality using any number of different characteristics. Some use debt/equity ratios, and assume that companies without debt are good companies, whereas others use the stability of earnings growth as a quality guideline. Return on equity, sales growth, earnings growth, and the dispersion of analysts' estimates (a measure of disagreement among analysts) are just a few others.

One of the most convenient and informative definitions of quality is the Standard and Poor's Common Stock Rankings. These rankings are based primarily on the stability and growth in earnings and dividends over a 10-year period (a more full description of the rankings is published in every issue of the Standard and Poor's *Stock Guide*). A company with an extremely stable earnings growth and dividend growth history would be ranked A+, whereas a company in bankruptcy would be ranked D. S&P calculates these rankings according to a computer algorithm, and there is little subjective interpretation. S&P has a largely unbiased quality measure on an extremely large universe of companies.

These rankings should not be confused with the better-known S&P Debt Ratings. The debt ratings are based on analysts' reviews of company fundamentals to determine a company's ability to repay its debt obligations. Some fixed-income researchers believe that the S&P Debt Ratings are subjective and can sometimes lag changes in fundamental data. The stock rankings are largely objective, and my studies on the stock rankings have shown that they have an immense amount of forward-looking investment information. Whenever the word *quality* is used in the subsequent chapters of this book, it refers to the S&P Common Stock Rankings.

Figure 8.1 shows the distribution of S&P Common Stock Rankings among the roughly 1,600 companies within the database I use (the actual universe of stocks that have S&P Stock Rankings is larger). The distribution

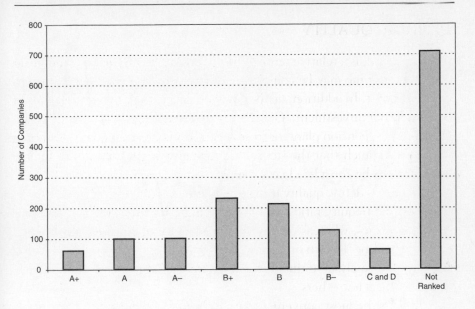

Figure 8.1   Distribution of S&P Common Stock Rankings

of companies is such that there are very few A+ and C and D stocks,[2] and many B+ and B stocks (i.e., the distribution is roughly normally distributed).

A very large proportion of the universe has no ranking at all, which implies that these companies have not been in existence for 10 years. New issues therefore dominate the not-rated universe. Small capitalization growth managers used to be the managers most interested in not-rated companies. However, the technology bubble changed that. The average market capitalization of the not-rated universe rose during 1998 and 1999 as the bubble inflated the market capitalizations of many young technology and telecommunications companies. As a result, many large capitalization stock investors have invested in these uncharted waters, some perhaps not realizing the risks involved.

We primarily focus on two rankings: the A+ and the C and D. We focus on the A+ stocks because these are typically considered to be the good companies and tend to exhibit the characteristics of "safe haven" investments. The Cs and Ds are the lowest ranked stocks, are often considered very risky, but actually outperform the other rankings through time. The not-rated universe is also interesting because stocks tend to be new and unknown and can potentially be the most influenced by investment noise.

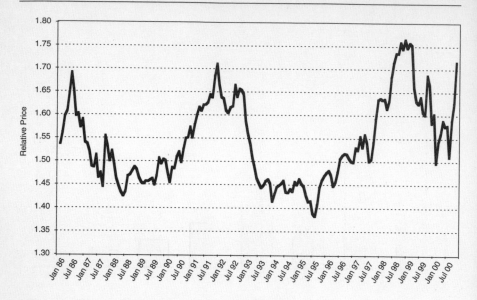

Figure 8.2   **Relative Performance of A+ Stocks**

GOOD COMPANIES, BAD STOCKS

Figure 8.2 shows the performance of an index of A+ companies relative to the performance of the Equal-Weighted S&P 500.[3] The A+ stocks actually barely outperform the overall market over the long term (here about 15 years). The A+ stocks' performance over the long term is surprising to many investors. They invest under the misperception that good companies (i.e., A+ companies) significantly outperform over the long term.

A WELL-DIVERSIFIED PORTFOLIO OF HIGH QUALITY STOCKS MIGHT SIMPLY BE AN EXPENSIVE INDEX FUND

There may be several reasons why good companies do not perform particularly well over the long term. First, although the absolute number of A+ companies is relatively small (there are only about 60 A+ companies in our database of 1,600 or less than 4% of the universe), the average market capitalization is quite large. Figure 8.3 shows that the market capitalization of the average A+ stock is nearly double that of the market capitalization of the average A stock. Because most accepted stock market indexes are market-capitalization weighted, a diversified portfolio of A+ companies will closely

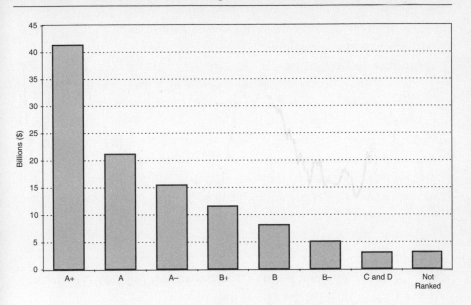

Figure 8.3   **Average Market Capitalization by S&P Common Stock Ranking**

resemble the performance of an S&P 500 index fund. In other words, A+ companies have historically performed as does the overall market because they are the overall market. If we were to expand the definition of higher quality companies to include both A and A– stocks, then the performance of higher quality issues and the overall market would appear even more similar.

Although A+ companies tend to perform similarly to the overall market through time, their performance is much more volatile. There are periods in which A+ companies perform well, and periods in which they do not. Their relative performance versus the overall market appears to be somewhat cyclical. We discuss the factors that influence that cyclical performance later in this chapter.

A possible conclusion from these data is that owning a diversified portfolio of A+ companies might simply be like owning an expensive index fund. The long-term performance of A+ stocks is similar to that of the overall market, so there is little performance benefit gained by investing in the subset of stocks. Their performance is more volatile than that of the overall market, meaning that you are taking more risk and not getting extra return. Finally, investing in them individually or by way of a fund that focuses on high quality stocks may be more expensive than would be investing in a low-expense index fund.

Another debatable point is whether so-called high quality funds are worth their costs. You could probably invest in a diversified portfolio of high quality stocks by yourself more cheaply than investing in a fund that invests in similar stocks. Investors are required to perform relatively little primary fundamental research on these companies because they are so well known that the amount of expertise needed to understand the companies is relatively small. Therefore, investors interested in high quality stock funds should investigate how much added value a high quality stock fund provides relative to an index fund, to the performance of A+ stocks, or to a universe of stocks that they would feel comfortable investing in by themselves.

IF YOU KNOW IT'S A GOOD COMPANY AND I DO, TOO, THEN EVERYONE PROBABLY KNOWS

Good companies tend to perform similarly to the overall market over the long term rather than outperform as most investors expect exactly because they are known as good companies. If you know a company is a good company, and I know it is a good company, then the odds are that most investors also know it is a good company. The valuation we will have to pay to invest in that good company might be higher than the valuation of other companies to reflect the company's superior quality. However, if the valuation is too high, then investors' expectations regarding the safety and quality of the company might be too high, and the probability is that investors will be disappointed. If the company's valuation is too rich, then the odds are that the stock is sitting around midnight on the Earnings Expectations Life Cycle.

The valuation of the consumer staples sector during the late 1990s is a perfect example of how investors can pay too much for the safety of higher quality issues. Figure 8.4 shows the price/earnings ratio of the consumer staples sector (i.e., industries such as foods, household products, beverages, supermarkets, personal care products) relative to that of the S&P 500. These stocks dominated the A+ universe during much of the 1990s. However, from 1995 to about 1998, the valuations of this group were the highest in the history of the data shown. The global economy was slipping into recession, and many investors thought these stocks and their stable earnings patterns would protect their portfolios against the "profits recession" that was forming globally.[4]

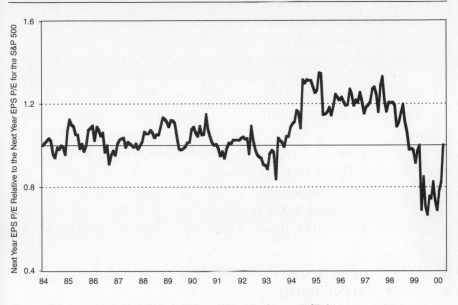

Figure 8.4 **Consumer Staples Next Year Relative P/E (August 1984 to November 2000)**
Based on data from Merrill Lynch Quantitative Strategy.

Figure 8.4 shows clearly that investors were paying too much for the quality of these well-known good companies during the late 1990s. The relative price/earnings ratio of the consumer staples sector was the highest in the history of the data during that time period. As a result, expectations were too high and the stocks disappointed investors during the next several years. In retrospect, these stocks were indeed at midnight on the Earnings Expectations Life Cycle. As an interesting aside, note that the valuations of the sector in 2000 were at their lowest levels in the history of the data. Some were suggesting in 2000 that the consumer staples stocks' prices had already discounted all the bad news associated with these formerly good companies, and the perception that the companies were "bad" was untrue. According to some investors, the sector was closer to six o'clock than to midnight during 2000.

BAD COMPANIES, GOOD STOCKS

Contrary to what most investors might expect, bad companies tend to make good stocks over the long term. Figure 8.5 shows the relative performance of C and D stocks since 1986, and this category of stocks has clearly

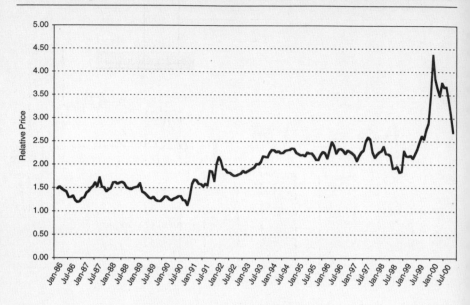

Figure 8.5   **Relative Performance of C and D Stocks**

performed much better than the A+ category. In fact, since 1986, C and D stocks have risen more than 800%, while A+ stocks have risen a relatively paltry 480%. Cs and Ds have almost doubled the performance of A+ stocks during the time period highlighted. It has not even been close.

Taking this analysis a step further, C and D stocks not only outperform A+ stocks through time, they are the best performing category. Figure 8.6 shows the absolute price performance of all the quality rankings since 1986. Cs and Ds are by far the best performers. Bad companies seem to make good stocks over the long term.

COMPOSITION OF QUALITY

Figure 8.7 shows the proportion of each economic sector that is comprised of higher quality stocks. Some of the results presented in this chart may be obvious, but some are not:

- The two sectors with the largest concentration of higher quality issues are utilities and consumer staples (foods, beverages, and the like). These sectors tend to have very stable earnings growth through time because of the relatively consistent need for the goods and/or

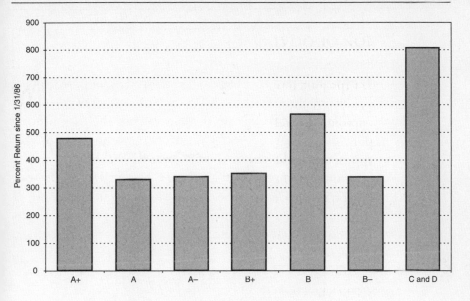

Figure 8.6   Performance of Quality Rankings

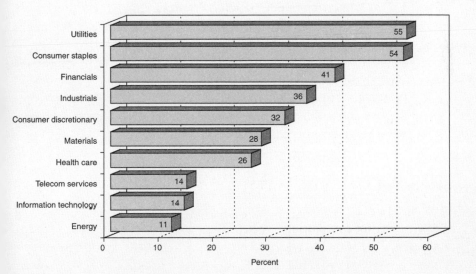

Figure 8.7   Percent of Higher Quality Stocks by Sector with S&P Common Stock Ranking of B+ or Better as of 11/30/00

MSCI™ (Morgan Stanley Capital International)–S&P sector classifications based on Merrill Lynch Quantitative Strategy Universe of approximately 1,500 stocks.

services the companies in these sectors produce. A simple economic reality is that no matter what goes on, we all still eat and we all still turn on the lights.

- Energy currently has the largest concentration of low quality stocks. That might seem obvious given the volatility in energy prices during the 1990s. However, that was not the case historically. The rankings of the stocks in the energy sector have drifted downward consistently during the last 10 to 15 years. Few investors today remember that energy stocks were considered growth stocks by the end of the 1970s because of the secular rise in energy prices during the decade. At that time, sectors such as consumer staples were actually considered income-oriented investments rather than growth investments.

- Perhaps most surprising to investors who got caught up in the technology bubble is that technology and telecom services rank just above the energy sector as low quality sectors. Less than 15% of these sectors is comprised of stocks with S&P Common Stock Rankings of B+ or better. Thus, these sectors are more cyclical than most investors believed during the bubble and probably still believe today.

- Many investors are surprised as well that health care ranks so low on the quality scale. Although the large pharmaceutical companies do indeed show very stable earnings patterns (most are ranked A+ or A), the broader sector does not. Political issues during the 1990s have significantly altered the growth patterns of several health care industries. For example, hospital management and nursing homes are two industries that have been hurt by the cutbacks in government reimbursement programs.

STILL NO FREE LUNCH, HOWEVER

It is important to emphasize that the outperformance of C and D ranked stocks is measured over many years. There are periods in which C and D stocks actually performed very poorly. Table 8.1 shows the year-to-year performance comparison between A+ stocks and C and D stocks. Investors interested in C and D stocks must be willing to hang on through good times and bad to reap the long-term performance these stocks offer. Here again is an example that there is no free lunch in the financial markets. Higher returns seem to be accompanied by higher risk.

Table 8.1   Annual Price Return of A+ and C and D Stocks

	A+ Stocks (%)	C and D Stocks (%)
1987	–3.5	20.5
1988	14.3	21.7
1989	23.4	–1.6
1990	–10.8	–20.5
1991	43.3	92.1
1992	7.4	22.7
1993	–1.4	33.2
1994	–2.3	6.3
1995	30.6	21.7
1996	19.1	21.7
1997	36.9	17.2
1998	19.8	–4.4
1999	–1.5	71.4
2000 (through October)	6.5	32.9

Let's examine some of the risk characteristics described in the earlier chapters for these categories of stocks. Table 8.2, which is based on monthly data rather than on annual data as in Table 8.1, shows the risk characteristics of these quality categories when defining risk either as the volatility or unpredictability of the returns (the standard deviation) or as the probability of losing money. In addition, the table shows the average 12-month return, median (middle) 12-month return, and the maximum and minimum 12-month returns.

Table 8.2   Comparative Risk/Return Statistics for A+ and C and D Stocks

	A+ Stocks (%)	C and D Stocks (%)
Standard deviation	14.6	26.4
Probability of a loss	19.3	18.1
Average 12-month return	12.4	22.1
Median 12-month return	11.1	18.2
Maximum 12-month return	50.0	113.3
Minimum 12-month return	–20.8	–29.9

Using the traditional definition of risk (the volatility or standard deviation of returns) C and D stocks appear much riskier than A+ stocks (14.6% for A+ stocks and 26.4% for C and D stocks). C and D stocks' returns are nearly twice as variable or unpredictable. The average, median, and maximum 12-month returns are higher as compensation to investors for the higher risk.

When defining risk as the probability of a loss, C and D stocks actually appear slightly safer than A+ stocks. Cs and Ds provide higher returns with less risk when compared to A+ stocks. C and D returns are more volatile than A+ returns, but the volatility has been skewed positively. Note that the two classifications' lowest 12-month returns are roughly similar (−20.8% for A+ stocks and −29.9% for C and D stocks), but the best return is meaningfully higher for C and D stocks (50.0% for A+ stocks and 113.3% for C and D stocks). To be fair, I should point out that the performance of C and D stocks was very positively influenced by the technology bubble. Prior to the bubble, the relative risk/return characteristics of C and D stocks were not quite as compelling.

ANALYZING TIME HORIZONS

As we did in Chapter 7, let's analyze what happens to the probability of a loss within quality rankings as we extend the time horizon used. The risk/return statistics shown so far have assumed a 12-month or calendar year holding period. Table 8.3 extends the time horizon to 3, 5, and 10 years. Similar to the statistics in Chapter 7, the probability of a loss is defined as the percent of the historical returns for the given holding period that were negative.

Table 8.3   **Probability of a Loss Using Varying Time Horizons**

	A+ Stocks (%)	C and D Stocks (%)
Twelve-month returns	19.3	18.1
Three-year returns	1.4	5.7
Five-year returns	0.0	0.0
Ten-Year returns	0.0	0.0

As we might expect from Chapter 7, the probability of a loss goes down for stocks in both quality ranks when the time horizon is extended. The probability of a loss in C and D stocks is typically 18.1% for a random 12-month period, but it declines to 0.0% when examining 10-year returns. Similarly, the probability of a loss in A+ stocks is typically 19.3% for a random 12-month period, but it is 0.0% for a random 10-year period. Note, however, that the probability of a loss in a 3-year period is higher for Cs and Ds than it is for A+s. Similar to some of the international stock data in Chapter 7, it appears as though medium-term losses for C and D stocks are smoothed out during longer time periods.

Despite such evidence, investors generally still tend to search for good companies rather than for good stocks. Several factors might contribute to that tendency, such as a lack of available research, lack of trading liquidity (an important factor for institutional investors), and psychological barriers.

NEGLECTED STOCKS

Considerable academic literature has been published on what has come to be known as the neglected stock effect. Researchers have shown that information is not uniformly available on all stocks. For larger, better-known stocks there is considerable information available daily. However, for smaller, lesser-known companies information may be sporadic at best. This lack of information is called "information asymmetry," and can present opportunities for those investors willing to do their own research on the ignored or neglected companies.

The studies on the neglected stock effect were an early version of the research on which this book is based. These earlier studies on neglected stocks were the first to examine the relationship between stocks' popularity and their performance. Investors seemed to pay a disproportionate amount of attention to those stocks that eventually underperformed, and ignored stocks that eventually outperformed. As might be suggested by the Earnings Expectations Life Cycle, these academic studies concluded that the correlation between investor attention and performance seemed inverse.[5]

Table 8.4 shows that the quality effect may be influenced by the neglected stock effect. The table shows the average number of analysts following companies grouped by S&P Common Stock Rankings. The average A+ company has about 17 analysts following its stock, whereas only about

Table 8.4　Analyst Coverage by S&P Common
Stock Rankings

S&P Common Stock Ranking	Approximate Average Number of Research Analysts
A+	17
A	14
A–	13
B+	12
B	12
B–	10
C	9
NR	8

9 analysts tend to follow the average C and D stock. It is perplexing that so many analysts follow A+ companies and so few follow Cs and Ds. A+ companies are those with the most stable earnings and dividend patterns; what is there to analyze? The analyst can simply extrapolate trend. However, few analysts research the companies for which only one question must be answered: Will the company survive? It is often a very difficult question, but a correct answer may give insight as to whether investors should buy or short the particular stocks and may yield tremendous returns.

Of course, the analyst who follows the A+ company has plenty to analyze regarding whether he or she should indeed extrapolate the trend-line in earnings and dividends, or should he or she be wary of some upcoming fundamental problem. Within the context of the Earnings Expectations Life Cycle, enthusiasm for a stock comes right as the stock's performance, expectations, and noise peak. Thus, most analysts believe that the good company's good fortunes will undoubtedly continue, and they simply extrapolate trend. The investor is left to wonder ultimately what happened to the performance of the so-called good company.

LIQUIDITY

Institutional investors tend to invest in stocks that have adequate trading liquidity. Trading liquidity refers to the amount of stock that trades for a given period of time, and is important to institutional investors because it allows them to gauge how large a position they can take in a stock and, in

Table 8.5 Trading Volume by S&P
Common Stock Rankings

S&P Common Stock Ranking	Average Weekly Trading Volume (000)
A+	2,284
A	1,099
A–	1,017
B+	1,121
B	1,373
B–	1,310
C	1,123
D	875
NR	931

Source: Reprinted from Richard Bernstein, *Style Investing—Unique Insight into Equity Management* (New York: John Wiley & Sons, 1995), 93.

some cases, how quickly they can get out of a position should something go wrong. Table 8.5, taken from a 1995 study, shows a simple measure of trading liquidity and trading volume across quality rankings. It demonstrates another potential reason why some investors gravitate toward higher quality issues. It is ironic that the need to escape from a stock position would decrease if investors simply searched for good stocks instead of good companies.

RISK AVERSION OR REGRET AVERSION?

Some academics[6] suggest another reason why investors tend to shun low quality companies. The academics hypothesize that portfolio managers, brokers, financial advisors, and the like are more regret averse than they are risk averse. Regret aversion is simply the fear of having to apologize to a client. They feel that if a manager recommends the stock of a good company or a financial advisor suggests the purchase of a good company, and the stock subsequently underperforms, then the manager or financial advisor can claim that it was not his or her fault. After all, the company was indeed a well-known good company, but some outside influence altered the investment returns from those that were expected. For example, the management of the company might have made bad corporate decisions or the market simply favored other sectors. However, if the financial advisor suggests purchasing a well-known bad company and it subsequently underperforms, then the risk of the financial advisor being fired goes up. It may appear to the client that everyone in the world knew that the company was a bad company except this one idiotic financial advisor. Thus, portfolio managers and financial advisors never want to face regret and tend to manage portfolios and recommend stocks accordingly.

BAD COMPANIES CAN MAKE BAD STOCKS

I mentioned earlier that bad companies make good stocks over the long term. As our risk/return study showed, there are shorter-term periods during which bad companies make very bad stocks. What are the factors that cause bad companies to actually perform like bad stocks instead of the good stocks that they are over the long term?

The prime factor that influences the performance of good companies and bad companies is the profits cycle. The profits cycle can easily be measured as the year-to-year percent change in S&P 500 earnings or simply S&P 500 earnings growth. One fundamental reason that bad companies outperform over the long term is that investors expect them to cease to exist. However, the secular trend in corporate profits in the United States is positive through time, and that secular profits growth supports these poorer quality companies. The companies, as a group, do survive, and investors are generally pleasantly surprised. It may not be the turn-around success of a particular company's management that causes the stock to outperform. Rather, it may simply be that a company has the "wind at its back."[7]

If the profits cycle is so important to the success of lower quality companies, then it makes sense that lower quality companies perform poorly when the profits cycle decelerates. When profitability decelerates, higher quality stocks tend to outperform lower quality ones. Higher quality stocks' stable earnings and dividend patterns seem boring or measly when the profits cycle accelerates because higher quality companies do not have the sensitivity to the economy that lower quality companies have. However, that lack of sensitivity and stable growth patterns pay off when the profits cycle decelerates. Secularly rising profits in the United States may therefore be one reason that lower quality stocks have outperformed over the long term.

NOISE AND QUALITY

Noise greatly influences investors' perceptions of company quality almost as much as it influences risk. Noise can make low quality companies appear to be of very high quality, and can make high quality companies appear to be of very low quality. As mentioned earlier in this chapter, companies are often judged as being *good* or *bad* because of their past stock performance, and not because of their superior or inferior fundamentals. If that assertion is indeed true, then investors must carefully scrutinize claims regarding a company's quality. We know that past performance is not necessarily indicative of future returns, so we should be careful not to judge a company's quality based on past stock performance. The next time someone says that company XYZ is a great company, ask him or her why he or she thinks so. My guess is that he or she might give reasons that are fundamentally based but will inevitably strongly emphasize the stock's outperformance.

A company's quality takes a long time to change, but it is easy to see within the context of the Earnings Expectations Life Cycle that *perceptions* of quality can change rapidly. Investment noise and hype do not actually alter the quality of companies, but they do affect investors' perception of the quality of those companies. The problem or opportunity for investors occurs when a company's true quality and the perception of quality are too far apart. Consensus might be that a company is of very high quality, yet it is a very cyclical one. Conversely, consensus might be that a company is in trouble, yet it is simply a stable growth company whose earnings growth cannot keep up with that of more cyclical companies when the profits cycle accelerates.

NOISE AND NOT-RATED COMPANIES

Not-rated companies may be particularly sensitive to noise because they are newer companies. Wall Street analysts sometimes hype newer companies in order to make the companies appear to be of significantly higher quality than they actually are. Because the companies are so new, and there are few alternative sources of information, it is difficult for investors to argue otherwise.

It is my experience that investors ignore S&P Common Stock Rankings when they find their favorite stock is not ranked or is ranked lower than they think it should be, showing clearly that noise and hype can powerfully influence investor behavior. Rather than accepting that their portfolios are perhaps riskier than was originally believed and adjusting the portfolio to better match their risk preferences, investors often blame the rankings as being inaccurate and meaningless. All I can say is don't shoot the messenger!

OBJECTIVE MEASURES OF QUALITY

Investors should be sure to use very objective measures of quality. Such measures should have the following characteristics:

- *Consistent numeric measure.* An objective measure of quality should be numeric rather than descriptive. Earnings growth might be stable, but how stable?
- *Systematic.* The calculation should be the same for all companies under consideration through time. The investor should not use one measure for one industry and other measures for other industries. Invariably, some investors will argue that the statistic does not apply to a certain industry. Do not believe it. Generally such arguments are made by those attempting to subjectively justify the purchase of a lower quality industry. Nor should investors believe that measures of quality are no longer appropriate because of the changing economic or stock market environment. Again, these are arguments typically used to support the purchase of lower quality companies.
- *Transparency.* The measure should be obvious and intuitive. Some analysts offer very complicated "black box" measures of quality in which the actual formula or theory is not divulged. I would avoid these measures. Measures should be simple and intuitive.
- *Verifiable.* The measure should have a significant history so that the investor can see if the measure is effective under varying economic and profits scenarios.
- *Free.* I am a firm believer that most investors should not pay for such data. It is rare that a service has proprietary data that is so insightful that an investor should pay for it (beyond normal data-

base costs). Always be skeptical regarding providers of data who claim to have exceptional models and statistics but do not manage money using them.

I use S&P Common Stock Rankings because they meet all the above criteria. They are numeric in that they follow a standardized formula. They are systematic in that all companies are calculated the same way.[8] Their information content is verifiable as demonstrated by the many studies other researchers and I have undertaken. Most important, there generally is no charge for the data above normal database costs. When looking for financial data, perhaps the grandest irony is that the S&P Common Stock Rankings have been around for decades, there is an immense amount of information in them, and yet few investors use them.

A RECENT EXAMPLE OF NOISE AND QUALITY: THE TECHNOLOGY BUBBLE

Some investors have wondered why renowned investors such as Warren Buffet do not invest in sectors such as technology and telecom. Buffet has commented many times that he refuses to invest in a company in which he does not understand the product. There are few of us, short of computer scientists and engineers, who completely understand today's technology and telecom companies' broad range of products produced and the uses of those products. We realize that technology plays a larger and larger role in our lives, but how many of us can decipher the competitive advantage of one grade of fiber optics from another, the reliability of one connector versus another, or the heat generation of one computer chip versus another?

Most investors hear about a technology company's cool product, and assume the company will succeed. Even Wall Street analysts have had difficulty deciphering the winners from the losers. By the time the technology hype was really percolating, most of the large brokerage firms' research departments followed over 500 technology companies around the world. Despite that huge number of companies, very few technology analysts used the word *competition* in their reports. They simply assumed that every company would be successful.

Why have brokerage firms' technology analysts not discussed competition, and why won't Warren Buffet buy technology stocks? My simple answer is noise. The more we know about a sector's or industry's business, the less susceptible we are to investment noise. We generally know a decent amount about toothpaste and soda, so it is more difficult to hype companies that produce those products (although it does happen). We generally know much less about fiber optics than we do about toothpaste. So, we can be told nearly anything about a company's prospects in that industry and it might sound exciting. We have no personal basis on which to compare.

Let's examine some of the hype and noise surrounding the technology sector during 1999 and 2000 that led investors to believe the sector was of much higher quality than it really was. As shown in Figure 8.7, technology is among the lowest quality sectors. Why were investors so far off in the perception of the sector's quality versus reality?

Quality Misperception #1: Confusing Cyclical with Secular

Perhaps the greatest misperception of the quality of the technology sector in 1999–2000 was that it was a stable growth sector. Not only did investors believe that the technology sector's earnings growth was the fastest of any sector, but they also were convinced that the earnings growth was more stable. The valuations given to technology stocks were exceptionally high because they incorporated assumptions regarding both tremendous growth and tremendous stability of growth. If there was going to be a so-called new economy, then investors must have felt it would not have the cycles that characterized every other economy in world history.[9]

Figure 8.8 shows actual S&P technology sector earnings and a log-linear trendline. There are two things in this chart that seem to be counter to the general perception of technology earnings. First, the cycles of technology earnings are larger than most might think. The technology sector has always been a very cyclical sector, and this chart reflects those cycles. Second, the long-term growth in earnings for the technology sector is much lower than most believe. The sector's historical earnings growth is not 20% or 30% as many believe. Rather, it is about 9%. Noise and hype led investors to believe that the technology sector was a very high quality, stable growth sector, when in fact it is a very cyclical, slower growth sector.

Why did investors in 1999 and 2000 believe that the technology sector was both a fast and stable growth sector? If the graph started in the

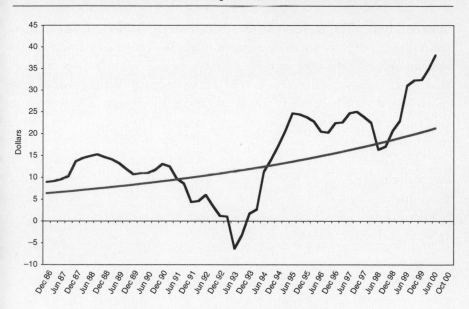

Figure 8.8   **Actual and Log-Linear Earnings for the Technology Sector (Trendline EPS Growth Equals 9% per year; R^2 Equals 15%)**
Based on data from Merrill Lynch Quantitative Strategy.

second quarter of 1998 rather than in 1986, then the trend in earnings growth was 62% per year, and the R^2 of the trendline (a measure of the consistency of earnings growth in which 100% means no variability) is about 95%. What investors seemed to forget was that S&P technology sector earnings growth was –34% as of the second quarter of 1998. Much of the world was in recession at that time, and technology sector earnings were hurt significantly by the slowdown in global growth.

It appears that investors confused a cyclical rebound in earnings with a secular trend. As technology sector earnings rebounded strongly from 1998's global debacle, investors assumed that the strong earnings growth was the emergence of the new economy. They incorrectly extrapolated the cyclical rebound that began in 1998 as a long-term trend. If the technology sector really could consistently grow earnings 62% per year, then it would probably be the highest quality sector known to mankind. Unfortunately, as with the earnings of most cyclical sectors, extrapolating short-term history proved dangerous.

Quality Misperception #2: The Only Sector That Was Growing

Because of the misperception of quality, many investors thought the technology sector was the only sector that was actually growing its earnings. The common thought was that no other sector could grow. Certainly, it was the fastest growing sector from the trough in the overall profits cycle in 1998 to the peak in the first quarter of 2000, but it was hardly the only sector that was growing. As Figure 8.9 shows, S&P technology sector earnings were actually growing slower than were those of the S&P 500 by the second quarter of 2000. In other words, despite all the attention the sector received in 2000, technology companies were inferior growers by that time! The hype led everyone to believe the sector was the only one that was growing when in fact the sector's earnings were growing slower than were those of the overall market.

As you can see, the technology sector was neither a stable growth sector nor was it the only sector that was growing. The misperception was that the sector was the highest quality sector because of those two misjudgments. The ramification was that the sector's valuation was one that might be given to an extraordinarily high quality sector (perhaps the highest quality ever), but, unfortunately, it was not.

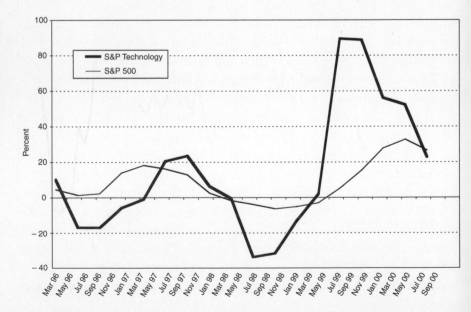

Figure 8.9   Comparison of S&P Technology and S&P 500 Earnings Growth

THE SERIOUSNESS OF THE MISJUDGMENT OF THE TECHNOLOGY SECTOR'S QUALITY

I have used three measures to attempt to measure how serious was the misjudgment of the technology sector's quality. The first, shown in Figure 8.10, measures the relative price/earnings (P/E) ratio of A+ companies (again using S&P Common Stock Rankings) versus B– companies. The data in this chart are calculated by simply dividing the average P/E ratio among all A+ companies by the average P/E ratio of all B– companies. From roughly March 1999 to March 2000, the height of the technology bubble, the A+ stocks were significantly devalued. By March 2000 to June 2000, the A+ stocks sold at about a 75% discounted valuation to the B– companies. Some of the highest quality companies in the world were actually selling at 75% discount to highly cyclical companies!

This amazing devaluation of high quality companies occurred because investors misperceived the quality of the technology sector. Figure 8.11 shows the proportion of technology companies within each S&P Common Stock Ranking when measured on both a market-capitalization basis and

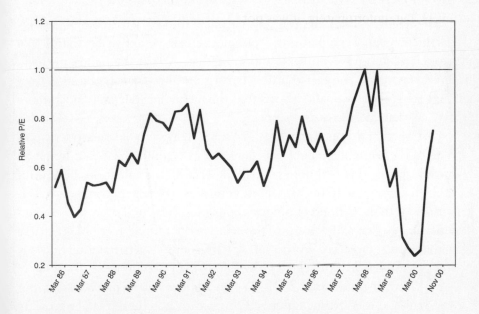

Figure 8.10   **Relative P/E of Merrill Lynch Quantitative Analysis A+ Index versus B– Index**
Based on data from Merrill Lynch Quantitative Strategy.

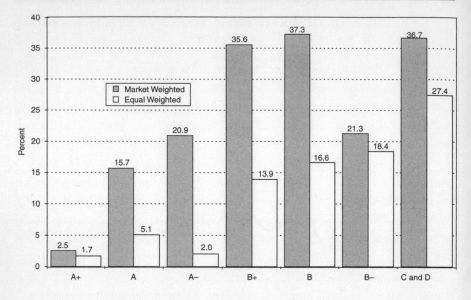

Figure 8.11 **Technology Weighting within Quality Indexes as of 11/30/00**
Based on data from Merrill Lynch Quantitative Strategy.

equal-weighted basis (simply a comparison of the size of the companies versus the number of companies). Technology stocks comprise less than 2% of the names in the A+ universe and more than 30% of the names in the C and D universe. The fact that the bars rise in the chart as you read from high quality to low quality shows that the technology sector is much more cyclical than most investors suspected.

The second valuation technique that attempts to measure the magnitude of the technology bubble is depicted in Figure 8.12. Some investors have suggested that technology stocks deserve higher valuations because of their superior growth, but this chart compares technology companies' valuations to those of nontechnology companies with similar growth characteristics. It specifically measures the relative P/E ratio of technology stocks with five-year projected growth rates of 20% or more versus nontechnology stocks with five-year projected growth rates of 20% or more.

In the first quarter of 2000, you would have had to pay between four and four-and-a-half times higher P/E ratio to purchase a super-growing technology stock rather than purchase a super-growing nontechnology stock. There is no explanation for this valuation difference except for the word *technology*. Investors were so enamored with the technology sector

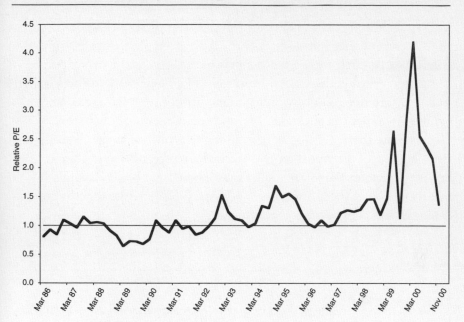

Figure 8.12   **Relative P/E of Technology Stocks versus Nontechnology Peer Group (Based on Five-Year Projected Growth Rates of 20% or Higher and Trailing P/E Ratios)**
Based on data from Merrill Lynch Quantitative Strategy.

that they actually ignored other super-growing stocks in other sectors. We have to seriously wonder whether it was worth four times the multiple to brag to friends at parties about the new technology stock we bought.

WHO CARES ABOUT THE TECHNOLOGY BUBBLE? BAD COMPANIES MAKE GOOD STOCKS, RIGHT?

Although it is true that bad companies make good stocks over the long term, investors should be careful not to dismiss quickly the magnitude or the financial market ramifications of such a serious misjudgment of quality. Subsequent to both the original "Nifty 50" in the early 1970s and the technology bubble that burst in 1983, the financial markets had extended periods of conservatism during which higher quality stocks dominated the market.

In addition, the misjudgment and the extraordinarily high multiples that resulted from the technology bubble allowed many companies to issue stock as an initial public offering or to issue additional stock to fund expansion. A current question is whether the "free money" that was given to the companies through these offerings has led to significant overcapacity in the sector. Already there have been signs of overcapacity in the Internet industry, Internet consulting, telecommunications services, telecommunications equipment, semiconductors, and component manufacturers.

Despite these warning signals, investors continue to spend an inordinate amount of attention on the technology sector because they cannot believe the sector is a lower quality one. There is no better example in the present-day markets of how noise and hype have led investors toward bad decisions and poor portfolio performance.

Chapter 9

What Makes a Good Analyst?

Has anyone wondered why financial reporters on television seem to know as much about companies as do the Wall Street analysts who follow the companies or the portfolio managers who hold them in their mutual funds? It seems to me that the analysts and portfolio managers should know a lot more about a company than do television reporters, but that does not always appear to be the case.

This chapter focuses on why the line between reporter and analyst has become so thin, and how you can recognize good analysts during the new age of media and hype. There certainly is no shortage of analysts, portfolio managers, and other "talking heads." The question is how to recognize who is really providing added value to the investor, and who is simply providing noise.[1]

THE THIN LINE BETWEEN REPORTING AND ANALYZING

Sadly, there is a very thin line between reporting and analyzing on Wall Street today. The difference should be very obvious. Reporting is conveying *what* has happened. Analyzing is attempting to decipher *why* it happened. To go one step further, forecasting is using the analysis to *predict what might* happen in the future.

183

Unfortunately, Wall Street has too few analysts and forecasters and too many reporters despite what title might appear on their business cards. Wall Street analysts increasingly are becoming mere reporters. They are excellent at retelling what the company said in a conference call or at a meeting, but they seem less able to delve through the myriad of statistics on a company's Form 10-Q or Form 10-K for data that might give clues about a company's future. Few have proprietary sources of information to double-check companies' claims, but rather rely on "guidance" from companies and accept the claims as fact.

Analysts who do not analyze and forecast contribute to the noise of the financial markets. I would even go so far as to say that analysts who report rather than analyze and forecast could be detrimental to investors' searches for true investment information. Investors need time and energy to sift through the noise, and louder levels of noise can lead to confusion, which increases the risk that investors will make bad decisions.

SEVEN CHARACTERISTICS OF A GOOD ANALYST

If my criticisms are correct, then how can you tell whether an analyst is a *good* analyst? I think the following characteristics are critical to good analysis and forecasting. This list should not be considered exhaustive, but my guess is that analysts who do not follow at least these traits will tend to sound more like reporters than like analysts.

Here are seven characteristics that I feel every truly good analyst will exhibit:

1. A good analyst does not tell stories or recite facts.
2. A good analyst realizes valuable investment information is not stating facts; it is stating intelligently derived opinions not shared by others.
3. A good analyst knows the difference between a fundamental opinion and an investment opinion.
4. A good analyst does proprietary research rather than accepting guidance from the company.
5. A good analyst avoids new, untested metrics and uses theoretically sound and tested fundamental ratios to analyze a company.
6. A good analyst does not put buy ratings on every stock under coverage.
7. A good analyst can take abuse and comes back for more.

A Good Analyst Does Not Tell Stories or Recite Facts

Every night before I go to bed I listen to one radio station's Far East financial report. The reporter comments on a sector in the region that is performing poorly or well that day. He invariably says some set of stocks were down because "investors felt the stocks' prices were too far ahead of fundamentals," or he comments on a sector that is performing well as one in which "investors felt the stocks were bargains relative to their fundamentals." I know it sounds crazy that the reporter is so inanely repetitive, but I now listen for the phrases every night, and the reporter has yet to fail me.

Wall Street analysts seem to have fallen into a similar rut. Good analysts do not tell stories about a company or recite facts to which everyone has access. Too many Wall Street reports merely recite facts about companies' new products or expansion plans without any significant analysis suggesting whether or why these products or plans will be successful. Strategists and economists frequently state the obvious about the market's condition without any insight as to whether the condition will continue. The terms *profit taking* and *bargain hunting* are very overused. Has there ever been a situation in which stocks that had appreciated were sold for reasons other than for taking profits?

I applaud analysts who openly state that a company's plans will not be successful. Better yet, how about an analyst saying that a company does not appreciate its own opportunities, and the stock will rise to levels even the company is not anticipating? Analysts who make comments such as these might be much more helpful to investors than the analysts who say "Company ZYX will be a leader in the next generation of the build-out of the Internet." Thanks for nothing.

Let's dissect the example about company ZYX and attempt to uncover some issues that might be of interest to investors interested in the company. Again, this is not intended to be an exhaustive list, just one to uncover how shallow the original statement actually is.

- ". . . will be a leader . . ."

    How many competitors are there in the business?
    How did the company gain the status as a leader?
    What is the company's market share?
    What are other companies doing to compete?
    How safe is the leadership position?

Is this a fragmenting or consolidating industry?
What advantages does the company have as a leader?

- "... the next generation ..."

  Was ZYX successful during the previous generation?
  Why is there a *next* generation?
  Are ZYX's earlier products obsolete?
  Will there be yet another *next* generation?
  Will ZYX's products be obsolete during that subsequent
    generation?
  How much is ZYX spending on R&D versus its competitors?
  When will the return on R and D occur?
  How much will the return be?

- "... of the build-out of the Internet."

  Is there a build-in? (Just kidding!)
  Is the build-out secular or cyclical?
  How is the build-out being funded?
  What is the anticipated capacity utilization of the build-out?

As you can see, a simple sentence that gives little or no information is given as a reason for purchase of ZYX stock. However, real analysis and forecasting would have at least answered the questions I have listed. Consider the answers to the following questions, and see if you would invest in ZYX:

Q: How many competitors are there in the business?
A: Twenty or thirty.

Q: How did the company gain the status as a leader?
A: Other companies' products became obsolete.

Q: What is the company's market share?
A: 5%.

Q: What are other companies doing to compete?
A: Spending a lot on R&D.

Q: How safe is the leadership position?
A: Safe for now.

Q: Is this a fragmenting or consolidating industry?
A: Fragmenting. Five new IPOs are due in the next week.

Q: What advantages does the company have as a leader?
A: Better sales and support for its products.

Q: Was ZYX successful during the previous generation?
A: Company did not exist.

Q: Why is there a *next* generation?
A: Previous products did not completely meet customer needs.

Q: Are ZYX's earlier products obsolete?
A: There were no earlier products.

Q: Will there be yet another *next* generation?
A: Yes.

Q: Will ZYX's products be obsolete during that subsequent generation?
A: Current products will probably be.

Q: How much is ZYX spending on R&D versus its competitors?
A: About 20% less of sales.

Q: When will the return on R&D occur?
A: Unknown.

Q: How much will the return be?
A: Unknown.

Q: Is the build-out secular or cyclical?
A: Showing signs of being cyclical.

Q: How is the build-out being funded?
A: Many companies are issuing stock.

Q: What is the anticipated capacity utilization of the build-out?
A: Huh?

The answers to these questions do not exactly instill confidence, do they? Alternatively, the answers to the questions could be as follows:

Q: How many competitors are there in the business?
A: None.

Q: How did the company gain the status as a leader?
A: Superiority of products put competition out of business.

Q: What is the company's market share?
A: 95%.

Q: What are other companies doing to compete?
A: Offering price discounts. Can't compete on product.

Q: How safe is the leadership position?
A: Essentially no competition.

Q: Is this a fragmenting or consolidating industry?
A: Consolidating. Smaller players going out of business.

Q: What advantages does the company have as a leader?
A: Better products, better sales, and better customer support.

Q: Was ZYX successful during the previous generation?
A: Company dominated previous market as well.

Q: Why is there a *next* generation?
A: Previous products did not completely meet customer needs.

Q: Are ZYX's earlier products obsolete?
A: Designed to be easily upgraded.

Q: Will there be yet another *next* generation?
A: Yes.

Q: Will ZYX's products be obsolete during that subsequent generation?
A: Current products are designed for upgrades as well.

Q: How much is ZYX spending on R&D versus its competitors?
A: About 20% more of sales.

Q: When will the return on R&D occur?
A: Estimated return on all projects is within two years.

Q: How much will the return be?
A: All projects expected to return at least 25–30%.

Q: Is the build-out secular or cyclical?
A: Showing signs of being cyclical.

Q: How is the build-out being funded?
A: Many companies are issuing stock.

Q: What is the anticipated capacity utilization of the build-out?
A: Huh?

Although the second version of the answers to the questions is certainly not perfect, the second version makes ZYX sound like a leader that is prepared for competition. The first makes ZYX sound like a company that fell into its leadership position and does not know how to prepare itself for the future. In which version of ZYX would you rather invest?

Most important, the original sentence, "Company ZYX will be a leader in the next generation of the build-out of the Internet," told us nothing about which version of the answers (or perhaps neither) we might expect to receive. The sentence sounded powerful, but was actually relatively meaningless to an investor. It was merely reporting something most people already knew.

A Good Analyst Realizes Valuable Investment Information Is Stating Intelligently Derived Opinions Shared by Others

Most analysts' opinions regarding the fundamentals of a company can best be summarized in the earnings estimates. We frequently hear or read analyst's estimates, but their value is not much more than the value of the sentence dissected in the previous section. I would argue that the earnings estimate is simply noise and actually provides very little investment information. "Company ZYX will be a leader in the next generation of the build-out of the Internet, and my earnings estimate for next year is $1.00." Again, thanks for nothing.

Instead of stating that the earnings estimate is $1.00, it might be more useful to investors if the analyst said the following: "The consensus estimate for ZYX is $1.00. However, my estimate is $1.10. Here are five factors that the Street is missing that explain why my estimate is $0.10 higher than the Street's."

The earnings estimate is not valuable investment information. However, the reasons for the difference between an analyst's earnings estimate and the consensus is very important. Reciting an earnings estimate is merely reciting a fact, and facts should theoretically be reflected in a stock's price. If an analyst raises or lowers an earnings estimate, that can be helpful information, but is not necessarily so because we do not know how other analysts are changing their earnings estimates. However, it is very valuable information if an analyst compares and contrasts his or her views with consensus.

Paying particular attention to the analysts' deviations from consensus can be a critical part of investment performance. Figure 9.1 shows the

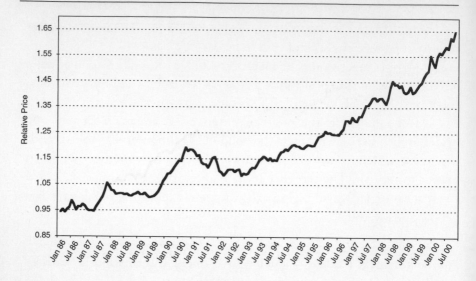

Figure 9.1 **Performance of Stocks When Analysts' Estimates Are Significantly Higher Than Consensus**

relative performance of a portfolio of stocks based on analysts' estimates that are higher than those made by their peers. A universe of analysts was chosen and the analysts' earnings estimates for the stocks they follow were measured versus the consensus estimate every month. Every month, stocks were ranked from 1 to 10. One signified a company for which the analysts' earnings estimates were substantially higher than consensus, whereas 10 signified a company for which the analysts' estimates were substantially lower than consensus. Figure 9.1 shows the cumulative relative performance of the portfolio comprised of stocks with ranks of 1 or 2 (i.e., estimates were significantly higher than consensus).

This portfolio performs exceptionally well. Since 1986, the portfolio has outperformed the S&P 500 by about 6% per year, and the Equal-Weighted S&P 500 by about 4.1% per year. Perhaps of more importance, given the discussion in Chapter 2, this portfolio does indeed outperform the market with less risk. Even more important, the original version of this study was in 1989. Thus, the strategy has continued to outperform the market while incurring less risk than the market for 11 years since the original study. That is a very robust out-of-sample test.

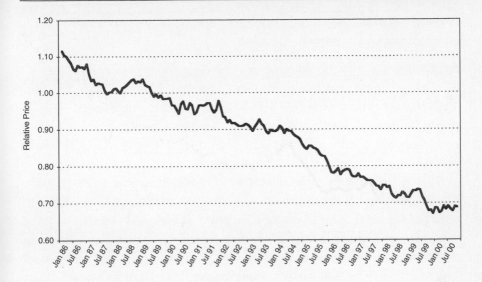

Figure 9.2   **Performance of Stocks When Analysts' Estimates Are Significantly Lower Than Consensus**

Figure 9.2 shows the opposite end of the study—the performance of portfolios comprised of stocks for which our analysts' estimates were significantly below consensus (i.e., ranked 9 and 10). These portfolios consistently underperform the S&P 500 by about 6.5% per year, and underperform the Equal-Weighted S&P 500 by about 4.0% per year. There appears to be valuable investment information when analysts' estimates are significantly different from consensus regardless of whether those estimates are significantly higher or significantly lower than consensus.

In essence, good analysts realize valuable investment information is not stating facts, it is stating intelligently derived opinions not shared by others. They realize that valuable investment information is what an analyst knows that he or she believes others do not know. Everything else is simply noise.

So, now our story about ZYX is:

Company ZYX will be a leader in the next generation of the build-out of the Internet. My earnings estimate for next year is $1.10, but the consensus is $1.00. There are five things that I think the Street is missing that support my higher earnings estimate.

A Good Analyst Knows the Difference between a Fundamental Opinion and an Investment Opinion

An analyst typically should have two opinions about a company: the fundamental opinion and the investment opinion. The fundamental opinion is whether the company is a good company. The investment opinion is whether the stock will make a good stock (see Chapter 8 for the differences between good companies and good stocks, if you have not already read it).

The fundamental opinion focuses on the quality of the company. The 18 questions that were reviewed earlier in this chapter focus on forming a fundamental opinion of the company. Go back and read through the questions, and you will note that there are no questions about how the stock will perform. Most interviews with analysts, and most Wall Street research reports for that matter, focus on the fundamental opinion of the company.

The investment opinion is a view of how the company's stock will perform in the future. Certainly, the fundamental opinion should influence the investment opinion, but the investment opinion is much more important. An incorrect assumption shared by many analysts is that good companies make good stocks. However, as we pointed out in Chapter 8 that is typically not the case. Actually bad companies perform the best over the long term. Good companies outperform when safety is needed, as it is during periods in which the profits cycle decelerates. All too often we hear analysts say something such as "This is a great company, and I would buy it here," when what we actually want to hear is something such as "This is going to be a great stock, and I would buy it here."

Our paragraph now reads as follows:

Company ZYX will be a leader in the next generation of the build-out of the Internet. My earnings estimate for next year is $1.10, but the consensus is $1.00. There are five things that I think the Street is missing that support my higher earnings estimate. The company may not be as good a company as some others in the sector, but I feel its stock will significantly outperform the others because of those factors the Street is overlooking.

A Good Analyst Does Proprietary Research Rather Than Accepting Guidance from the Company

"We are waiting to change our investment opinion and estimates until after the company gives some guidance on their 11 A.M. conference call." Translation: "I do no primary research. I merely repeat what the company says. They will tell me what to say at 11 A.M." Need I say more?

Primary research is that which is done directly by the researcher. The researcher has a theory, gathers the necessary data, and tests the theory to see if it is viable. Some of the theories presented in this book are based on my own primary research.

Secondary research is that which is gained from others' primary research. If I am studying relativity theory, the history of the White House, or what makes a pitcher's curve ball curve, the odds are I will not do my own primary research and will rely on a compilation of other people's research. If you are studying how noise effects the financial markets, you might use the primary research in this book as secondary research.

Good analysts rely on primary research more than on secondary research. To a certain extent, Wall Street analysts must rely on some secondary research because they must get some information from other sources. For example, financial information from companies and industry and segment information from industry associations are necessary sources of secondary information. However, many analysts double-check company and industry forecasts with their own proprietary information. Proprietary surveys of customers, sales representatives, or manufacturers, self-testing of goods and services, and proprietary industry supply/demand models are just some examples of how good analysts undertake their own primary research.

One mutual fund company clearly understands the difference between primary and secondary research and attempts to convey the difference in its advertising. The mutual fund company's advertising highlights that its analysts are out in the field separating myth from reality regardless of whether the company in question is an Internet company, a restaurant chain, or a telecommunications company. This ad campaign may be a takeoff on a similar mutual fund advertisement from about 10 or 15 years ago in which an analyst was tasting the cheesecake of a bakery company.

I find it amazing that analysts admit to waiting for *guidance* from companies. The analysts effectively tell their audience that their analytical work is superfluous, and that everyone should simply listen to the conference call. Of course, everyone does not have time to listen to every conference call that goes on in a day, so analysts have reduced their roles to reporters and representatives who merely report what took place in the conference call.

Let's look at how our paragraph now stands. I think you will agree we are now getting some pretty serious investment information.

> Company ZYX will be a leader in the next generation of the build-out of the Internet. My earnings estimate for next year is $1.10, but the consensus is $1.00. There are five things that I think the Street is missing that support my higher earnings estimate. The company may not be as good a company as some others in the sector, but I feel its stock will significantly outperform the others because of those factors the Street is overlooking. My proprietary customer survey shows that users are beginning to strongly favor ZYX's product over those of the competition. I'm not sure the company even realizes how strong the demand for their product will be.

A Good Analyst Avoids New, Untested Metrics and Uses Theoretically Sound and Tested Fundamental Ratios to Analyze a Company

I am certainly not a linguist, but I think Wall Street's newfound use of the word *metric* is rather interesting. Analysts seem to use it as a synonym for the word *measure*, but the connotation is that a metric is more rigorous than a measure. A measure sounds like something you bake with, but a metric sounds like important investment information. As a quantitative strategist, I am now often asked to define the *metric* that I used in a study.[2] On the other hand, the term *fundamental ratio* seems not to have been used in years.

Although some might consider this ranting, I think there is a connection between the use of the word *metric* and the decay in the quality of Wall Street research. New metrics pop up frequently, but few are tested. Analysts assume new metrics have importance but lack the data and research to support their claims. I think a good analyst realizes the difference between metrics and sound fundamental ratios.

I will not even give credibility to some of the Internet-related metrics, such as *eyeballs*, by discussing them. However, there are many metrics about which I think investors should be wary. Some of the most controversial work I have done has been to refute these widely accepted metrics. We'll start with the most controversial.

For readers who might not be familiar with the income statement of a company, it is the accounting statement that shows the results of a period's (i.e., a quarter's or a year's) operations. The top line of the income statement is the period's sales. Various expenses are then subtracted from sales to eventually arrive at net income and earnings. Reported earnings are those at the very bottom of the income statement, that is, earnings after all subtractions. Operating earnings are generally those that include all subtractions except various one-time, nonrecurring charges. Cash flow is typically earnings plus depreciation. EBIT stands for earnings before interest and taxes. EBITDA stands for earnings before interest, taxes, depreciation, and amortization. As one moves from reported earnings to operating earnings to EBITDA to EBIT to sales, one is figuratively moving up the income statement.

In addition, there tends to be a tug-of-war between the company and the investor, with the company's valuation and income statement as the rope. Companies prefer that investors value them as far up the income statement as possible because it virtually assures them of getting a higher valuation (and a cheaper cost of capital) than it would if they were valued on earnings. In simple terms, sales are larger than earnings, so a valuation of 20 times sales will give a company a higher market capitalization than will a valuation of 20 times earnings.

Operating Earnings

I may be the only person left on Wall Street who believes reported earnings, and not operating earnings, give investors the most investment information. As mentioned, the main difference between the two is that reported earnings include all expenses even if they are nonrecurring. The main difference between my view and my colleagues' is that I believe there is important information in those one-time charges. The important information is that the reported earnings of a company that takes one-time charges will not be as stable as the company that does not take charges.

Most investors discuss the cyclicality of a company's earnings. I prefer to discuss the variability of a company's earnings. The variability in earnings can be attributed to the economic cycle or to one-time charges. As pointed out in Chapter 8, quality is largely dependent on a company's stability of earnings. Thus, anything that disrupts that stability (whether it be the overall economy, weather, bad management, etc.) is important because it lowers the predictability of earnings and the quality of the company. Companies clearly prefer analysts not to include one-time charges because an earnings stream that does not include the charges will obviously appear more stable through time than one that does include the charges. The more stable the earnings stream appears, the higher the quality of the company will appear as well, which may be the reason that the S&P Common Stock Rankings use reported earnings.

A study completed several years ago uncovered that strategies that employed operating earnings tended to underperform identical strategies that used reported earnings.[3] The study found that the conclusion held for both growth and value strategies. Figure 9.3 shows the performance of low P/E strategies and earnings momentum strategies when the definition of earnings was reported earnings versus that when the definition of earnings was operating earnings. From 1981 to 1998, low P/E strategies based on reported earnings outperformed the same strategy based on operating earn-

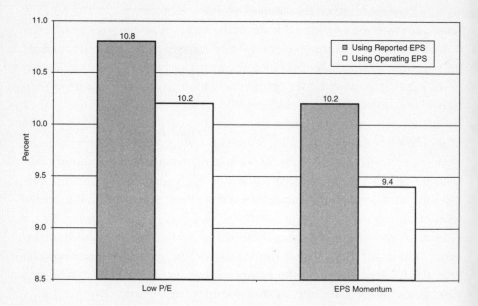

Figure 9.3   **Reported versus Operating Earnings per Share in Growth and Value Strategies (Compound Annual Price Return, 1981–1998)**
Based on data from Merrill Lynch Quantitative Strategy.

ings by about 0.6% per year. Earnings momentum strategies based on reported earnings outperformed the same strategy based on operating earnings by 0.8% per year.[4]

The researchers of that study not only found that using reported earnings rather than operating earnings increased the returns of a strategy as shown, but did so without incurring more risk. Using the directional analogy we have been using within the risk/return charts previously shown, strategies that used reported earnings typically were north of those that used operating earnings.

Economic Value Added (EVA)®

The return on an investment should always be compared to the cost of the capital invested. Everyone would invest in one-year T-bills if T-bill rates were 6% and borrowing costs for one year were 5%. Under such conditions, you could receive a guaranteed 1% return for a year without even touching your own money. For that reason, such an opportunity does not exist. The markets are not that stupid.

Without realizing it, some people have been borrowing funds at 15% to 20% in order to invest in the stock market. As mentioned in Chapter 4, they are not actively making this decision. Rather, they are investing in the stock market but refusing to consume less in order to save. They therefore end up running up credit card bills to maintain their standards of living. The long-term average return on equities in the United States is about 8% to 9%. Borrowing at 15% to receive 9% obviously has little probability of being successful over the long term.

These are simple examples, but companies regularly must make decisions based on the differences between their return on investments and their cost of capital. If a company consistently earns a return on invested capital that is lower than its cost of capital, the firm will eventually cease to exist.

Economic Value Added, or EVA®,[5] is a proprietary measure of the consulting firm Stern Stewart that examines the spread between companies' returns on capital and their costs of capital. The measure has helped corporate managers allocate capital and make better corporate decisions (i.e., anything from building or closing a plant to taking over another company). As a result, Stern Stewart's clients are many of the leading corporations.

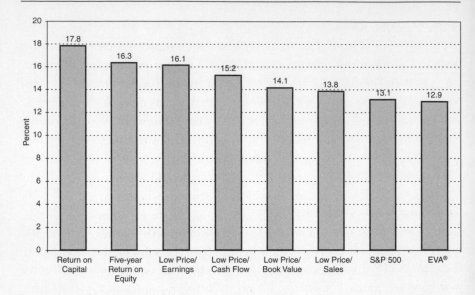

Figure 9.4   Twelve-Month Price Returns (February 1987 to October 1997)
From Richard Bernstein and Carmen Pigler, "An Analysis of EVA®," *Merrill Lynch Quantitative Viewpoint*, 19 December 1997.

Some Wall Street analysts have recently attempted to apply EVA® to individual stock selection. Companies that generate exceptional levels of EVA® are generally good companies, and these analysts believe that good companies will make good stocks. Of course, we have already discovered that bad companies make good stocks over the long term.

Figure 9.4, taken from a 1997 study,[6] further confirms that good companies do not make the best stocks over the long term. The chart shows the performance of strategies from 1987 to 1997 based on various stock selection techniques. Notice that a strategy based on EVA® slightly underperforms the market (12.9% average 12-month return versus 13.1% for the S&P 500), whereas strategies based on simple fundamental ratios, such as low price/earnings (16.1%), low price/cash flow (15.2%), and low price/book value (14.1%) outperform. EVA® may be an excellent tool for corporate management, and it has received substantial publicity as such, but it is not a very effective method for picking stocks when compared to more traditional fundamental ratios.

Price/Sales Ratio

Recently, Wall Street has valued technology companies using price/sales ratios. I've mentioned before that there is a figurative tug-of-war between investors and companies. Investors typically want to value companies based on the lower end of the income statement, whereas companies want to be valued based on the upper portion of the income statement. When investors value companies on price/sales, there is no tug-of-war. Investors have simply handed the rope to the company.

It is inconceivable to me why investors would want to value companies based on sales. As an equity owner in the company, it is in the investors' best interest for the company to generate earnings. Higher sales growth can obviously lead to higher earnings growth, but recent investors have forgotten the latter part on earnings growth. Sales growth is relatively meaningless if investors are willing to value the company on sales. For example, I can easily form a company that has tremendous sales growth. I will sell Rolls Royce cars for $1,000. My company will lose money, but I will gain tremendous market share if Wall Street is willing to continue to fund my company. I could add a little creative accounting, as some Internet companies did, and book the difference between the list price of the Rolls Royce and $1,000 as marketing expenses. Then my *gross margin* would be quite high. However, my company will go out of business the day the Street decides it does not like my business plan and stops funding me. It is not sales that are important, it is earnings growth and positive cash generation that make a company viable.

A 1994 study found that strategies based on valuing companies on earnings or simple cash flow (earnings plus depreciation) outperformed those based on sales.[7] In other words, strategies based on low price/earnings ratios and low price/cash flow ratios outperformed those based on price/sales through time. The study further found that this was true not only in the United States, but also in several major equity markets around the world. Figure 9.5 shows the results for the United States.

I do not mean to imply that every new valuation measure, sorry, *metric*, is a waste of time. The point is that analysts should test the efficacy of any valuation metric before employing it. In fact, some of my colleagues at Merrill Lynch have come up with their own proprietary measures of success in the industries they cover. In most cases, the analysts have indeed tested

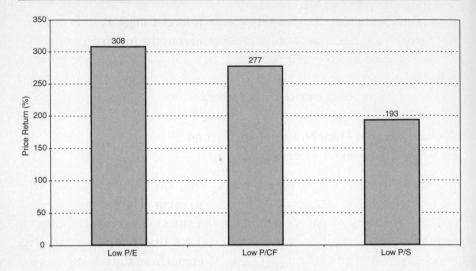

Figure 9.5   **Comparison of Low P/E, Low P/CF, and Low P/S Strategies in the United States (February 1986 to June 1996)**
From Richard Bernstein and Markus Barth, "Analyzing Global Valuation Techniques," *Merrill Lynch Global Quantitative Viewpoint*, 14 August 1996.

their measures' efficacy, and, as a result, provide investors with immense added value.

Let's now update our paragraph again:

Company ZYX will be a leader in the next generation of the build-out of the Internet. My earnings estimate for next year is $1.10, but the consensus is $1.00. There are five things that I think the Street is missing that support my higher earnings estimate. The company may not be as good a company as some others in the sector, but I feel its stock will significantly outperform the others because of those factors the Street is overlooking. My proprietary customer survey shows that users are beginning to strongly favor ZYX's product over those of the competition. I'm not sure the company even realizes how strong the demand for their product will be. The Street is valuing the company on its price/sales ratio, and it does not appear attractive based on that measure. However, our historical analysis suggests that earnings growth is a better predictor of this industry's future performance.

Thus, our proprietary earnings growth model suggests that the stock should be one of the best performers in the industry during the next 12 to 18 months.

Now we're really getting somewhere!!

A Good Analyst Does Not Put Buy Ratings on Every Stock under Coverage

It is well known that there are more *buy* ratings on Wall Street than there are *sell* ratings. Many factors cause this bias to occur. The pat answer is that analysts are scared to put sell ratings on the stocks of investment banking clients of their firms. To a certain extent that is true, but perhaps the bigger pressure not to put sell ratings on stocks comes from the buy side of Wall Street. Portfolio managers and individual investors do not take it well when a major holding is reduced to a *hold* or a *sell* and the stock price plummets. Given that the many polls that rate analysts on the value they add have become so powerful on Wall Street that analysts are probably more fearful of alienating their firm's clients than they are of the alienating investment bankers within their firms.

Relative strength of stocks has an influence over analysts' buy/hold/sell ratings as well. Analysts tend to have buy ratings on stocks that go up, and lower ratings on stocks that go down. Thus, one factor that has contributed to the dearth of hold and sell ratings has simply been the bull market.

The influence of the bull market and the magnitude of the issue has become quite significant. Figure 9.6 shows the percent of a brokerage house's stocks under coverage that received the brokerage house's highest rating through time. In 2000, approximately 20% of the stocks in the brokerage house's universe received the highest rating. Note that less than 5% of the universe received the highest rating in 1991 and 1992 when investors were generally more bearish than there were in 2000.

So, let's update our paragraph again:

Company ZYX will be a leader in the next generation of the build-out of the Internet. My earnings estimate for next year is $1.10, but the consensus is $1.00. There are five things that I think the Street is missing that support my higher earnings estimate. The company may not be as good a company as some

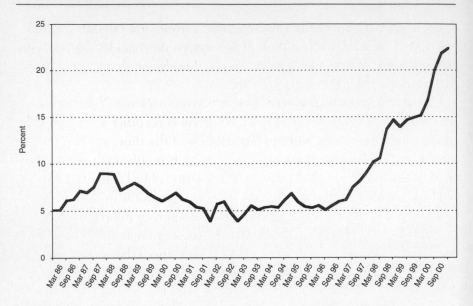

Figure 9.6   **Percentage of Research Universe with Highest Rating**

others in the sector, but I feel its stock will significantly outperform the others because of those factors the Street is overlooking. My proprietary customer survey shows that users are beginning to strongly favor ZYX's product over those of the competition. I'm not sure the company even realizes how strong the demand for their product will be. The Street is valuing the company on its price/sales ratio, and it does not appear attractive based on that measure. However, our historical analysis suggests that earnings growth is a better predictor of this industry's future performance. Thus, our proprietary earnings growth model suggests that the stock should be one of the best performers in the industry during the next 12 to 18 months. This is the only stock that I follow that I have rated as a buy.

Getting pretty gutsy, wouldn't you say?

A Good Analyst Can Take Abuse, and Comes Back for More

Good analysts don't mind taking a punch. If the goal is to express intelligently derived opinions not shared by others rather than reciting facts, then some people will always disagree. Nothing can upset a buy-side portfolio manager more than when a Wall Street analyst downgrades the portfolio manager's largest holding. I can assure you that *that* analyst will not be on that portfolio manager's Christmas list.

Part of being a good analyst is sticking your neck out. Your head may get chopped off every now and then, but there is no other way to provide added value. No analyst will be correct 100% of the time, and it is unreasonable for anyone to expect so. Too often high-profile analysts are criticized in the media for a bad call or a recent string of bad calls. The articles rarely point out how the analyst came to be so high profile in the first place. I strongly doubt that it was by giving clients consensus information.

The key to providing added value is whether an analyst was correct more often than the investor would have been without the analyst's aid. Of course, this is nearly impossible to measure, but I think the thought process is important. It is not whether the analyst buys low and sells high every time. It is whether the analyst correctly suggested buying low and selling high more often than the investor did.

Let's update our paragraph one final time:

Company ZYX will be a leader in the next generation of the build-out of the Internet. My earnings estimate for next year is $1.10, but the consensus is $1.00. There are five things that I think the Street is missing that support my higher earnings estimate. The company may not be as good a company as some others in the sector, but I feel its stock will significantly outperform the others because of those factors the Street is overlooking. My proprietary customer survey shows that users are beginning to strongly favor ZYX's product over those of the competition. I'm not sure the company even realizes how strong the demand for their product will be. The Street is valuing the company on its price/sales ratio, and it does not appear attractive based on that measure. However, our historical analysis suggests that earnings growth is a better predictor of this industry's future performance. Thus, our proprietary earnings growth model suggests that the stock should be one of the best performers in the industry during the next 12 to 18 months. This is the only stock that I follow that I have rated as a buy. I might be the only analyst on the Street who has this opinion.

Bravo!! (Brava?) What a difference from the original statement that was basically meaningless.

An analyst who used to work at my firm seemed never to have an earnings estimate that agreed with consensus. He also never seemed to agree with company management. Some portfolio managers complained that the analyst simply loved to destroy stocks. Others used to praise him as being incredibly insightful. Whenever he still comes up in discussion, I point out two things: (1) everyone remembers his name; and (2) he still comes up in discussion despite no longer being a Wall Street analyst. Some hated him, some loved him, but he made everyone think, and everyone wanted to know what he was saying. As a result, no one has forgotten him. To me, he epitomized a *good* analyst.

Chapter 10

Growth and
Value and Noise

Style investing has become very popular during the last 20 or so years. Although many general equity funds remain, the number of specialized growth and value funds has mushroomed. According to Merrill Lynch Mutual Funds Research, there are presently about 1,700 dedicated growth funds and about 1,500 dedicated value funds out of a total universe of about 4,600 equity mutual funds (excluding sector and index funds). Thus, when excluding sector and index funds, roughly about 70% of all mutual funds in the United States are classified as either growth or value funds.

Whether you should invest in a growth fund or a value fund or whether you should attempt to pick stocks using growth or value strategies depends on many factors. We have already discussed how time horizon and risk preference can alter an investor's style allocation. This chapter focuses more on the basic concepts and style performance under varying economic conditions.

As you might expect by Chapter 10 of this book, noise can indeed greatly influence investors' decisions regarding growth and value investing. There are dramatic examples of noise incorrectly influencing investors with respect to choosing a style in which to invest. Neither style is immune to the effects of investment noise.

WHAT ARE STYLES?

Simply put, styles are segments of the equity market. They are stocks with like characteristics that tend to perform similarly. For example, stocks with low price/earnings (P/E) ratios or stocks with high projected growth rates tend to perform as a group through time. There are many such segments within the equity market. Small capitalization stocks, large capitalization stocks, value stocks, growth stocks, and traditional industry and sector groupings are all examples of market segments.

Some academics used to argue that equity markets could not be segmented because it would suggest inefficiencies, or opportunities within the equity market of which investors could take advantage. They believed if those opportunities existed, investors would quickly find them, bid up the prices of the stocks involved, and remove the potential effect. If these segments existed for long periods of time, then it would suggest that the stock market's investment opportunities are long-lasting. The market's discounting mechanism, therefore, would be slow and inefficient.

WHY IS THE MARKET SEGMENTED?

I think there are three main reasons why stock markets are segmented. First, there are structural reasons. Many professional investors are prohibited or restricted from investing in some parts of the equity market because of their investment charters with their clients. For example, some investment managers are prohibited from investing in lower quality stocks such as those ranked B or worse according to S&P Common Stock Rankings. Some are prohibited from investing in stocks below a certain market capitalization, whereas others are prohibited from investing in stocks above a delineated market capitalization. Some are prohibited from investing in certain sectors because of moral or ethical issues. The increased use of style delineation has further compounded this segmentation issue and made the stock market potentially even less efficient.

Second, an information asymmetry exists within the equity market. Those who believe the stock market is truly an efficient discounting mechanism believe that all information is assimilated, interpreted, and acted on by all investors instantaneously and simultaneously. Clearly, that is not the case. Not all investors receive information at the same time,[1] not all investors interpret information identically, and not all investors act at the same time. If the stock market matches buyers and sellers, and the theory of the Earnings Expectations Life Cycle is accurate, then by definition investors must be interpreting information differently. Someone must still consider the stock that is truly at midnight to be attractive, otherwise no transaction would occur.

Third, regret aversion might drive investor behavior more than risk aversion. As mentioned in Chapter 8, regret aversion means not wanting to tell a client you are sorry. If an investment manager or a stockbroker buys a well-known, good company and the stock performs poorly, the investor will typically not fault the broker or manager. The management of the company or the overall market might be at fault, but the manager or broker did the correct thing in buying a good company. However, if an investment manager or a stockbroker buys a well-known bad company and the stock performs poorly, the investor will think the broker or the manager is stupid. The investor knew the company was a bad company, and the poor performance suggests to the investor that the broker or manager is a poor one. The performance might have been poor regardless of whether a good or a bad company was purchased. It is a question of who takes the blame for the poor performance, the broker/manager or the company/market. Thus, regret aversion and the fear of taking the blame for poor performance lead many investors to avoid low quality stocks and those stocks that are at six o'clock on the Earnings Expectations Life Cycle.

GROWTH INVESTING

As mentioned in Chapter 3 on the Earnings Expectations Life Cycle, growth investors tend to be those that search for stocks about which expectations are high. They tend to define stocks based on very visible statistics such as profits growth or return on equity. A relatively newer breed of growth investors, momentum investors, tends to use statistics that are even more visible such as revisions in earnings estimates, earnings surprises, and relative strength (stock price momentum).

Table 10.1 shows the performance of some of these strategies since 1987.

Table 10.2 shows risk measures for the selection of growth-oriented strategies. The first set of figures, based on the volatility or standard deviation of returns, shows that these strategies span the risk spectrum. Some growth strategies such as earnings surprise are relatively safe, whereas others such as relative strength are quite risky. The volatility of the returns associated

Table 10.1   Price Performance of Selected Growth Strategies (1987 to 2000)

Growth Strategy	Average 12-Month Price Return (%)
Five-year projected earnings growth	17.8
Earnings momentum	14.3
Earnings surprise	16.1
Estimate revision	17.0
Relative strength	24.3
Return on equity	16.7

Note: Estimate revision returns begin in 1990.

with a typical relative strength strategy is more than 50% higher than that of a typical earnings surprise strategy. The second set of statistics are based on the percent of the historical 12-month returns that were negative (i.e., the probability of a loss). Using the second definition of risk, strategies such as relative strength appear to be much safer. The returns of some of these strategies appear, therefore, to be positively skewed.

Figure 10.1 puts these two tables together and shows the risk/return scatter for these selected growth strategies using the standard deviation of returns as the measure of risk. Note that the earnings surprise strategy sits northwest (i.e., higher returns with less risk) or at least west (less risk regardless of return) relative to most of the strategies listed.

Figure 10.2 shows a risk/return chart for growth strategies based on the probability of a loss as the measure of risk. The relative risk/return characteristics of the strategies do not change meaningfully, but it is clear that the volatility of these strategies is generally skewed upward (i.e., generally more positive returns than negative).

Table 10.2   Risk Statistics for Growth Strategies (1987 to 2000)

Growth Strategy	Standard Deviation (%)	Probability of a Loss (%)
Five-year projected earnings growth	18.5	15.1
Earnings momentum	14.0	13.9
Earnings surprise	12.4	8.4
Estimate revision	14.9	11.1
Relative strength	21.1	10.8
Return on equity	16.7	15.4

Note: Estimate revision statistics are based on data that begin in 1990.

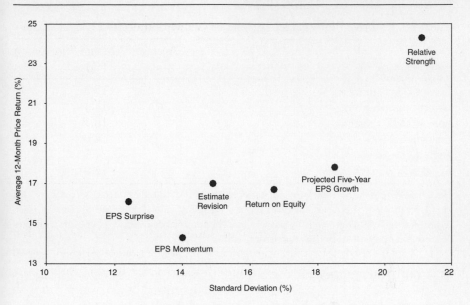

Figure 10.1   Growth Strategies' Risk/Return—Risk Defined as Volatility

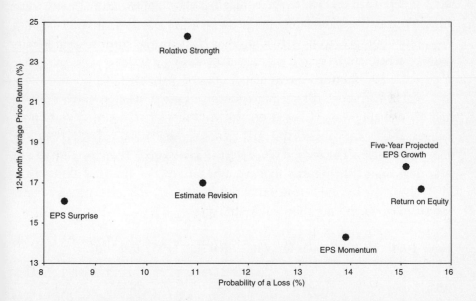

Figure 10.2   Growth Strategies' Risk/Return—Risk Defined as Probability of a Loss

Table 10.3   **Price Performance of Selected Value Strategies (1987 to 2000)**

Value Strategy	Average 12-Month Price Return (%)
Low price/earnings	15.3
Low price/cash flow	15.1
Low price/book value	12.7
Low price/sales	12.8
High dividend yield	7.7
Dividend discount model	12.0

Note: The figures in this table measure price returns of the strategies. Stocks' dividend yields play large parts of the stock selection process for many value strategies. Measuring price returns for value strategies may negatively bias the returns versus those of growth strategies because most growth stocks have little or no dividend yield.

VALUE INVESTING

Value investors tend to be those who search for low expectations stocks. They define stocks based on fundamentals that suggest the valuation of the stock is depressed relative to the company's earnings and growth potential. They frequently use fundamental ratios (such as price/earnings, price/cash flow, price/book value, and dividend yield) in combination with a lack of positive sentiment to search for attractive stocks or sectors.

Table 10.3 shows the performance of some of these strategies since 1987.

Table 10.4 shows risk measures for the selection of value strategies. The first set of figures, again based on the volatility or standard deviation of returns, shows that these strategies generally are more volatile than are growth strategies. The second set of statistics are based on the percent of the historical 12-month returns that were negative (i.e., the probability of a loss). Using the second definition of risk, strategies such as relative strength appear to be much safer than value strategies.

Table 10.4   **Risk Statistics for Value Strategies (1987 to 2000)**

Value Strategy	Standard Deviation (%)	Probability of a Loss (%)
Low price/earnings	17.8	17.5
Low price/cash flow	21.2	19.9
Low price/book value	19.1	25.3
Low price/sales	21.7	27.1
High dividend yield	13.5	28.3
Dividend discount model	14.1	18.1

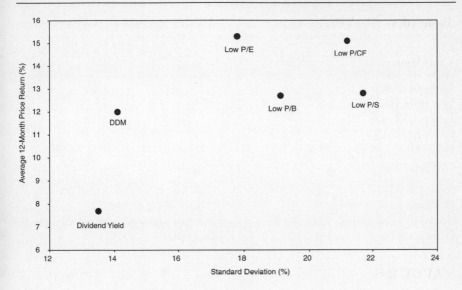

Figure 10.3   Value Strategies' Risk/Return—Risk Defined as Volatility

As we did for the growth strategies, Figure 10.3 and Figure 10.4 put the value strategies' two statistical tables into two risk/return scatter diagrams. Figure 10.3 incorporates the volatility of returns as the measure of risk, whereas Figure 10.4 uses the probability of a loss as the definition of risk.

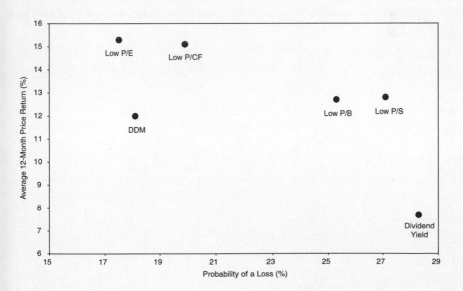

Figure 10.4   Value Strategies' Risk/Return—Risk Defined as Probability of a Loss

GARP INVESTING

Some investors prefer to mix growth and value strategies to form what are typically called growth at a reasonable price (GARP) strategies. The theory behind GARP investing is simply that diversification of strategies is less risky than following a single strategy. Chapter 5 on diversification stressed that putting all of your assets in a single strategy or stock historically has generally been an unwise decision. Investors are increasingly realizing that investing in a single strategy can also be riskier than originally anticipated. Thus, some investors now look for an optimal combination of growth and value to form a single strategy that better matches their risk/return preferences.

Perhaps an easy method for explaining the rationale of GARP strategies is to return to the Earnings Expectations Life Cycle. In Chapter 3, we reviewed that good investors tend to buy and hold stocks that are on the right side of the life cycle or that have rising expectations. If we only used expectations to pick stocks, then we would never know if our stocks were at 6:00 on the life cycle or at 11:59. Because investors only know that expectations are rising and little else, there is no way to tell how much longer the stock might appreciate. Think of all the growth/momentum stocks that disappoint and instantly underperform dramatically during every earnings-reporting season. We know that value stocks tend to reside in the lower half of the life cycle. Thus, GARP strategies combine measures of rising expectations with measures of valuation in order to attempt to purchase stocks that tend to be closer to 6:00 than to 11:59.

I have data for two GARP strategies. The first, price/earnings (P/E)-to-growth, is perhaps the best known GARP strategy. P/E-to-growth is a simple approach that measures stocks' valuations relative to their projected growth. If a stock had a P/E ratio of 20 and a projected five-year earnings growth rate of 10%, then the P/E-to-growth would be 2.0 (20 divided by 10). The ratio would be the same for a stock with a P/E of 40 and a projected growth rate of 20 (40 divided by 20 equals 2.0). A stock with a P/E of 20 and a growth rate of 20 would be cheaper than the two examples just given because the P/E-to-growth would be 1.0 (20 divided by 20 equals 1.0).

There are many different ways to calculate P/E-to-growth. Some analysts use price/earnings ratios based on the latest 12 months of earnings, whereas some use price/earnings based on forecasted earnings. The growth rate is typically the five-year projected earnings growth rate. More recently, some analysts have begun to calculate price/sales relative to five-year sales growth rate in order to justify the lofty valuations of stocks that have no earnings. According to the most extensive study I have ever seen on P/E-to-growth, the most successful combination appeared to be the ratio of P/E based on trailing 12 months of earnings relative to projected five-year earnings growth.[2]

Figure 10.5 shows how combining strategies can indeed reduce risk. The chart shows a risk/return scatter diagram that includes the risk/return characteristics of a strategy based on high five-year projected earnings per share (EPS) growth, a strategy based on low P/E ratios, and a strategy based on low P/E-to-growth ratios. The low P/E and high five-year projected growth have roughly the same risk, although the high five-year projected growth strategy has a higher average 12-month return. The risk/return combination for the growth strategy sits almost due north of the one for the value strategy.

Because one strategy is north of the other, you might think that combinations of the two strategies will lie somewhere north of low P/E, but somewhere south of high projected five-year earnings growth, but that is not the case. Low P/E-to-growth is west of the two other strategies. Higher returns could not be achieved by combining the two individual

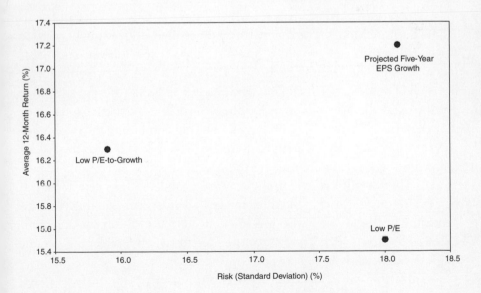

Figure 10.5   **Risk/Return Analysis for P/E-to-Growth**

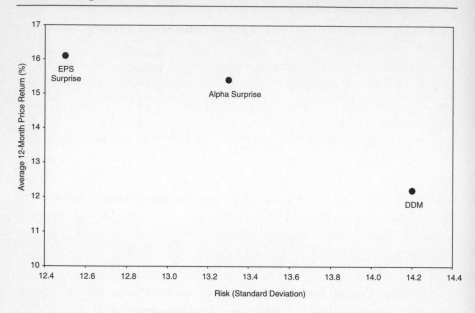

Figure 10.6   **Risk/Return Analysis of Alpha Surprise GARP Strategy**

strategies, but the risk of the GARP strategy is more than 10% lower than that of either of the other two strategies alone.

The other GARP strategy for which I have data is the Merrill Lynch Alpha Surprise Model. The theory that a diversified strategy might provide better risk/return than would a single strategy is the foundation of this model as well. The Merrill Lynch Alpha Surprise Model is a weighted combination of the Merrill Lynch Dividend Discount Model (the alpha or value portion) and the Merrill Lynch Earnings Surprise Model (the surprise or growth portion). Figure 10.6 similarly shows that combining the two strategies into the Merrill Lynch Alpha Surprise Model does reduce the risk of following the single strategy using the Merrill Lynch Dividend Discount Model. The Merrill Lynch Earnings Surprise Model did, in fact, have the best risk/return statistics of the three models, so diversification might not be appealing to the investor who was solely using the EPS surprise approach followed by this model. The user of the Merrill Lynch Dividend Discount Model would clearly have benefited by diversifying.

Table 10.5 shows the summary risk/return statistics for the two GARP strategies analyzed. The returns are competitive with those of the growth and value strategies. The risk of the strategies is generally less than that

Table 10.5   **Summary Risk/Return Statistics for Selected GARP Strategies**

	Average 12-Month Return (%)	Standard Deviation (%)	Probability of a Loss (%)
P/E-to-growth	14.5	15.7	15.3
Alpha surprise model	13.9	12.6	10.2

associated with most of the growth or value strategies alone because of the diversification of the strategies.

THE CYCLES OF STYLE INVESTING

Some analysts claim that growth outperforms value over the long term. Others claim value outperforms growth. Which assertion is correct depends on the measures of growth and value we use and the time period used in the analysis. We can get very different performance results by using different measures for different time periods. My work has attempted to address this issue in as unbiased a fashion as possible. I am not a dedicated growth or value investor and have no investment bias to support. This book has pointed out two important points: The two styles' performances are remarkably similar over the long term; and there are distinct cycles of style investing within those long-term statistics.

Figure 10.7 shows the relative performance between a select group of growth mutual funds and a similar group of value funds. These funds were chosen in 1990 because they were fairly representative of growth and value investing. Growth outperformed value during periods in which the line went up in the chart, and value outperformed during periods in which the line fell. It is very clear from this chart that there are distinct periods in which growth outperformed value and vice versa.

In some cases, the relative performance reverses significantly from period to period. On average, the periods of outperformance last about three to five years. Over the long term, though, they performed similarly. When measured on a total return basis (the chart depicts only changes in net asset value), the value funds used in the study outperformed the growth funds by an annualized average of only 0.19% per year during the 30-year period (13.33% versus 13.14%).[3]

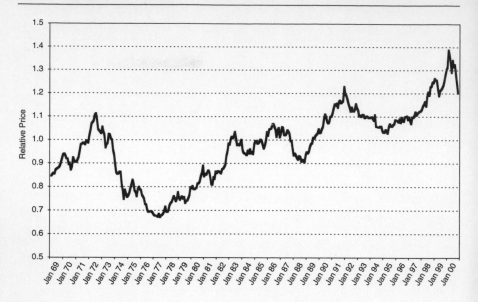

Figure 10.7   The Cycles of Growth and Value Investing

MORE ON RISK AND RETURN
AND GROWTH AND VALUE

Figure 10.8 shows the risk/return combinations for the growth and value funds' returns series. The horizontal axis in the figure measures risk as the standard deviation of 12-month returns, and the vertical axis shows the average 12-month return. Growth funds' returns might be higher than value funds' returns, but growth funds' returns also appear riskier. Figure 10.9 leads us to the same conclusion despite the definition of risk being changed to the probability of a loss. The conclusion here is somewhat different from that presented from the risk/return characteristics of the individual growth and value strategies. It is difficult to pinpoint why that is the case except to say that the strategies are not true managed portfolio returns, whereas the mutual fund returns are indeed actual portfolio returns.

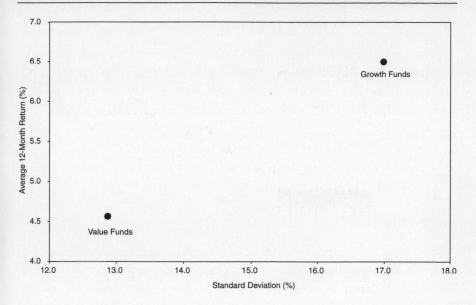

Figure 10.8   Risk/Return for Growth and Value Based on Standard Deviation as Risk

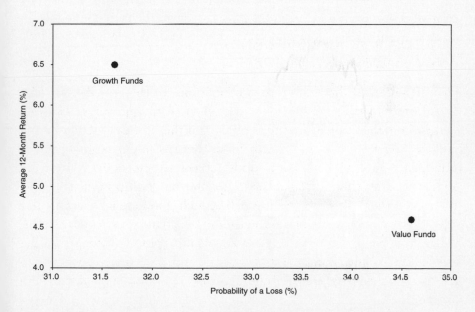

Figure 10.9   Risk/Return for Growth and Value Based on Probability of Loss as Risk

WHAT INFLUENCES STYLE PERFORMANCE?

The two most important factors that influence the relative performance of growth and value stocks are the profits cycle and long-term interest rates. Understanding these two key factors will lead investors to ask the following three questions when deciding whether to invest in growth or value:

1. How much earnings growth will I receive?
2. How many choices do I have to receive earnings growth?
3. When will the earnings growth occur?

The Profits Cycle

The profits cycle is perhaps the single most important variable used in determining the cycles of relative performance between growth and value. Figure 10.10 shows the same cycles of style relative performance as in Figure 10.7 overlaid on the profits cycle. The profits cycle is defined simply as the year-to-year percent change in S&P 500 reported earnings per share.

There is a significant inverse relationship between growth and value relative performance and the profits cycle that spans the period from roughly 1975 until early 1999. For example, the profits cycle decelerated from 1995

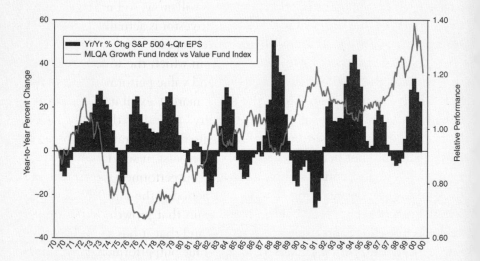

Figure 10.10   **Growth Versus Value—Relative Performance and S&P 500 EPS Momentum**
Based on data from Merrill Lynch Quantitative Strategy.

to 1998, and growth outperformed value. Prior to that in the early 1990s, when the profits cycle was accelerating, value outperformed growth.

This inverse relationship between growth and value and the profits cycle seems to be based on a very simple economic principle. When the profits cycle decelerates, earnings growth within the overall economy becomes increasingly scarce, and investors react by bidding up the price of that scarce resource. In other words, they expand the P/E multiples on the stocks that can maintain their earnings growth. A value manager will not typically pay a very high multiple to get a stock with potential growth, so value managers' performances tend to lag the growth ones during such periods. However, note that value outperforms growth when the profits cycle accelerates. When the profits cycle accelerates, growth becomes increasingly abundant. As it becomes increasingly abundant, investors become comparison shoppers for growth. A comparison shopper is often called a value investor.

Contrary to popular belief, growth investors are basically pessimists and value investors are optimists. Growth investors essentially believe that only a few companies will significantly grow their earnings, so they must find those few stocks and pay whatever price is necessary to hold them. Value investors believe everything will grow, so they comparison shop among all these healthy companies for the cheapest one. Thus, the growth investor is a pessimist (only a few companies will grow, so I must pay a premium for those that do), whereas the value investor is actually the optimist (everything will grow, so I have to find the cheapest).

There are two periods in Figure 10.10 in which the inverse relationship between the profits cycle and growth and value performance does not hold. Both are periods in which the stock market exhibited speculative bubbles. The first is the original "Nifty Fifty" period of the early 1970s. Notice that growth outperformed value despite the acceleration in the profits cycle during that period. When the bubble burst, it was followed by an extended period of conservatism, and value outperformed growth despite the profits cycle decelerating. The second period is the late 1990s, which was the recent technology bubble. Note again that growth outperformed value despite the profits cycle accelerating, and that it has so far been followed by another period of conservatism. Value outperformed growth during 2000 despite the profits cycle decelerating. Later in this chapter we discuss the details of how the technology bubble and its related noise skewed the normal relationship between growth and value stocks.

Long-Term Interest Rates and Duration

If a 30-year zero-coupon bond is held to maturity, all of the total return of the bond will be received in the 30th year. If a 30-year coupon-bearing bond is held to maturity, you will have received the interim coupons during the 30-year period. Only the principal and the last coupon are received at the end of the full term of the bond.

Duration is a measure of the interest rate sensitivity of a bond and is based on both the amount of return an investor might expect from a bond, and when the investor can expect to receive it. By definition, the 30-year zero-coupon bond has a duration of 30 years. All the return is received in year 30. A 30-year coupon-bearing bond has a shorter duration because some of the return is received during years 1 through 29.

Other factors also influence a bond's duration. Higher yielding bonds have shorter durations than do lower yielding bonds because more of the bond's total return is paid in interim coupon payments. Shorter maturity bonds have shorter durations than do longer maturity bonds for the obvious reason that shorter maturity bonds' lives are shorter and their total return must be delivered to the investor during that shorter time period.

Financial theory suggests that short-duration bonds outperform long-duration bonds when long-term interest rates rise. Long-duration bonds outperform when interest rates fall. During periods of inflation and rising interest rates, it is typically preferable to immediately receive as much total return as possible in order to reinvest in another investment that might provide a higher rate of return and keep up with inflation. In addition, rising interest rates negatively affect the present value of any future payment. A payment that I might receive in a year is worth less if I can invest in a T-bond yielding 5% instead of 4%, but that extra 1% return is probably not enough to entice me to sell my bond. However, a payment that I might not receive in 30 years looks less attractive because compounding that extra 1% for 30 years might be a sizeable difference. Thus, long-duration bonds are more sensitive to changes in interest rates than are short-duration bonds.

Duration and Growth and Value

The concept of bond duration can be applied to growth and value stocks and helps to explain why growth stocks are more sensitive to changes in interest rates than are value stocks. A simple characterization of a growth stock is one with a high P/E ratio and a low dividend yield. The high P/E ratio means that investors are discounting earnings very far into the future, and the low dividend yield means that there are little or no interim income payments. A value stock might be characterized as one with a low P/E ratio and a higher dividend yield. The low P/E ratio suggests that investors are discounting earnings for a short time period, and the higher yield indicates a higher level of interim payments. Thus, growth stocks' long time horizons and little interim income look more like long-duration bonds. Value stocks' low P/E and high dividend yield look more like short-duration bonds.[4]

If growth stocks resemble longer duration bonds and value stocks resemble shorter duration bonds, then it would follow that growth tends to outperform value when interest rates fall, and that value tends to outperform growth when interest rates rise. Figure 10.11 shows that the equity duration theory appears to be true. The thick line in the figure is the relative performance of the growth and value funds mentioned earlier. The thin line depicts long-term interest rates. Growth funds do tend to outperform value funds when long-term interest rates fall, and value funds tend to outperform growth funds when interest rates rise.

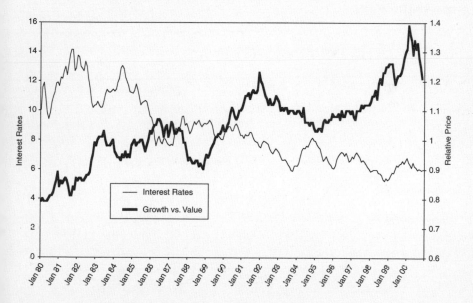

Figure 10.11   **Interest Rates and Growth versus Value (1980 to November 2000)**
Correlation is –0.81.
Based on data from Merrill Lynch Quantitative Strategy.

From these two factors, we can conclude that growth typically outperforms value when profitability is slowing in the economy and interest rates are falling. Value outperforms growth when profitability is accelerating and interest rates are rising. As said before, bad news on the economy is generally good news for growth investors. Some analysts have said that bond investors love bad news because interest rates fall as the economy weakens. The same is true of growth stock investors. A slowing economy, profits recession,[5] or economic recession means slower profits growth, which means a scarcity of earnings, lower long-term interest rates, and a great environment in which to be a growth investor.

Value investors, however, live in fear of such profit recessions and economic recessions. Those periods typically are so-called value traps. Some stocks P/E multiples may appear cheap during the early stages of an economic slowdown, and value investors are enticed by such stock valuations. However, the stocks' P/E multiples eventually expand by earnings going away rather than by profits going up. Value investors typically perform well during periods of rising rates and accelerating earnings growth, whereas this scenario would typically be a nightmare environment for growth investors.

BACK TO THE THREE QUESTIONS

We can now answer the three questions posed earlier:

1. *How much earnings growth will I receive?* Check the earnings growth forecasts for the company. Regardless of growth or value, we should at least start with a company that is expected to grow faster than the overall market.
2. *How many choices do I have to receive earnings growth?* Check whether the profits cycle is accelerating or decelerating. If it is accelerating, there are many growth companies, and investors might take a value-oriented approach. If it is decelerating, there are fewer growth companies, and a growth strategy might be more appropriate.
3. *When will the earnings growth occur?* Check whether this is a long-duration or short-duration story. Check whether the company is currently profitable or whether it is forecasted to be profitable sometime in the future. If interest rates are expected to rise, look for

current rather than future profitability and favor value over growth. If interest rates are expected to fall, look toward future profitability and favor growth over value.

NOISE AND GROWTH AND VALUE

I mentioned earlier that the inverse relationship between growth and value performance and the profits cycle held from about 1975 until early 1999. Growth outperformed value from early 1999 until early 2000 despite that the profits cycle was accelerating sharply. This growth outperformance was the influence of the noise and hype of the technology bubble.

Noise and hype encouraged investors to believe that the technology sector was the only sector that offered potential growth, but nothing could have been further from the truth. At the peak of the profits cycle, S&P 500 earnings were growing 33%, and the average company was growing earnings between 25% and 30%. Regardless of that fact, investors behaved as though only a few companies could grow their earnings. They paid higher and higher and higher price/sales multiples for companies that had no earnings.

Instead of paying exorbitant price/sales multiples, they should have been paying lower price/sales multiples for these stocks. Investors incurred several risks when investing in these stocks, and they should have demanded compensation for these risks. The first risk was that investors were giving up 25% to 30% current earnings growth for a promise of growth in the future. Second, the promise of growth did not promise how much growth would actually occur. Third, the promise of growth never defined when exactly the growth would occur. Thus, by paying higher and higher price/sales multiples, investors were actually paying to take risk, instead of demanding lower valuations and being compensated for the risk.

In addition, interest rates were rising because the economy was gaining momentum. As was previously discussed, investors typically should shift to shorter-duration assets during periods of rising interest rates. The goal during periods of rising interest rates is to look for stocks that are expected to have substantial near-term earnings growth to offset the effects of rising rates. Instead, the technology bubble led investors to some of the longest duration assets investors will ever see in our lifetimes. Imagine investing in a 100-year zero-coupon bond when interest rates are rising.

NOISE AND THE COST OF CAPITAL
AND GROWTH AND VALUE

Many people observed that the technology bubble was causing extreme valuations, but few discussed that the companies were beginning to run their businesses differently because of those high valuations. A lofty valuation to an investor is a cheap cost of capital for a company. If a company issued stock at 5 times earnings, the proceeds from that issuance would obviously be one-tenth of that from stock issued at 50 times earnings. By March of 2000, so much money was flowing toward the technology sector that the companies' cost of capital was essentially free. Their stocks were so overvalued that many companies began to use it as *currency* instead of cash. They used stock instead of cash to buy other companies, to pay their employees, and in some extreme cases, to pay for their office furniture and coffee machines.

Smart investors do not simply look for cheap growth stocks that will appreciate; they look for companies whose cost of capital is artificially high. Companies whose cost of capital is artificially high are figuratively starved for capital. The investor who provides capital to a capital-starved company will tend to receive higher returns because of simple supply/demand dynamics (i.e., not a lot of capital providers, and a capital-starved company). Noise and hype during the technology bubble encouraged investors to provide more and more capital to a sector that was already awash in capital. Using this theory, it should not be surprising that technology investors' returns were ultimately subpar.

NOISE AND QUALITY AND GROWTH AND VALUE

I have mentioned that investors typically pay for safety and want to be compensated for taking risk. However, as pointed out in Chapter 8 on quality, during the technology bubble investors actually were paying for risk and could be paid for safety. The result of this misperception of risk is that value universes subsequent to the bubble were more defensive than were growth universes.

Growth historically outperformed value when the profits cycle decelerated largely because higher quality companies tended to be in the growth universe. Investors valued the safety these companies offered, and the stocks' multiples tended to be higher. Riskier stocks tended to be in the value universe because investors were more fearful of them and demanded compensation for their riskiness in the form of lower multiples. Stable growth, therefore, was a growth characteristic, whereas cyclical growth was a value characteristic.

The technology bubble changed all that. Because investors believed that the technology stocks were the safest despite their inherent cyclicality, they bid up the multiples of risky stocks. The growth universe became unusually cyclical. Figure 10.12 and Figure 10.13 show the proportion of the S&P/Barra Value and Growth Indexes in the fourth quarter of 2000 that were high and low quality (defined as B+ or better for high quality and B or worse for low quality). Amazingly, the value universe at the end of 2000 was more defensive than was the growth universe. This explains why value began to outperform growth during 2000 despite the profits cycle decelerating.

The general perception that growth is safer than value remains. However, noise and hype have significantly altered the traditional performance relationships between these styles. The growth universe now appears to be unusually speculative because riskier stocks are still commanding higher multiples (at least as of this writing), but the value universe now appears to be unusually safe. Getting paid for safety sounds like a better strategy to me than does paying to take risk. We will have to see how long that situation lasts in the equity market.

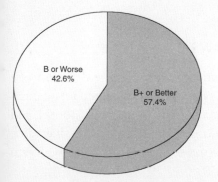

Figure 10.12   S&P/Barra Value Index by Quality Ranking
Based on data from Merrill Lynch Quantitative Strategy.

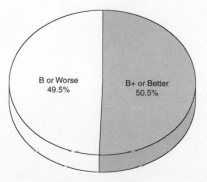

Figure 10.13   S&P/Barra Growth Index by Quality Ranking
Based on data from Merrill Lynch Quantitative Strategy.

Chapter 11

A Preflight Checklist

Before pilots begin to fly they go through a rigorous preflight checklist to make sure all parts of the airplane are functioning properly. These routines do not completely prevent mechanical difficulties from occurring, but many malfunctions are spotted and can be repaired before the airplane ever leaves the hangar. No pilot would fly without doing a preflight check first and would consider doing so a foolish risk.

I think investors should also have a preflight checklist, so to speak. Before investing, you should answer a set of questions, checks, or requirements to help reduce the probability of a foolish risk. Nothing can prevent investments from turning sour just as no preflight checklist can spot every mechanical malfunction in an airplane. However, going through a preinvesting checklist might help avoid major investment catastrophes.

Here is a set of questions derived from the chapters in this book that I think investors should answer before ever making an investment decision. These questions attempt to filter noise and hype, and to make the investor think more completely about the investment before acting. As I have said many times before in this book, this is not a how-to book. However, consistently asking these questions before making an investment decision might actually alleviate the need for a how-to book.

QUESTION #1: WHY DO YOU THINK IT IS A GOOD INVESTMENT?

The most important question to ask: Why is this investment better than any other investment right now?

If you cannot answer this question quickly and succinctly, I would suggest that you start over and perhaps find a new investment. If you find you repeatedly cannot answer this question, then perhaps you should look at mutual funds or other managed investments because you probably do not know enough about investments to successfully invest totally on your own.

There is nothing wrong with admitting that you do not know enough to invest on your own. I am an investment professional, and I often use managed products to invest in areas in which I have little experience or do not have the time to properly evaluate. Most professional investors I know do the same. A good analogy would be that well-known oncologists probably do not attempt to diagnose and treat their own health problems that are not cancer-related. It is impossible for anyone to know everything about every possible investment.

QUESTION #2: WHAT LED YOU TO THE INVESTMENT?

How did you find out about this investment?
Did a friend tell you about it?
Did a broker call you with the idea?
Did you think of it yourself?
Did you hear someone talk about it on television, radio, or read about
    it in the newspaper?

It is important to evaluate whether the source of the idea is truly credible. Obviously, this can be difficult if you are not an investment expert. Some sources are obviously not credible. Your Uncle Ned who runs a very successful restaurant supply business is probably not the one to give insight on the fiber optics market, but you actually might want to ask him about restaurant supply companies and their businesses. A portfolio manager on television who talks excitedly about a company that coincidentally happens to be the largest holding in his or her portfolio probably is not credible either. I doubt anyone would say anything critical of a company if the company's stock was the largest holding in the speaker's portfolio. Ask your barber or hairdresser for his or her opinion on personal care products but don't ask for his or her opinion on natural gas distribution.

Lots of people have lots of expertise in their own industries, and I would encourage you to search them out. However, you should be critical of the self-proclaimed expert who knows everything there is to know about the latest hot industry.

QUESTION #3: HOT OR NOT?

Very simply, is this a hot investment? Remember that noise tends to focus on hot investments. You should consider whether the investment truly has merit or whether it is simply a hot investment that is being driven by noise and hype. The investment might appreciate in the short term as many people are drawn to the siren's song. However, history suggests that hot investments turn cold faster than most investors appreciate.

Using the temperature nomenclature, room temperature or lukewarm might be best. Cold investments might soon be frozen solid, and frozen investments probably need time to thaw.

QUESTION #4: WHERE IS THE INVESTMENT ON THE EARNINGS EXPECTATIONS LIFE CYCLE?

One institutional investor I know has a picture of the Earnings Expectations Life Cycle on his wall. He attempts to pinpoint where a stock might be on the cycle before making every buy and sell decision. He claims the life cycle is a very simple way to add discipline to his investment process.

As stated earlier, the best place to attempt to purchase stocks might be about seven o'clock on the life cycle if you think of the cycle as a clock. It is extremely difficult to buy stocks at six o'clock, and being even slightly early can significantly hurt performance. Attempting to buy at seven o'clock means the stock has already begun to appreciate, but it is not close to being a hot stock. Hot stocks reside closer to ten and eleven o'clock. It obviously takes more work to find stocks at seven o'clock, and such stocks typically will not be featured on investment shows or in investment magazines. If you feel unsure about your ability to ferret out such situations, again perhaps you should consider managed alternatives.

Using the life cycle as a check will work only if you are honest with yourself and attempt to be objective when investing. If you find yourself rationalizing about where the stock might be on the life cycle, stop immediately and return to Question #1.

QUESTION #5: HOW DOES THE INVESTMENT FIT IN WITH YOUR EXISTING PORTFOLIO?

The definition of diversification should be "an important concept typically ignored by investors."

Remember to consider the diversification of your total assets. Is your job in the same industry as that of the company in which you are investing? Compounding the situation further, are you partially paid in stock by your company? If you already own three technology stocks, you probably do not need a fourth or fifth. If you own a drug stock, a drug store stock, a nursing home stock, and a medical products stock, then you probably do not need to purchase another stock in the health care sector. If you own high yield or junk bonds, you probably do not need to buy lower quality stocks as well. The portfolio already has a heavy concentration in lower quality assets.

Here is a very simple rule of thumb: If the market's volatility worries you or keeps you up at night, then your portfolio is not properly diversified. It is that simple. Day-to-day, week-to-week, or month-to-month market volatility should have no impact on your psyche if your portfolio is properly diversified. If properly diversified, then you will probably consider short-term market swings to be nonevents.

QUESTION #6: DO YOU THINK THE INVESTMENT IS RISKY?

Why do you think it is risky?
Should you be investing in it at all if you think it is risky?
Do you already hold a lot of assets that you also consider risky?

Don't fall into the trap of thinking that you must take risk to get higher returns. Of course, it is true that investors who take more risk over the long term are rewarded with higher returns, but short-term investors sometimes attempt to apply that axiom to shorter time periods. In addition, people often rationalize that underperforming investments are worthwhile because investors have to take risks to get returns.

On a free afternoon, I might want to have some fun. I could go parachuting or I could do arts and crafts with my daughter. I prefer arts and crafts. High risk is good for some people but not for all people. Investors should not feel compelled to invest in risky assets.

QUESTION #7: HOW DO YOU KNOW THE INVESTMENT IS RISKY OR SAFE?

Do you think the investment is risky or safe because of perception or because you have actually examined the numeric risk characteristics of the investment. The risk surveys earlier in the book were designed to show you how difficult it is to determine what exactly is a risky investment and whether you want to tolerate such risk.

Do you define risk as the probability of a loss, and have you determined risk by past performance statistics alone? Remember that strategies that outperformed for a three-year period had a greater probability of underperforming during the subsequent three-year period than did strategies that underperformed during the first period. An investment that has a great track record could turn out to be more risky than you thought it would. Be sure to examine long time horizons of performance and the variability of that performance through time. A good 10-year performance statistic could be the result of 4 years of outstanding performance and 6 years of slightly poor performance. Could you tolerate 6 slightly down years out of 10?

QUESTION #8: GOOD COMPANY OR GOOD STOCK?

Do you really care if it is a good company? You do if the economy is slowing and profits are falling, but you don't if the economy is strengthening and the profits cycle is gaining momentum. Remember that bad companies make better stocks than do good companies over the long term. If you are unsure as to how to spot bad companies that will make good stocks, then you should probably investigate managed alternatives that invest in such turn-around or undiscovered situations.

QUESTION #9: IS THIS A HIGH OR LOW QUALITY COMPANY?

Do you know? It is pretty difficult to answer Question #8 if you do not know the quality of the company whose stock you are about to buy. Check the S&P Common Stock Rankings to see if the stock you are considering matches your intuition about the company. If it does not, and you thought the company was of higher quality than it truly is, then do not shoot the messenger and do not rationalize that there is something wrong with the rankings. Rather, you should probably consider investing in a different company.

QUESTION #10: IS IT TIME FOR HIGH OR LOW QUALITY COMPANIES?

What are the present economic and profits conditions and will economic and profits conditions be better or worse one year from now? You have to make a simple judgment as to whether economic and profits conditions will be better or worse one year from now. If the answer is better, then typically lower quality stocks are preferable. If the answer is worse, then higher quality stocks are preferable. Try not to get caught up in the minutiae of economic forecasts (i.e., GDP growth, inflation, productivity, etc.). These statistics are indeed important, but they can overwhelm the most important question: Will conditions be better or worse one year from now? You will not see too many economists on television simply saying, "My forecast is that conditions will be better one year from now. Good-bye."

After Question #1, Questions #11 and #12 are the next two most important questions. If you insist on shortening your preflight checklist, make sure it contains Questions #1, #11, and #12. Ignoring these three questions would practically make reading this book worthless.

QUESTION #11: WHAT DO YOU KNOW THAT EVERYONE ELSE DOES NOT?

If you are investing on your own, then you are playing the roles of both the analyst and the portfolio manager. Remember that good analysts realize that true investment information is not reciting facts, but rather it is expressing intelligently derived opinions that are not shared by others. What is your intelligently derived opinion that is not shared by others?

If you do not have one, then start over. If you do not know how to form one, then investigate managed alternatives. Answering this question is the key to separating outstanding investors from those who allow noise and hype to lead them around.

QUESTION #12: ARE YOU ATTEMPTING TO FORECAST SATURDAY NIGHT'S WEATHER?

In the Introduction, I mentioned that there are forecasts that have a very high probability of being correct, but most people would consider those forecasts to be silly or obvious. I used the five-day weather forecast as an example. Despite that we know the probability is low that Monday's forecast for Saturday's weather will be correct, we stay awake to watch the five-day weather forecast on Monday to see if our plans for the weekend will materialize. I mentioned that television stations are quite aware of our affinity for the five-day weather forecast and typically hold it until late in the program in order to keep up viewer ratings as long as possible.

I also offered a weather forecast that I thought would be accurate 100% of the time. It will be cold in January in Minneapolis. It is an obvious and silly forecast, but I bet my forecast will have a better track record than will the Monday forecasts for Saturday's weather. Similar forecasts can be made for the stock market, but people ignore them because they seem silly and obvious.

Are you holding a well-diversified portfolio with a long-term time horizon (Minneapolis in January) or are you day trading in the latest hot sector (Monday's forecast for Saturday's weather)? We examined that the probability of losing money in an investment increases as the time horizon decreases. Day traders who focused on minutes and hours were generally bound to lose money. Investors who kept their day jobs and had a well-diversified portfolio with a long-term time horizon probably are performing better than are day traders. Sure, some hot day traders will appear on television and in magazines because they turned into gazillionaires, but nobody wants to interview a boring long-term investor? Ratings do not get higher, eyeballs do not increase, and subscriber bases do not increase from boring stuff like that.

This preflight checklist of 12 questions does not cover all aspects of the investment decision-making process, nor is it intended to do so. I simply offer 12 questions that I am guessing most investors have never asked before investing. I think they are 12 questions that, if regularly answered before investing, will significantly help people navigate the noise and invest in the new age of media and hype.

Glossary of "Noisy" Terms

The new age of media and hype has coined some fascinating terms that did not exist or were used very differently when I started on Wall Street in 1981. I list just a sample of them here with my, admittedly sarcastic, translations to plain English.

Build-out   A term used to describe infrastructure building in technology industries such as the "build-out of the Internet." This used to be called construction, but that term sounds too cyclical or industrial for technophiles. No one described the construction of the interstate highway system as a build-out. They called it construction.

Currency   This used to refer to the dollar, deutsche mark, pound sterling, and so forth. It now refers to an expensive stock that everyone wants so badly that a company has no use for dollars or deutsche marks or pounds. They literally trade their stock for goods and services.

EBITDA   Acronym for earnings before interest, taxes, depreciation, and amortization. Actually this is a standard accounting term. On Wall Street, however, investors now believe EBITDA is more important than E (just plain old earnings). I would love to apply for a loan or a mortgage on a second house using my personal EBITDA. If you exclude all my existing obligations, my financial position looks *really* strong.

Eyeballs   A term that was applied to Internet websites to refer to the number of people who looked at a website page. I think it is similar to "page views," but am not sure. Either way, I once heard someone suggest that a stock was cheap based on a price-to-eyeballs ratio. (You can't make this stuff up!!)

Glass   Slang term that refers to fiber optics. The phrase "laying glass" means to lay fiber optic cables, which everyone seems to be doing these days with reckless abandon.

Gross Margin   Another boring accounting term that Wall Street now loves. Accountants have found creative methods for keeping up gross margins by deciding what expenses to subtract and where to subtract them on companies' income statements. Somehow it is unimportant that companies that have huge gross margins do not have earnings and have a lot of competitors.

Guidance   Companies tell analysts what to say. Others have used many animal analogies to describe how analysts follow company guidance (sheep, lemmings, penguins, etc.).

Hard Landing   Used to be called recession. Clients of Wall Street firms do not like it when Wall Street analysts use the r word, so Wall Street has come up with the term *hard landing*.

Metric   Used to be called measure. Measure sounds like something used in baking, but metric sounds very rigorous. What actually constitutes a sound and rigorous metric is quite interesting. See Eyeballs.

New Economy   This term is used to describe some mythical economy in which there are no cycles and in which the technology, media, and telecom sectors are the only ones whose earnings grow. I think there are two problems with the so-called new economy. First, there has been technological evolution since year one, and economic cycles have remained. Somehow, everyone thought the new economy would not be cyclical. Second, if only technology, media, and telecom companies were going to grow, and other companies' businesses were expected to decline, then who was supposed to buy all the technology, media, and telecom?

Old Economy   The portion of the economy that was supposed to go out of business. I prefer to call it the real economy. The new economy is actually part of the old economy, but please don't tell anyone. Technology stocks' valuations might crumble if you did.

Pharma   A term used to refer to the pharmaceutical industry. I am not sure when the drug industry became the pharmaceutical industry because the AMEX Drug Index is still called the AMEX Drug Index and still uses ticker symbol DRG. Evidently, pharmaceutical is too long a word, so it has been shortened to pharma. Isn't "drugs" shorter still than "pharma"? My guess is that "drugs" reminds investors too much of LSD, and not enough of the companies' research and development.

Pre-Revenue   A term that refers to companies that have ideas but have not sold anything. Believe it or not, some companies have actually come public during the past several years on a pre-revenue basis. I have a lot of ideas for new companies. Hmmm.

Soft Landing   Again, no one likes the *r* word. Thus, instead of forecasting a hard landing, economists sometimes forecast soft landings, which refer to periods in which economic growth slows but a recession does not occur. Portfolio managers like soft landings because interest rates tend to fall during such periods, but they do not like hard landings because stocks tend to fall during such periods. The reality is, however, that the adjective that accompanies the word *landing* is relatively immaterial. Defensive stocks tend to outperform other groups regardless of whether the landing is hard or soft.

Space   This is similar to *universe*. However, space has more specific connotations than does universe. We might refer to the universe of companies in a database, but would not refer to the space of companies in a database. Space connotes an industry or sector. For example, we might say that company ZYX is the leader in the space, rather than saying ZYX is the leader in the industry. Given that many industries thought they could operate in a vacuum without concern about the overall economy, space may be the appropriate term. "Space: the final frontier" has taken on new meaning for some now defunct dot-com companies.

TMT   Stands for technology, media, and telecom. Was supposed to be a cute play on words with TNT. I doubt the originators of the term thought these stocks would ever "blow up."

Notes

Chapter 1—What Is Noise?

1. Commentary on National Public Radio, 30 July 2000.
2. Jim Rutenberg, "'Big Brother' Host Seeking Credibility," *New York Times*, 7 August 2000.

Chapter 2—The Risks of Do-It-Yourself Investing: What You Don't Know Could Hurt Your Performance

1. Ian K. Smith, M.D., "Ginseng Surprise—An Independent Report Finds That What's Listed on a Supplement's Label Is Not Always What's Inside," *Time Magazine*, 31 July 2000.
2. Patrick McGeehan and Danny Hakim, "Online Funds, Built to Order," *New York Times*, 13 August 2000.
3. I have omitted the names of the strategies from the chart so as not to mislead the reader and imply that the superiority of certain strategies will necessarily continue.
4. One should never underestimate the power of human psychology. A professor of mine once described the "I got an A, he gave me an F" syndrome. When children score well on an exam, they rush to tell their parents they got an A. However, if they score poorly, they complain to their parents that the teacher gave them an F. This occurs quite frequently in life in that we like to take personal credit for good outcomes, but blame bad outcomes on others. I personally find it astounding that this particular hedge fund is able to again raise funds by blaming its past faults on the markets' unusual behavior. I suppose those who are investing with the fund must believe that the markets will never

239

again behave unusually, thus limiting the potential for these hedge fund managers to perform poorly.

5. Mark Hulbert, "In the Data Mine, There Is Seldom a Pot of Gold," *New York Times*, 1 October 2000.

6. James P. O'Shaughnessy, *What Works on Wall Street: A Guide to the Best-Performing Investment Strategies of All Time* (New York: McGraw-Hill, 1997).

7. David Gardner and Tom Gardner, *The Motley Fool Investment Guide: How the Fool Beats Wall Street's Wise Men and How You Can Too* (New York: Simon & Schuster, 1996).

8. Because the S&P 500 is a weighted index, performance of the S&P 500 is dominated by larger companies. By using the Equal-Weighted S&P 500 as a benchmark rather than using the actual S&P 500 we remove any potential biases of comparing large companies to smaller ones. All companies, regardless of market capitalization, received the same weight within the Equal-Weighted S&P 500. Therefore, the relative performance shown in the chart is more likely to be attributable to the particular strategy rather than to the relative performance between larger and smaller companies.

9. Many thanks to Steve Spence at Merrill Lynch, who has developed one of the most comprehensive back-testing capabilities I have ever seen.

10. Statisticians will realize this depends on the distribution of returns of a particular strategy. It is possible that the distribution is skewed such that the mode is almost equal to the best return. Such strategies are few, although naive investors might envision a new strategy's mode and best returns to be similar. If the distribution of returns is more normally distributed or simply skewed less than is assumed, the odds will increase that a naive investor will be disappointed with the outcome.

Chapter 3—Noise and Expectations: What Goes Around, Comes Around

1. See Richard Bernstein, "Revisiting the Earnings Expectations Life Cycle," *Merrill Lynch Quantitative Viewpoint*, 13 August 1991.

2. Richard Bernstein, *Style Investing—Unique Insight into Equity Management* (New York: John Wiley & Sons, 1995).

3. Interestingly, analysts cited "business models" as failing rather than the business. This might have been an attempt to deflect attention away from their poor analysis of the company. The analysts seemed to take credit when they chose stocks that appreciated in value, but blamed the downfall on failed business models (i.e., we all knew the Internet was the wave of the future, but the companies' managements ruined the opportunity).

4. I heard an interesting anecdote that demonstrates exactly how far out of favor the technology sector was subsequent to the 1983 bubble. A technology analyst was encouraged to take a job as Director of Research in 1990 because his managers suggested that there was no future in being a technology analyst. No one ever anticipated that analysts following the sector would be in such demand during the next decade.

5. Those who wrote articles suggesting that bonds were riskier than stocks seemed to forget one rather basic tenet of investing: Equities are subordinated relative to debt.

6. The portfolios are rebalanced monthly and are equal-weighted. Their performance is measured versus the Equal-Weighted S&P 500 for reasons cited in Chapter 2.

7. Admittedly, one confounding variable in this analysis might be the number of brokerage firms in existence. Bull markets, in which IBM's stock price would probably appreciate, would tend to increase the number of brokers, whereas bear markets would cause the opposite to occur. However, the results of this study would have changed only marginally had we controlled for the direction of the overall stock market and measured IBM's returns in relation to those of the S&P 500.

8. Kari E. Bayer and Richard Bernstein, "Can the Market Predict Long-Term Earnings Growth and Performance—Part I," *Merrill Lynch Quantitative Viewpoint*, 15 September 2000.

9. One of the best-performing value managers during 1999 was widely criticized by his value-oriented peers for doing exactly that. He evidently bought America Online at a very low price when the company was out of favor. He subsequently continued to hold the stock despite that it moved into the growth universe.

Chapter 4—Noise and Long-Term Investment Planning

1. I am sure that many psychologists could explain why I chose the second highest yielding fund rather than the highest yielding fund. However, the important point remains that the factor I ultimately used to make my choice was historical yield. There was no forward-looking analysis.

2. There is a slight flaw in this analysis in that education costs are measured only since 1993, whereas asset returns are measured over a longer time period. Unfortunately, data for the CPI for Education begin only in 1993. I think this analysis errs on the side of conservatism because asset returns since 1993 have been extraordinarily good.

3. Of course, there is an issue of dividend reinvestment that I am ignoring in this simplified example. However, I do not think it is unrealistic to assume that most investors searching for the next Microsoft are not very interested in dividend-paying stocks.

4. An interesting sideline to this thought is whether college financial aid causes what is called a "moral hazard" among parents seeking to save for college. A moral hazard is a situation in which people take inordinate risks because they realize that there is a safety net. In other words, certain forms of guaranteed insurance might actually encourage excessive risk taking. Some people might argue that parents of smarter students are encouraged to take unusual risks when saving for college because their children are likely to receive financial aid if their investment does not pan out and they cannot pay for college. The risk is ultimately very small that their children will not be able to attend college. Thus,

some parents may speculate instead of invest because if they cannot pay for college, then someone else will. My guess is if colleges stopped offering financial aid, parents would be much more conservative with their investments.

Perhaps the most famous moral hazard issue of recent times was the FDIC, FSLIC, and the savings and loan scandals of the late 1980s and early 1990s. Some heads of savings and loans took terrific amounts of risk in their businesses, and totally abused their positions because they felt that the government would bail out depositors if their schemes failed. They were correct.

Curiously, few have talked of the moral hazard issue with respect to some plans to privatize social security. A successful privatization must not have a so-called safety net. If it does, then individuals will be encouraged to take excessive risks and will ultimately ruin their retirement savings. The government would then be left with no social security system and the need to bail out retirees. Of course, removing the safety net is politically unfeasible. In my opinion, the current proposals to privatize social security are destined for ruin because of the inclusion of the safety net. It is also curious that such privatization plans are emerging after an 18-year bull market. The cries for privatization were mute in 1979 when equity returns were terrible. Predicting future demographic trends has not produced different results from those produced 20 years ago. Only the allure of the stock market has increased.

5. The authors of these studies made a very common error. They confused *ex post* returns (those studied after the fact) with *ex ante* expectations (those made before the fact). *Ex post* data do suggest that there are periods in which stocks are less risky than bonds. However, a prime reason that stocks can generate such superior risk-adjusted returns is that investors are generally fearful of stocks. The higher *ex post* returns are the compensation for that risk. If investors' *ex ante* fears of the stock market subside, then we should expect lower returns from the asset class. As previously mentioned, articles claiming that stocks were safer than bonds were written just in time for bonds to outperform stocks. Essentially, *ex ante* expectations dropped for bonds, bonds were perceived to be riskier, and bonds provided superior *ex post* returns.

Chapter 5—Noise and Diversification

1. For statisticians, the correlation between the returns of the two hypothetical assets is −0.77.
2. You might suggest that I invest in gold because it tends to be inversely correlated with the stock market. However, as I mentioned, I am not particularly bearish on the long-term prospects for the financial markets. An active investment in gold would be a very bearish strategy. If I were that bearish, a better question might be why am I working on Wall Street at all?
3. See Richard Bernstein and Steve Kim, "The Paradox of Private Equity: Diversification or Information," *Merrill Lynch Quantitative Viewpoint*, 12 July 1995.

4. For perhaps the most complete and best source I have found on the topic of small stock investing, see *Small Stock Dynamics*, written by my colleague at Merrill Lynch, Satya Pradhuman. Bloomberg Press published it in 2000.

Chapter 6—Noise, Risk, and Risk Assessment

1. Even with a U.S. Treasury bill there is not complete certainty. There is the extremely remote possibility that the government could default on its short-term obligations. However, this risk should not be taken lightly when investing in the short-term obligations of other nations, particularly those of the emerging markets. Again, there is no free lunch in the financial markets. If short-term obligations have higher yields, there is probably additional risk.
2. I am assuming a payout to only one winner, and no partial payouts for partially picking the correct lottery number, and so forth. There is clearly some probability that the lottery player might get all or part of his or her $1,000 back.
3. It seems to me that some stocks are typically removed from the point-gain lists every day because of their large prices. For example, I rarely see Berkshire Hathaway on the point movers list despite that its stock price and price changes are measured in thousands. If these stocks were left in the charts, the charts would be very repetitive, and not very exciting. Thus, a little editorial license appears to sometimes be used.

    Also, it would be helpful if media charts were presented in logarithmic form. The difference between a logarithmic chart and a standard price chart is that two sets of equidistant points measure the same return on a logarithmic chart, whereas they measure the same point difference in a standard price chart. By using logarithmic charts, the chart of a stock whose price went from $90 to $100 would look similar to the chart of a stock whose price went from $9 to $10. Using standard charting practices, the $90 to $100 move would look much more dramatic. In both cases, however, the return is identical.
4. You might also criticize this discussion because the table refers to strategies rather than individual stocks. However, buying an individual stock is a one-stock active strategy. The probability of future outperformance should not be influenced by the size of the portfolio.
5. This is yet another example of the "I got an A, he gave me an F" syndrome. The class became openly hostile to me when the results clearly showed that they could not assess their own risk tolerance. As financial consultants whose job it is to assess clients' risk preferences, they viewed the results as a poor grade, rather than as a constructive exercise. In the end, this class was a great lesson to them in how client relationships can deteriorate by a simple misperception of risk.
6. A Dividend Discount Model attempts to value stocks in a manner similar to the method used to price bonds. An investor knows the bond's current price, knows the stream of future coupons from the bond, and knows when the principal will be returned. A bond's yield-to-maturity is the discount rate that equates today's

price to the present value of the future stream of coupons and principal. There are many types of Dividend Discount Models, but most value stocks using this relationship. An investor knows the stock's price today, and knows how analysts expect the earnings and dividends of the company to grow. The Dividend Discount Model searches for the discount rate that equates today's price to the stream of estimated future dividends.

Chapter 7—Investment Losses, Time Horizon, and Risk

1. Defining risk in this manner is merely a very simplified version of the more sophisticated concepts of semivariance and pension fund shortfall.
2. A dividend-paying stock should be thought of as a portfolio of stock and cash, whereas a stock that does not pay dividends should be thought of as an all-stock portfolio. Because cash returns have little or no volatility or uncertainty, a portfolio that combines stocks and cash will always have a lower volatility than will an all-stock portfolio of the same stocks.

    Also, you can think of a dividend-paying stock as a coupon-bearing bond, whereas a stock that does not pay dividends is a zero-coupon bond. Zero-coupon bonds are generally considered riskier than are coupon-bearing bonds because zero-coupon bonds' prices are more sensitive to changes in interest rates, their returns are more volatile, and the probability of losing money is higher.
3. Again, this assumes that it is highly unlikely that the United States would default on its debt. Federally insured CDs are not quite as riskless, as there is the possibility of the individual bank defaulting. Even federally insured CDs are not guaranteed above certain very large amounts.

Chapter 8—Don't Search for Good Companies, Search for Good Stocks

1. See Hersh Shefrin and Meir Statman, "A Behavioral Framework for Expected Stock Returns," Santa Clara University working paper, October 1993.
2. C & D stocks are grouped together because there are no D-rated stocks at certain points in the economic cycle. The risk of bankruptcy declines when profits growth is extremely strong in the overall economy, and the number of D stocks is sometimes zero. Thus, C-rated and D-rated stocks are combined.
3. As was done in previous chapters, the relative performance charts in this chapter include the Equal-Weighted S&P 500 as a benchmark rather than the S&P 500. This has been done for two reasons. First, the quality indexes are equal-weighted—each company in the index receives the same weight within the index. The actual S&P 500 is, for all practical purposes, market capitalization-weighted. Second, comparing an equal-weighted index to a market capitalization-weighted index tends to accentuate the performance of smaller capitalization companies. Thus, we can observe a more pure quality effect by comparing an equal-weighted quality index to the equal-weighted S&P 500.

4. A profit recession is not an economic recession. An economic recession is defined as two or more consecutive quarters during which Real Gross Domestic Product (GDP) growth is negative. A profit recession is one in which S&P 500 earnings growth is negative for two consecutive quarters. Profit recessions occur more frequently than do economic recessions, but profit recessions always have accompanied economic recessions.

5. For those interested, in my opinion the two best early studies on the neglected stock effect are Avner Arbel, and Paul Strebel, "The Neglected and Small Firm Effects," *Financial Review*, 1982, 17(4): 201–218; and Avner Arbel, Steven Carvell, and Paul Strebel, "Giraffes, Institutions and Neglected Firms," *Financial Analysts Journal*, 1983, 39(3): 57–63.

6. See note 1 above.

7. I emphasize at this point that the studies performed on lower quality companies were done as a portfolio. Individual lower quality companies sometimes do declare bankruptcy or completely go out of business. These studies do not examine the probability of success when picking an individual company of extreme low quality.

8. Standard and Poor's appears to have begun to subjectively give rankings to an increasing number of companies that do not have 10 years of history. Although their literature on the rankings does mention that some subjectivity can be applied to the process, these companies would typically be "not rated." However, we have found that S&P has assigned quality rankings to some technology companies that have not been in existence for 10 years. We can only suspect that the technology bubble has influenced S&P's rating scheme. S&P may be confusing market capitalization with viability and quality. It is hoped that they will soon end this practice.

9. It is curious that the advocates of the so-called new economy seemed to forget that economies are cyclical. Technological evolution is nothing new. Unless we live in an agrarian society tending vegetables, some form of technology has always become a larger part of GDP and enhanced productivity. If we are discussing the 1950s, perhaps technology would be aluminum manufacturing. Today, it is information processing and electronics. Despite technological evolution, economies remain cyclical. The fact that many investors missed this simple point again demonstrates how the bubble altered people's thought processes.

Chapter 9—What Makes a Good Analyst?

1. I realize that I am one of the many "talking heads" that appear on television and in the print media and that I, too, help create noise. I do, however, try extremely hard to abide by this chapter's description of the characteristics of a *good* analyst.

2. See the Glossary of "Noisy" Terms at the end of the book for other similar word distortions.

3. See Richard Bernstein and Kari Bayer, "An Analysis of Earnings: Reported vs. Operating," *Merrill Lynch Quantitative Viewpoint*, 9 February 1999.

4. The Bernstein and Bayer study points out that the differences in the strategies' performances might not be statistically significantly different, but that such lack of statistical significance supports their contention that operating earnings do not provide any additional investment information. The authors claim that the results at worst show there is no advantage to using operating earnings. Similar results were found when other definitions of earnings were used, although the authors admit that earnings before interest, taxes, depreciation, and amortization (EBITDA) has some effectiveness within growth-oriented strategies.
5. Economic Value Added and EVA® are registered trademarks of Stern Stewart & Company.
6. See Richard Bernstein and Carmen Pigler, "An Analysis of EVA®" *Merrill Lynch Quantitative Viewpoint*, 19 December 1997.
7. See Richard Bernstein, Markus Barth, and Satya Pradhuman, "Analyzing Global Valuation Techniques," *Merrill Lynch Quantitative Viewpoint*, 14 August 1996.

Chapter 10—Growth and Value and Noise

1. The Security and Exchange Commission's new Regulation Fair Disclosure (Regulation FD) is an attempt by the SEC to make sure that information is distributed by companies to investors in a manner in which all investors receive important information at the same time. Previously, companies were allowed to disclose information selectively. Regulation FD now prohibits that practice.

   Although Regulation FD attempts to ensure that investors receive identical information at the same time, there remains no guarantee for the efficient markets enthusiasts that all investors interpret the information the same way.
2. See Donald Peters, *A Contrarian Strategy for Growth Stock Investing* (Westport, CT: Quorum Books, 1993).
3. This may be a confusing point because the growth and value cycles chart seems to imply that growth outperforms value over the long term. The cycles chart incorporates the funds' changes in net asset value (or price appreciation), whereas this study is based on the funds' total returns (price appreciation plus distributions). On a change in net asset value (NAV) basis, growth funds outperformed value funds. On a total return basis, value funds outperformed growth funds by a very small amount as noted.
4. Of course, one problem with this equity duration concept is that the interim cash flows from stocks are not fixed as they are with bonds. The economy is often strengthening when interest rates rise, and it is not uncommon to see dividend payments rise during those periods as corporate cash flows strengthen. Conversely, dividend payments sometimes fall when interest rates fall because the economy weakens and corporate cash flows suffer. Thus, an equity's duration is a moving target.
5. I define a profits recession as two consecutive quarters in which S&P 500 earnings growth is negative. Economists define an economic recession as two consecutive quarters in which real gross domestic product growth is negative.

Index